Illuminate
Publishing

WJ...

A

S

Christine Bell
Consultant: Barbara Connell

D0415668

Published in 2013 by Illuminate Publishing Ltd, P.O. Box 1160, Cheltenham, Gloucestershire GL50 9RW

Orders: Please visit www.illuminatepublishing.com
or email sales@illuminatepublishing.com

British Library Cataloguing in Publication Data

A catalogue record for this book is available from the British Library

ISBN 978-1-908682-01-7

Printed by Ashford Colour Press Ltd., Gosport, Hampshire

09.13

The publisher's policy is to use papers that are natural, renewable and recyclable products made from wood grown in sustainable forests. The logging and manufacturing processes are expected to conform to the environmental regulations of the country of origin.

Every effort has been made to contact copyright holders of material produced in this book. Great care has been taken by the authors and publisher to ensure that either formal permission has been granted for the use of copyright material reproduced, or that copyright material has been used under the provision of fair-dealing guidelines in the UK - specifically that it has been used sparingly, solely for the purpose of criticism and review and has been properly acknowledged. If notified, the publisher will be pleased to rectify any errors or omissions at the earliest opportunity.

This material has been endorsed by WJEC and offers high quality support for the delivery of WJEC qualifications. While this material has been through a WJEC quality assurance process, all responsibility for the content remains with the publisher.

Editor: Geoff Tuttle
Design and layout: Nigel Harriss

Cover photograph: © Andrei Tsalko / fotolia.com

Acknowledgements

The author and publisher wish to thank:

Barbara Connell for her thorough review of the book.

Lucy Alice Williams and Daryl Smith for allowing their MS3 work to be included.

Dedication:

In memory of my Mum and Dad.

Contents

How to use this book

The contents of this study and revision guide are designed to guide you through to success in the WJEC Media Studies A2 level examination. This book has been written specifically for the WJEC A2 course you are taking and includes useful information to help you to perform well in the examination and the internally assessed unit.

There are notes for the following elements of the A2 Media Studies specification:

MS3 – Media Investigation and Production

MS4 – Media – Text, Industry and Audience

The first section of the book aims to prepare you for the MS3 internally assessed unit. This considers approaches to the planning and writing of the Research Investigation, completing the production piece including advice on how to demonstrate technical and creative skills. There is also support to help you to write your evaluation and complete your cover sheet. In this section you will also find examples of 'real ' student's work, this will give you an idea of what is expected at this level.

The second section of the book aims to prepare you for the MS4 examination. This section:

- Covers all of the main industries including background information, their organisation and how they are regulated.

- Presents a detailed case study of one text for each of the industries covering the main areas of genre, narrative, representation and audience. This will give you a formula to allow you to investigate your other texts.

You will also find additional support so that you can develop your work:

- Examples of how to analyse a range of media texts including relevant terminology.

- Definitions of key terms and their application to help you in your revision.

- There are Quickfire questions designed to test your knowledge and understanding of the material.

- Tips based on the experience of marking this paper over a period of years and designed to help you to improve your examination technique.

- Tasks to encourage you to apply the knowledge outlined in the guide to develop your understanding of the examples you have studied in class.

- We have also highlighted key figures and research to broaden your knowledge and make you aware of the theorists behind the key theories relevant to this subject.

- At the end of each section there is a summary page to help you to structure your revision.

It is important to remember that this is a guide and, although there are examples of texts to help you, it is more important that you gain the knowledge to allow you to demonstrate your understanding of the texts and the industry that produced them. The idea is that you will apply the knowledge and understanding of the industry gained in this book to the other media texts you have studied in class.

Exam practice and technique

The **third section** of the book covers the key skills for examination success including the important skill of essay writing and how to structure an examination response. There are examples of how to deconstruct examination questions and there are also some sample answers to possible types of questions that may appear in the examination. These are not model answers and you should not attempt to learn them. They offer a guide as to the approach that is required, and the commentary will explain the strengths and weaknesses of the responses. You will be offered advice on how to structure your writing to produce an effective examination response.

Finally, at the end of the book you will find a glossary of key media terminology to aid your learning and develop your analysis

Most importantly, you should take responsibility for your own learning and not rely on your teachers to give you notes or tell you how to gain the grades that you require. You should look for additional notes to support your study into WJEC Media Studies.

You can look at the WJEC website www.wjec.co.uk. In particular, you need to be aware of the specification. Look for specimen examination papers and mark schemes. You may find past papers useful as well.

AS revision – a quick reminder!

It is important that you transfer the skills acquired at AS level into your A2 year. The final MS4 examination is synoptic and the expectation is that you will bring to it all the knowledge and skills you have learned over the whole course. The AS Media Studies course provided you with knowledge and understanding of the key concepts underpinning the subject. This knowledge enabled you to analyse a range of media texts using media terminology. The AS course also introduced you to technical and creative skills that facilitated the production of high quality media artefacts. These skills are also highly relevant at A2 and must be developed and refined.

Genre – what can you remember?

This is a way of categorising media texts through a set of easily recognisable conventions or repertoire of elements. These genre conventions are repeated over time and are therefore familiar to audiences. Categorising media texts in this way is not always straightforward – some media texts belong to **sub-genres** and some are **hybrid genres**. Genre conventions can be divided into key areas:

- Narrative – this is the structure of the particular genre, how its story is told. Some narratives have a straightforward linear structure, some are more complex incorporating multi-strand narratives that challenge and hold the interest of an audience. In discussing and analysing narrative it is important to be aware of how that narrative is constructed through a range of techniques.

- Characters – specific genres tend to have recognisable characters that help to establish the genre. Audiences become familiar with these 'stock' characters and can predict their role within the narrative and how they will behave. Stars may become associated with a specific genre through playing the same or a particular type of role. This can help in the promotion of the text.

- Setting and iconography – certain genres are recognisable through the use of setting. Establishing shots can be used to quickly transmit information about where a programme/film is set through the use, for example, of iconic landmarks. Certain genres have specific objects linked to them, these help to establish the genre for an audience. Print texts will use iconography to establish genre, for example the front cover of a heavy metal music magazine.

- Technical and audio codes – some genres employ a particular style of filming that makes them recognisable, for example the slow editing and tense non-diegetic music of a thriller. Signature tunes for television programmes, for example *Dr Who*, may have been modernised but have remained constant over a period of time because they are recognisable to audiences. Particular shots are associated with specific genres, for example the use of the close-up in tense emotional situations in a soap opera or drama.

Key Terms

Sub-genre = This is where a large 'umbrella' genre is sub-divided into smaller genres each of which has their own set of conventions. For example, television genre can be sub-divided into teen drama, hospital drama, costume drama, etc.

Hybrid genre = These are media texts that incorporate elements of more than one genre and are therefore more difficult to classify. *Dr Who* is a science fiction/fantasy television drama.

How will I use this knowledge at A2?

Genre as a media concept may be an area you will focus on for your MS3 Research Investigation. It may also be the focus of a Section A examination question for MS4.

① How can the front cover of a magazine establish the genre?

Task

Choose a media text from a specific genre. What are the main genre conventions contained within this text?

Key Terms

Back story = This is part of a narrative and may be the experiences of a character or the circumstances of an event that occur before the action or narrative of a media text. It is a device that gives the audience more information and makes the main story more credible.

Suspend disbelief = Here, an audience may be aware that where they are positioned by the camera, for example, is impossible, but they do not challenge and instead believe it because it enhances their involvement in the story.

How will I use this knowledge at A2?

Narrative as a media concept may be an area you will focus on for your MS3 Research Investigation. It may also be the focus of a Section A examination question for MS4.

Narrative – what can you remember?

All media texts, whether they are fictional or fact, print or audio-visual, have a narrative structure. The producers of media texts employ a range of narrative techniques to develop the story arc and hold the attention of the audience. These may include the following.

Narrative techniques in audio-visual texts

- **Manipulation of time and space** – the narrative can move the audience around within a given time frame. For example, a crime drama may employ a non-linear narrative where it starts with the discovery of the crime and then moves back in time to show the lead-up to the crime.

- **Three-strand narratives** – this is the most common form of narrative structure whereby three different storylines are introduced in the beginning and then these narratives interweave throughout the programme/film. Some will begin and end in one episode, others will continue on. In this way both loyal and one-off audiences gain some pleasure from the programme.

- **Flexi-narrative** – this is a more complex narrative structure that is consequently more challenging for an audience. Here the narrative is made up of a series of interweaving storylines involving complicated scenarios and plot situations. There will often be narrative twists and enigmas until the final exposition.

Narrative conventions in audio-visual texts

- **Flashbacks** – these are often used to give an audience the **back story** and can serve to develop the audience understanding of a character or their motivation within the storyline. Audiences are given clues when time and space are being manipulated, for example a change in clothing, iconography or the style of the filming.

- **Point of view shot** – this helps to involve the audience in the narrative as they view the action from the point of view of a particular character.

- **Audience positioning** – this is where the camera or the audio codes place the audience in a particular position. This may be literally, for example as the murderer stalking the victim, or emotionally where the music may cause the audience to feel tense or sad.

- **Apparently impossible position** – this is another type of audience positioning whereby the camera places the audience in an unusual position to view the action. For example, viewing the operating table from the ceiling in *Casualty*. Audiences will **suspend disbelief** if their involvement in the narrative is enhanced.

Exam Tip

Analysing the narrative of a media text does not mean re-telling the story. You must ensure that you approach a discussion of narrative in a more sophisticated way considering how the narrative is constructed using a range of different techniques.

GoodMood Photo/Shutterstock.com

- **Privileged spectator position** – here the audience is involved in the narrative as the camera 'shows' them what other characters cannot see. This allows the audience to anticipate how the story will unfold.

- **Enigma codes** – these are evident in both audio-visual and print-based media texts. They are a way of restricting the narrative information given to the audience, the purpose being to make the audience watch or read on. For example, the use of teaser trailers that divulge minimal narrative clues is a main technique in film production.

- **Action codes** – something a character does allows the audience to anticipate how the narrative will develop. For example, the writing and delivering of a letter giving important information.

- **Voice-over** – this can be used in certain media texts to fill in gaps in the narrative or give clues to what an audience may expect from the storyline, for example in a film trailer.

- **Dialogue** – a conversation between two characters, for example, can be a rapid way of filling in background information and establishing character motive within the narrative. Dialogue may also serve to give the audience expectations about how the narrative will unfold. Selected **sound bites** of dialogue are used in film and television trailers to give clues to the narrative.

Key Term

Sound bites = These are short clips of dialogue or music taken from a longer text in order to communicate the essence of the narrative to an audience.

Narrative conventions in print-based texts

Print texts also have a narrative structure. In this format narrative refers to the codes and conventions that are recognisable to audiences as belonging to that text. These include:

- **Headlines** – in quality newspapers the headline gives information about the story that is to follow. In the popular press these may be more dramatic than informative. The purpose of both is to encourage the audience to read on.

- **Cover lines** – in magazines these appear on the front cover and suggest the content. They usually contain enigmas and the audience has to buy the magazine to get the full story.

- **Images and captions** – the purpose of images used in print-based texts is usually to suggest or develop a narrative. The caption that accompanies the image interprets the meaning for the audience. For example, advertisements use images and copy to place us within a particular, often aspirational, narrative in order to persuade us to buy the product.

- **Language and mode of address** – this can give information about the genre and what the audience may expect. The written information on the back of a DVD cover will encapsulate the narrative of the text, often using genre-specific language, in order to draw the audience in.

- **Enigma codes** – these are also a feature of print texts. They appear in tag lines, headlines and cover lines. Their purpose is to restrict the narrative – the audience have to access the text in order to read the whole story.

© Walter McBride/Corbis

② Outline the narrative structure of a newspaper.

Representation – what can you remember?

Understanding the concept of representation is essential, this understanding must be developed at A2 and must go beyond a simplistic discussion of, for example, positive and negative representations in media texts. In order to analyse representation in media texts you must be aware of both the context and the purpose of the representation contained within the text. There are key questions you need to consider:

- How is the world represented in the media text constructed?

- Who is in control of the text and how are their ideas and values communicated in the text?

- Who is the target audience of the text? How may different audiences respond to the representations contained within the text? Who will accept and who will challenge?

- What messages are contained within the text? How might these messages impact upon the audience? For example, lifestyle magazines represent women as thin, beautiful and desirable. What effect might that representation have upon a young female reader?

Oleg Gekman/Shutterstock.com

What do I need to understand about representation as a media concept?

- The producers of a media text encode ideas and messages within the text through representations. The aim of the producers of the text will be to communicate their ideology to the audience. Audiences then decode the messages and respond to them in different ways.

- All media texts are constructed and all representations contained within the texts are constructed. This gives an illusion of reality which some audiences will accept as the truth without challenge.

- Representations are constructed through technical and audio codes, layout and design, and language and mode of address.

- The context and purpose of the representation is important. The representation of young people in *The Inbetweeners* is constructed to make an audience laugh because it is a situation comedy.

- Stereotypes are constructions which are made up of over-exaggerated and easily recognisable character traits. They are used to convey information rapidly as audiences will have expectations of how certain stereotypical characters will behave. Not all stereotypes are negative.

- All media texts go through a process of **mediation**. They are not **windows on the world**. Through construction and selection the texts are interpreted for us and the representation of the issue, event and social group is presented in a particular way through this process.

Key Terms

Mediation = This is the way in which a media text is constructed in order to represent the producer of the text's version of reality. This is constructed through selection, organisation and focus.

Window on the world = This is the idea that media texts, particularly those that present aspects of reality, for example news programmes, are showing the audience the real world as it happens.

How will I use this knowledge at A2?

Representation as a media concept may be an area you will focus on for your MS3 Research Investigation. It may also be the focus of a Section A examination question for MS4.

③ Give an example of a positive stereotype.

Audience – what can you remember?

No media text can be analysed without considering the concept of audience. Unlike previously thought, audiences are not mass, they are made up of individuals whose responses are influenced by a range of factors. All media industries are aware of the importance of the audience and use a range of strategies to attract and maintain them.

Consider the following.

Who is the target audience of the text? How do media texts target and appeal to an audience?

This is a **text out** approach and addresses what the particular text does to attract an audience. In order to understand how the text appeals to an audience you must be aware of the target audience of the text. Different texts will adopt different approaches – some texts **narrow cast** and others will try to attract a broad audience. The techniques used to attract audiences include:

- Technical and audio codes
- Language and mode of address
- Construction
- Context
- Positioning.

How do media texts position audiences?

Texts place audiences in a particular position in order to encourage and manipulate them into accepting the messages contained within the text. This is achieved through:

- **Technical and audio codes**. A close-up of a character's face in an emotional scene involves the audience and encourages them to empathise with the character. Tense music in a thriller combined with a shot from the point of view of the main protagonist will also make the audience feel more involved in the action.
- **Language and mode of address**. The way in which the text 'speaks' to the audience will place them in a particular position. The chatty, colloquial style of the teenage magazine makes the young reader feel part of the magazine's community.
- **Construction**. Media texts, through their construction, are said to create an idea of their audience or user. For example, certain magazines and documentary television programmes tell the audience what is important and how they should like their lives.

How and why do different audiences respond in different ways to media texts?

An audience is made up of individuals who will respond to media texts and the messages contained within them in different ways according to:

- **Gender**. Men and women may respond differently to certain media texts. Some texts may alienate a particular gender through, for example, images and terminology.
- **Age**. The age of the audience may evoke different responses. For example, younger people are said to be more desensitised to horror and violence in certain media texts.

Key Terms

Text out = This relates to the strategies the text uses to attract an audience rather than the 'audience in' which refers to how the audience may respond.

Narrow cast = This is where a text, for example a magazine about sea fishing, will target a very specific, narrow audience.

④ Give an example of how gender may affect how an audience may respond to a media text.

How will I use this knowledge at A2?

It may be appropriate for you to engage in some form of audience research for your MS3 Research Investigation. Audience will also be the focus of Section B examination questions for MS4.

© Juice Images / Alamy

- **Ethnicity**. The upbringing and beliefs of different ethnic groups may affect their response to, for example, a news report on the fighting in Syria.

- **Culture and cultural experience**. The upbringing and the ideologies of the audience as well as life experiences will affect how an audience responds to a text. The text itself may also shape the experience of the audience. For example, you may have never been to America but your perception of it may be formed by what you have seen in films, newspapers and television.

- **Cultural competence**. This also links to age, experience and gender. Some audiences may have different cultural competencies than others. For example, older people may be less comfortable with accessing information through digital technology.

- **Situated culture**. Where you are and who you are with will affect how you respond to a text.

⑤ Why might certain media industries find demographic profiling of audiences useful?

How can audiences be categorised by different media industries?

Media industries categorise audiences in order to make them easier to target. This is particularly true of the magazine and advertising industries as they are usually selling a clearly defined product and so need to be accurate about the target audience. There are two main ways in which audiences are categorised by these industries:

- **Demographic profiling**. This is the division of consumers into bands from A to E according to, for example, their income, occupation, household size and marital status. A and B are the wealthiest members of society and are therefore assumed to have the most disposable income. Magazines will use this information to inform possible advertisers of the audience demographic.

- **Psychometric profiling**. This defines an audience by their values, attitudes and lifestyle and is seen to be more relevant in relation to today's consumers. This method was developed by Young and Rubicam, an American advertising agency. Audiences were split into categories according to their motivational needs, for example aspirers, explorers and reformers.

Exam Tip

Many students misuse audience categorisation. These ways of defining audience are very specific to the magazine and advertising industry, they should not be applied to other media industries.

How are audiences constructed by media texts?

This is a more complex question and suggests that media texts themselves are responsible for constructing an idea of their audience. This is achieved through the images, language and representations contained within the text. This tends to be who the producer of the text wants their audience to be. For example, *Cosmopolitan* woman is a construction, but if the magazine can convince the reader of her existence and that she is 'normal', then that reader may buy into the world of the magazine in order to aspire to be that woman.

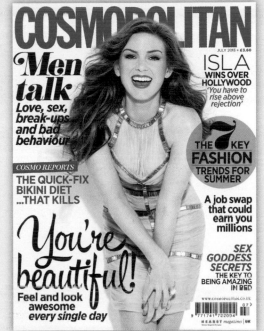

Cosmopolitan © Hearst Magazines UK

Useful audience theories

There are several theories written about audiences and how they respond to media texts. It is important that when you are discussing audiences, you apply the correct theory to support what you want to say.

The uses and gratifications theory

This was one of the first theories to challenge the **hypodermic needle** effects theory and to suggest that audiences are active and use different media texts in order to gratify certain needs. This theory stated that audiences chose texts for:

- Entertainment and diversion – the text allows them to escape the mundanities of everyday life into another world created by the text.

- Information and education – some texts are chosen by audiences because they want to find out or learn about something. This may make them feel better about themselves and up to date.

- Social interaction – some media texts are discussed on a daily basis and audiences watch them in order to be a part of that discussion.

- Personal identity – some texts offer audience pleasures because they can compare what is happening in their own lives with the narrative in the media text.

David Gauntlett's pick and mix theory

This theory also suggests that the audience are active and discerning and counteracts the idea that they will be adversely affected by what they read and see. He suggests that audiences are sophisticated and will select the aspects of the text that best suits their needs and ignore others.

Two-step flow and opinion leaders

This theory was another challenge to the hypodermic needle model. This suggested that an audience's response to a media text will be influenced by the opinions of others. The audience may have not had direct contact with the text themselves, this is how the 'two-step flow' idea works, but may be influenced by opinion leaders like, for example, parents, friends, politicians or celebrities. Examples of this theory are celebrity endorsement of products, and film reviews. The audience will need to decide whether to trust the opinion leader and they may not always agree with their viewpoint.

Key Term

Hypodermic needle model
= This is generally acknowledged to be an out of date theory which suggests that an audience will have a mass response to a media text. The idea is that the media injects an idea into the mind of an audience who are assumed to be passive and as a result they will all respond in the same way.

Task

Choose a magazine cover and consider how it constructs the idea of an audience.

Task

Visit David Gauntlett's website and read in more depth his ideas about how audiences respond to texts: www.theory.org. This will help you to develop the more sophisticated media knowledge needed at A2.

quickfire

⑥ Give a specific example of how the two-step flow/opinion leader's theory works in practice.

Audience reception theory

Stuart Hall, a cultural theorist, explored the concept of how audiences make sense of media texts. Like other theorists, he accepted that audiences were active, not passive and may decode the ideologies of a text in different ways:

- Preferred reading – here the audience will accept the meaning encoded in the text and intended by the producer of the text. This is usually the case when the text reflects the ideas and opinions of the target audience.

- Negotiated reading – here an audience may accept some of the messages contained within the text and reject others. This links to Gauntlett's pick and mix theory.

- Oppositional reading – here the audience will reject the messages encoded in the text. This may be because of a range of factors including cultural experience, age or gender.

MS3 Media Investigation and Production

Internally assessed work: introduction

MS3 is the internally assessed unit of the A2 course. It will be completed in your centre and is assessed by your teachers. A sample of the work from your centre is then sent to an external moderator whose job is to ensure that the standard of assessment in your centre is the same as in other centres nationally. The objective of this unit is to develop the practical, analytical, technical and creative skills introduced at AS. It is also designed to demonstrate the importance of research in informing the production of media texts. A key element of this unit is independent study. You will be given a free choice of assignments or be able to select from a range of options set by your teacher. This is not a taught unit although you will use some of the skills you learned at AS. The role of your teacher is to supervise and guide you. You will be expected to take responsibility for your work in this element of the course.

For this internally assessed work you will be required to demonstrate:

- Individual and independent research skills

- The ability to use this research to inform a media product

- High level technical and creative skills

- The ability to evaluate the final product exploring the validity of the research undertaken.

Content – What will I have to produce for MS3?

- A Research Investigation of 1400–1800 words

- A production piece that is informed by the findings of the Research Investigation

- An evaluation discussing the links between the Research Investigation and the Production.

A Research Investigation

You will be required to undertake an individual investigation of 1400–1800 words into a specific area of study that is of interest to you. The focus of the investigation must be one of: **genre, narrative or representation.** This piece of work is an academic research-based study which will allow you to explore an area of the media of your choice in detail. Your research should be taken from a range of **primary** and **secondary sources** and must be properly referenced. As this is an 'investigation' the assumption is that you will reach some conclusions that will then inform your production piece. Choose an area to research that you are interested in and want to find out more about. You will spend a lot of time with your chosen media texts so make sure that you like them and have enough to say about them!

Key Terms

Primary sources = This will be the specific media texts that you choose to analyse, for example two horror films or two music videos.

Secondary sources = These will be academic texts that will support your investigation. They must be from a range of different formats including books, articles, websites, for example.

Exam Tip

Two texts should be enough; this will allow you to make comparisons. For some areas you may need more, for example print-based adverts where two examples may not give you enough material to discuss.

7 What is the purpose of using both primary and secondary texts in your Research Investigation?

What is primary research?

This is the analysis of your main primary texts. These may be music videos, print-based advertisements or opening sequences from films, for example. The main body of your investigation should consist of detailed primary research supported by secondary sources; your focus must be on your **chosen concept** in relation to your main texts. Primary research allows you to give your opinions or to challenge the opinions of your secondary sources. As stated earlier, two primary texts should be enough. In your primary research it is important that you have chosen texts that allow you to demonstrate your ability to engage in sophisticated analysis related to genre, narrative or representation.

- Texts that are too similar will encourage repetition of points. If you are analysing, for example, the genre conventions established in the opening sequence of horror films, then choosing an older and a more modern film will allow you to examine the texts within a sociological context and to draw conclusions regarding whether the conventions have changed over time.

- Texts that are too different, for example from different genres, will make comparison difficult to demonstrate.

- In your analysis make sure you link the concept focus to the analysis in a sophisticated way. If the focus is representation of gender, for example, avoid simplistic judgements about positive and negative and consider how the representations are constructed and mediated using technical and audio codes.

- Remember that if you are analysing audio-visual texts, it must be evident that you are dealing with moving image texts; your analysis must include reference to shots, angles, editing, etc.

- If you have chosen primary texts that are films or television programmes then you need to select key scenes that best demonstrate your focus. You cannot discuss complete texts effectively within the word limit.

- If your focus is narrative, this does not mean that you retell the story of the text. You must be able to analyse specific narrative techniques employed that are relevant to that genre.

- No matter which texts you choose to analyse, the expectation is that you are able to employ relevant media terminology and analytical vocabulary.

- The findings from your research will influence the decisions you make when creating your own production artefacts. You will be expected to refer in detail to your primary texts in your evaluation and to demonstrate clear links between the two.

Exam Tip

Narrowing down the amount of texts you choose to analyse will ensure that you engage in the sophisticated level of analysis expected at this level. Use your secondary sources to support the points you make.

⑧ Why is it important to have a balance between primary and secondary texts in your investigation?

ducu59us/Shutterstock.com

What is secondary research?

In preparation for completing your investigation you must engage in structured, relevant secondary research. This could be:

- Websites – there are a range of sites that offer valid media information. The advantage of these is that they are regularly updated.

- Articles from newspapers – *The Guardian* and other quality newspapers have regular sections on the media that can be used for research. Particular columnists have up-to-date media knowledge in particular areas; for example, Laura Barton writes regularly on the music industry, and Charlie Brooker on television.

- Books – there are books that will give you more detailed information about your key focus: genre, narrative or representation. There are other books related to theories you may want to use. Further texts may have a specific focus related to your study, for example 'Women in action films'. You will need to spend some time reading to gain understanding; you then may be able to take direct quotations to be used in your work.

- Audience research – it may be relevant to your study that you engage in audience research. However, this will not be relevant for all investigations and remember you have a lot to discuss within the word limit. If you are considering using audience research then avoid questionnaires that will usually only give you **quantitative data**. Focus groups with a narrow brief allow you to be more in control and can provide **qualitative data** that is more detailed and specific.

Task 1

Compile an annotated catalogue of 10 items of research covering your main concept (genre, narrative or representation) and your area of study, for example women in action films. Your items must come from a range of sources, for each source you need to write a brief description of why it will be useful for your study.

Task 2

Complete the 'Proposal Form' (example on next page) outlining your initial ideas.

Task 3

Check the deadlines you have been given. Create a time plan to ensure that you meet those deadlines.

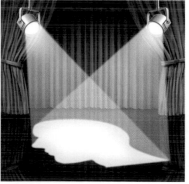

Lightspring/Shutterstock.com

A2 MEDIA STUDIES

MS3 COURSEWORK – MEDIA INVESTIGATION AND PRODUCTION

PROPOSAL FORM

NAME:

POSSIBLE IDEAS FOR RESEARCH INVESTIGATION

BRIEF IDEAS FOR RESEARCH TO BE UNDERTAKEN IN PREPARATION

IDEAS FOR PRODUCTION (include details of your contribution to group work if relevant)

MS3: Detailed plan

It will help you to structure your Research Investigation if you use a structured plan.

Introduction

- Briefly introduce your area of study, e.g. magazines or action films.
- Briefly introduce your research focus, e.g. representation of women.
- Be clear about your reasons for your investigation and choice of texts.

Part one

Introduce and demonstrate your understanding of your key concept, e.g. representation, genre, narrative. This is essential to demonstrate your broad understanding of the media.

Here you should begin to draw upon your research into key theories/theorists associated with your concept. You should be quoting from key media experts and a range of sources, commenting on these secondary sources and their relevance to your investigation.

Introduce your primary texts generally, e.g. action films. This will demonstrate your understanding of your media area of focus. You should not discuss your key texts in detail yet.

Main body

Here you move on to and concentrate on your primary texts. You should have selected key examples from those texts that best suit your area of investigation.

Explain why you have chosen them and their relevance to your study.

Analyse your texts in detail. If you are using films and TV programmes you cannot analyse the whole text – you must select key scenes that best illustrate your points. If you are analysing print texts, ensure that you choose 'rich' texts that allow you to present a detailed analysis.

Relate your analysis to your research title.

Remember to use the initial secondary research you discussed earlier in your essay and apply it to your texts using the sources to support your analysis. This may mean that you reintroduce relevant theories/theorists.

Detail should include filming techniques, camera angles, audio codes, portrayal of character, layout and design, language, visual codes, etc. Remember to analyse the effect of the techniques employed.

Avoid description/narrative and use analytical and media terminology. Include **quotations** from secondary sources to reinforce your points.

Conclusion

Remember the focus of your study.

What have you found out or proved through this research?

Sum up your findings and relate this back to your original title.

The Research Investigation: Examples of titles and opening sections

Example 1

Are women represented in a sexualised way in music videos? With close reference to Snoop Dogg *Sexual Seduction*, Rhianna *Umbrella* and Beyonce *If I Were a Boy*.

Commentary

The title is appropriate and focused. It contains the concept and the main texts.

The opening paragraph clearly sets out the aims of the investigation and the subject area. Relevant media terminology is employed which relates to the concept of representation.

The student does not rush straight into their key texts but establishes the industry context first.

The first secondary source is clearly related to the point they want to make about construction and is used to support this view.

Audience research in the form of a focus group has been used effectively here without taking up too much of the word count. The findings have been summarised in one pertinent quote selected because it relates to the points being made.

The student goes on to develop their argument about representation of women. Their second source is a quote about sexual objectification; the student has been able to apply it to what they want to say about music videos and to broaden the argument about the social implications of negative media representations.

Only after establishing this broad knowledge do they discuss their primary texts.

My area of study is gender representation in music videos and my investigation will focus on women being constructed and mediated by the text and represented in a sexual way when they are a primary or secondary artist. In my view there is a very significant sexual theme regardless of the role played in the video. In order to discuss this issue further it is useful to consider the function of a music video.

'Its main function is to act as advertising for the record. It also serves and contributes to the image of an artist or band and to maintain a visibility of performances in the absence of personal appearances.'

This is a useful quote as it refers to the image of the artist and I believe it is a widely held view that, in the case of women, this image is mainly sexual and this prompts us to ask if the use of women's sexuality is justified in order to achieve an artist's high profile. Having discussed this issue with a focus group the typical views can be summed up in this response:

'Generally I feel women are shown as an add-on to the main artist to provide sex appeal, they are seen as sex objects, especially in rap music videos. When they are the main female artist they can choose how they want to be represented and the portrayal can be different, almost seen as powerful, but still in a "risky way".'

This is a commonly expressed view showing that audiences have a perception that women in music videos are constructed in a sexual way. In order to discuss the representation of women in music videos, it is important to understand what is meant by representation. Representation is the way in which a text is constructed for an audience. In the music industry the artists themselves are the text and they are constructed in a certain way to sell their product to an audience. Those who construct the texts know that sex sells so therefore women are represented in a highly sexualised way. In this way they are constructed for the male gaze, but also women aspire to be like them. This representation is created through visual and technical codes and women are shown as objects to be looked at. This representation has wider social implications:

'Objectification contributes to social problems. These problems include: sexual violence and other violence against women. When women are portrayed as objects without subjectivity it may be easier for someone to justify violence against them. If a woman is just a "thing" to be looked at, her feelings and concerns might seem less important.'

This quote supports the negative view of women being represented in a sexualised way and can be applied to the music industry.

I have chosen three main music videos to illustrate how this industry represents women.

The Research Investigation: examples of titles and primary analysis:

The main body of the Research Investigation must focus on the analysis of the chosen primary texts. The secondary research sources will be used to support this analysis.

Example 2

An exploration of how youth is represented in British cinema with specific reference to extracts from *Billy Elliot* and *Eden Lake*.

These are extracts from the student's investigation which focuses on textual analysis.

The first clip I examined is a scene from Eden Lake, this scene, when scrutinised, shows how Watkins represents youth. Initially, we are introduced to the gang of youths. The audience assumes they are a gang as a result of the visual codes employed – by dressing youths in similar costumes they are defined as a gang. This diminishes their sense of individuality and identity. The costume selection for the gang of youths is representative of recognisable iconography associated with teenage characters in the horror genre, they wear casual clothing and 'hoodies' that provide a stereotypical presentation of youth. Diegetic sound within the storyworld is also disturbing in its representation of youth, the dialogue is aggressive and uses violent language. Cinematography can be commented on as a low angle tilt is used with point of view shots looking up at the youths to make the adults appear subservient and the youths dominant. These elements are part of the construction of the representations within the text and enhance the viewing experience for the audience.

Example 3

An analysis of the representation of women in horror films with specific reference to a series of posters for *Jennifer's Body*.

In the second poster an extreme close-up shot is used of Jennifer licking her lips, which connotes sex and the close-up emphasis on it makes it a key factor for selling the film. The blood – which connotes an element of danger – reinforces the horror and vampire genre. Her red glossy lips against her pale skin challenges the stereotype of the usual horror virginal characters and represents Jennifer in a different way. She has lost her innocence. The narration elements suggest that she is the control character; possibly a killer. The image raises enigmas and challenges the idea of her being a typical sex object. If she is the killer, would the targeted audience really want to see her in a sexual way? In a world where the horror genre is known for representing women as the victim to the 'distinctly male killer', Jennifer's Body challenges this stereotype. Jennifer appears to be the challenging 'young and beautiful' victim stereotype suggested by Clover – and seems to be using her body and her sexuality.

Commentary

Both these examples have appropriate titles and have selected texts that allow the student to engage in detailed textual analysis.

Example 2 has selected an extract from the film which best illustrates their point, as a focus.

The student avoids description, the scene is analysed in detail with references to clothing, sound and technical codes and their purpose and effect. There is a clear understanding about how the representation is constructed.

The focus remains very clearly the representation of young people but there is also a broader awareness of genre conventions.

Example 3 has a range of print texts as a focus. It is often necessary to analyse more than two print texts to develop the investigation. The choice of a range for the same film works in this essay as the posters are quite different – this may not be the case for all film posters.

The concept focus is again clear, technical terminology is used confidently and secondary texts are use to support the assertions. The student engages in detailed analysis of the chosen text in the context of the chosen concept.

Key Terms

Harvard referencing = A specific style of citing and acknowledging sources used in academic essays.

Bibliography = A list of the books, articles and websites that you have used in order to help you write your investigation. You should include items in this list even if you have not directly referenced them in your essay.

Notes = This is the method by which you acknowledge the texts you have referenced specifically in your investigation. You can include footnotes or notes at the end of the essay.

Plagiarise = To plagiarise is to use the language and thoughts of another author without their permission and to then represent them as if they were your own.

Exam Tip

You will be given more credit for referencing your sources that pretending than they are your own.

MS3: Style guide

The MS3 unit is an academic, research-based study – you must engage in relevant research around your key concepts, e.g. representation, and your chosen texts. Within your essay it is essential that you acknowledge and reference the secondary texts you have used. It is not important which referencing style you use, as long as it evident that you know how to do this accurately, although you may wish to use an accepted method, for example **Harvard referencing**.

All writing should be clear, coherent and articulate. All spellings should be checked for typing errors .

Although you will do this work independently, you will be able to hand in a rough draft of your investigation to your teacher who will advise you on how to improve your work. It is important that you take note of the advice given by your teacher.

All Research Investigations must include notes acknowledging sources and may also include a **bibliography**.

You must acknowledge all sources as notes when you use them. There are two ways to do this:

- Write a number next to the quote

- At the bottom of the page detail the source as a footnote OR

- Include a page of **notes** in chronological order at the end of your essay.

When you acknowledge a source you can use the following style:

Hall, Matthew, *Teaching Men and Film*, BFI Education, London, 2005

(author, title in italics, publisher, place of publishing, date of first publishing)

Miller, Rob, www. mediaedu.co.uk, *The Representation of Masculinity in Men's Magazines* – include as much information as you can, just giving the website address is not enough.

Cochrane, Kira, The Guardian, *UK Feminista founder Kat Banyard: 'It's staggering retailers sell lads' mags'*, 23 June 2013 (include as much information as you can).

Quotations – If the quotation is less than two lines long, incorporate it into the body of your work, in quotation marks e.g. As David Gauntlett suggested *'many of the academic books on "masculinity" are disappointing as they dwell on archetypes from the past and have little to say about the real lives of modern men.'* If the quotation is longer, double space and set it out separately, in quotation marks.

You must always acknowledge quotations – **DO NOT PLAGIARISE**!

All names of texts, e.g. films, TV programmes, etc., must be written in italics.

A production

There is a distinct difference about the production work completed at A2 compared with AS. A2 production work must develop from and be informed by the findings of your Research Investigation. It can be in any form but there are some rules:

- You must work in a different form from AS. For example, if you produced a magazine at AS you cannot also produce a magazine for your A2 production. However, you can work in the same medium in both years; for example, if you produced an opening sequence for a television crime drama at AS, you can produce the trailer for a film at A2.

- Audio-visual productions must be up to 4 minutes in length.

- Print-based productions and their digital equivalent must be a minimum of three pages.

- Non-audio-visual digital media and print-based productions must be completed individually. Audio-visual productions can be produced individually or as part of a group of no more than four.

- Everyone within the group must have a clear **technical role** and make an individual contribution.

- The development from A2 should be evident – the completion of the Research Investigation ensures that you have a conceptual understanding of the texts you are producing.

Examples of individual linked work

Example 1:

- How are women represented in music videos with reference to Beyonce's *If I Were a Boy* and Rhianna's *Te Amo*?

- A music video focusing on a specific female representation.

Example 2:

- How typical are the genre conventions of music magazines with reference to *Kerrang!*, *We ♥ Pop* and *NME*?

- A front cover and double page spread for a new music magazine reflecting specific genre conventions.

Example 3:

- How is narrative constructed in the opening sequences of gangster films with reference to *Goodfellas* and *Reservoir Dogs*?

- The opening sequence of a new gangster film demonstrating narrative techniques.

A word about group work

You can work as a group only if you intend to produce an audio-visual production piece. However, this needs careful planning as each group member must be able to demonstrate links between their Research Investigation and the joint production. The group will need to decide what they want to create for the production and then ensure that each group member researches the same media area but refers to a different concept and different primary texts in their Research Investigation.

Examples of group linked work

Research titles 1

The representation of women in two music videos

How is narrative constructed in two different music videos?

An examination of the genre conventions employed in popular music videos.

Production

A music video for a new band

Key Term

Technical role = For the purpose of this specification, this refers to filming, editing and sound. Where sound is taken on as a technical role the expectation is that you will be able to demonstrate a range of complex skills comparable with filming and editing. This may be, for example, dubbing, audio editing, lip synching, managing the recording of external dialogue, post production audio, etc.

quickfire

⑩ How can you aim to demonstrate development from AS in your A2 production artefact?

Research titles 2

An examination of the genre conventions in two documentaries.

How are teenagers represented in documentaries? A close study with reference to two texts.

An exploration of the narrative structure in two documentaries.

Production

An opening sequence or trailer of a documentary about issues related to teenagers.

Key points to remember

- In your production work you can choose to **subvert** or **replicate** your findings. For example, if your Research Investigation was into the representation of women in music video and your findings indicated that women tended to be sexually objectified, you could make a music video showing sexual objectification or you could subvert your findings and make a video showing a representation of a strong, independent woman.

- Your production work can be a combination of audio-visual and print. For example, a Research Investigation into genre conventions in action films could result in a production which included pages of a website for the film in which was embedded a teaser trailer.

- From your Research Investigation findings you will, in some cases, have an option of producing an audio-visual or a print-based production piece. For example, if you have looked at representation of gender in action films you could make a trailer for a new action film or a DVD cover and a poster promoting the film, both of which would allow you to demonstrate your research findings.

Production approaches: Creating an audio-visual artefact

This production must have a direct link to your research findings but must also demonstrate technical and creative skills relevant to the chosen format. If you are part of a group you need to have a clear technical role.

Tips for creating an audio-visual text

- If you are working as part of a group to produce an audio-visual piece, be clear from the start what your technical role is and how you will demonstrate your research findings. There are different ways in which you can divide the responsibilities: each group member can have a separate distinct role, for example editing. Alternatively, different sections of the film can be filmed and edited by individuals or each group member can produce a different edit of the filmed footage, one that best highlights their specific research findings.

- Planning is essential. Although you will not be awarded marks for a pre-production storyboard, you still need to consider the shots you will use. Be aware of the concept focus of your investigation and your main findings and how you will demonstrate these. For example, how will you film your lead character if you want to construct her as a strong female in the music video? What shots will you use?

Key Terms

Subvert = In this sense it means that you can use your findings to create a product that uses the conventions of the text in a different way. For example, you may find, after researching the representation of women in horror films, that they are usually victims. You may decide to subvert these findings by producing a trailer featuring a woman 'villain'.

Replicate = In this context this means that you would create a text that follows closely the findings of your Research Investigation.

Exam Tip

If you aim to produce a music video using music from an existing artist, you must select a track that does not already have a music video associated with it. The alternative is to use a school band or singer with original music.

- Consider not only how to illustrate your research findings but how you will demonstrate creative skills and show understanding of the codes and conventions for your chosen format. For example, if you decide to create a film trailer, your finished piece must demonstrate the relevant generic codes and conventions.

- Make sure that you film in enough time – editing always takes longer than you think! Build in time in case you need to re-shoot a scene or lose footage. Always have a back-up copy of your edit, just in case!

- Equipment – consider what you will need to produce your audio-visual text. For example, if you intend to record external dialogue you will need a **boom microphone**. To produce a more sophisticated edit you may need to use more than one camera.

- Sound is very important and is often not given the attention it needs by students. Think carefully about where you are filming and what audio tracks you may need to dub as part of the post production.

- Lip synching for music videos needs careful consideration. If you are going to dub the soundtrack on afterwards then it is important that your 'singer' sings along to the track playing while you are filming and doesn't try to mime. This will make the post production process much easier.

Key Term

Boom microphone = This is a directional microphone mounted on a long pole. It is very sensitive, can block out extraneous noise and can be positioned to pick up specific sound, for example dialogue in a busy street.

Luminis/Shutterstock.com

MS3 Production approaches: Creating an audio-visual artefact

This production artefact is a music video and was produced after investigating if women were represented in a sexualised way in music videos. As a result of the findings the student decided to create a music video featuring a strong woman who was in charge in a relationship. The chosen song was *Time After Time* by Cindi Lauper.

Key Points

▶ There is clear evidence in the music video that the research findings have been used.

▶ The student has used a positive representation of a woman artist. This is constructed through clothing; she is not dressed in a provocative or sexual way but in normal, everyday clothes.

▶ The external settings are natural and the lighting is low key. The studio settings are edited into black and white to suggest sophistication, producing a representation that is not focused on body image or sexuality.

▶ However, in the use of the iconography of the music studio, the session musician and the instrument, there is also demonstrated an awareness of the codes and conventions of this style of music video. These have been used creatively.

Key Points

▶ In one shot she is walking confidently ahead of the man who looks to be the one left behind.

▶ The range of shots, lip synchronisation and post-production techniques also demonstrate technical and creative ability.

Work by Lucy-Alice Williams featuring Beth Macari, both of Heaton Manor School

MS3 Production approaches: Creating a print artefact

The print production you choose to create must reflect your research findings and must be an individual piece. Print texts can include DVD covers, film posters, CD covers, magazine pages, etc. You must produce a minimum of three pages.

Tips for creating a successful print text:

- You must demonstrate your ability to plan and construct a print media product. You must also demonstrate your technical and creative skills – your artefacts must look as professional as you can make them.

- If you are working in the print medium you must choose a format that will best demonstrate your research findings. For example, the front covers of television listings magazines would not be an appropriate text in which to illustrate narrative in crime drama; a DVD cover and a poster would be better and give more opportunities to demonstrate the focus. This is particularly relevant where you are using a print medium to demonstrate the research findings of audio-visual texts.

- Whatever the print text you choose to produce you must use your own original photographs. You cannot be given credit for photographs you have not taken, even if you manipulate them digitally. Using a good quality camera and planning your photographs carefully will mean you have less post-production editing to do. Think about where you will take your photographs and the composition of your images. Consider whether you may need extra light, for example.

- For editing, using a program like Adobe Photoshop, for example, will give you much more professional results as it allows you to create layers and achieve a range of photographic effects. You may have to take some time learning how to use it but the benefits to your production will be worth it.

- Be aware of the codes and conventions of your chosen format and genre. For example, a DVD cover should incorporate the typical features of the text. Don't forget the smaller details, the design of the spine, for example, or the industry information on the back cover.

- The back of a DVD cover is as complex in its layout and design and use of images as the front. For this reason and for the purposes of this unit, a DVD cover counts as two pages.

- Remember to use the texts analysed in your Research Investigation as a guide. Do you intend to subvert or replicate your findings? Consider how you intend to do this.

Exam Tip

Plan the time you have to create your production texts carefully. Build in time to sort out possible problems and to become familiar with the technology.

MS3 Production approaches: Creating a print artefact

The posters here were produced as a result of the findings of a Research Investigation focusing on the representation of women in horror films. The primary research was a series of posters for the film *Jennifer's Body*.

Daryl Smith of Cardiff and Vale College

Key Points

▶ There is clear evidence that the research findings have been used to create these posters. The student has chosen to replicate the codes and conventions of the posters for *Jennifer's Body* analysed in the Research Investigation.

▶ The iconography, visual codes and technical codes all clearly signify the horror genre.

▶ The construction of the main images featuring the female character replicate the representation constructed in the film posters for *Jennifer's Body*. A range of images is used and replication is avoided. In the evaluation the inclusion of these images alongside those of the poster for *Jennifer's Body* would demonstrate clearly how the research findings had impacted upon this production.

▶ The technical and creative skills demonstrated are sophisticated. There is particularly creative use of font style and language establishing the genre effectively.

▶ The photographs are original and there is evidence that the composition has been well planned for maximum effect.

▶ There is also evidence of post-production editing, for example the blood on the posters, further emphasising technical competence.

An evaluation

The A2 evaluation is very different in content and structure from the report completed at AS and you must be aware of this and establish the correct focus. The evaluation is NOT an evaluation of process, but an evaluation of the link between the Research Investigation and the production. The evaluation must focus on the key decisions that you made as a result of your Research Investigation findings and how they impacted upon your production work. For example, the evaluation may focus on your key findings and then highlight examples within your production or it may focus on key elements used within the production and relate these back to your research findings.

How do I demonstrate the links between the Research Investigation and the Production?

- Think of four or five key elements that you found out as a result of your investigation. This will help to focus your evaluation.

- Identify clearly how you then used these in your own production. These could be: particular camera shots, editing techniques, layout and design, narrative construction, genre codes and conventions including visual codes and iconography.

- It is helpful to visually demonstrate the links, for example including an image of your magazine front cover alongside the magazine cover you analysed in your investigation, or including screenshots from your opening sequence to illustrate how you used similar shots to the investigation texts.

- If you worked as part of a group, you must focus on how you demonstrated the findings of your Research Investigation in the production text.

- It may be relevant to refer to the secondary sources you used in your Research Investigation.

Exam Tip

The evaluation must be 500–700 words in length. You must therefore be consise and clear. Do not exceed the word limit.

Example of an opening of an evaluation

For my MS3 coursework I conducted an investigation into the representation of youth in British films. This investigation was focused on two texts: Billy Elliot and Eden Lake. As a result of my investigation I discovered:

- *the effect of selected mediation and construction techniques on the representations in the films*

- *the determination of representation based upon genre*

- *the issue of youth representation as a product of stereotypical ideologies of youth culture.*

To present my findings I produced a trailer for a social realist film focusing on two young men trying to make their way in the music business. I aimed to create a product that conformed to the conventions of its genre whilst challenging the traditional representations of young people apparent in this genre.

Exam Tip

Starting your evaluation with a short bullet pointed list of your key findings will help to focus your evaluation.

MS3 Summary

Research Investigation

- Must be 1400–1800 words – it is important that this word limit is adhered to. It is worth 45 marks.

- Must focus on one of: narrative, genre, representation.

- The investigation must include primary and secondary research. The best essays will achieve a balance between the two.

- Secondary research must be drawn from a range of sources including books, articles, Internet sites, etc.

- You must be discriminating in the sources you use and remember that this is an academic essay.

- All sources must be correctly acknowledged and referenced either in footnotes or a page of notes at the end of the essay.

- The Research Investigation must be written in continuous prose and demonstrate an ability to structure ideas in a logical and coherent manner.

Production

- This must develop from and be informed by the findings of the Research Investigation.

- It must be in a different form from the AS production.

- Audio-visual productions can be completed as part of a group and should be up to four minutes in length. Each member of the group must have a technical role and be able to demonstrate their research findings.

- Print productions must be completed individually and should be a minimum of three pages.

Evaluation

- This must be 500–700 words in length and is worth 10 marks.

- This has a clear focus – it must explore how the production has been informed by the research findings. It must not be a discussion of the production process or of strengths and weaknesses.

- It can include bullet points and annotated images to support the points made.

- The research findings and primary research texts must be referred to throughout the evaluation.

You will also need to complete a cover sheet MS3/1. See the example at the end of this section. Here you will outline the main points from your Research Investigation, explain your production including your individual technical contribution if you worked in a group and state the main areas of your evaluation. Both you and your teacher must sign this sheet. You are signing to say that it is your own work. The detailed completion of this sheet is very important.

To be completed by the candidate
AS Production: indicate what you produced for your AS production (MS2)
I produced an opening sequence of a new television crime drama.
Research Investigation: title
Are women represented in a sexualised way in music videos? With close reference to Snoop Dogg Sexual Seduction, Rhianna Umbrella and Beyonce If I Were a Boy.
Production (including details of your contribution to group work where relevant)
For my production I decided to create a music video that incorporated a range of generic devices including direct mode of address from the artist, narrative interpretation of the song lyrics and footage of the artist in performance. I worked on my own and I was responsible for planning, filming and editing the video. I used a track by Cindi Lauper as it seemed to suggest a more positive and powerful female representation.
Evaluation: brief summary of how research informed production
I analysed a range of different music videos to investigate how women were represented in a sexual way. In Sexual Seduction women are represented as objects and accessories to the male artist, they are secondary performers and overly sexualised. This was also true of Rhianna who, as a main performer and supposedly in control of her image is still represented in a very sexual way in order to promote her music. Beyonce, in If I Were A Boy offers a more thoughtful and challenging representation that contains a message about women in society. As a result of my findings I decided to produce a music video that constructed a more positive representation of a female artist who is not sexualised and who is in control of her life.

NOTICE TO CANDIDATE
The work you submit for assessment must be your own.

If you copy from someone else, allow another candidate to copy from you, or if you cheat in any other way, including plagiarising material, you may be disqualified from at least the subject concerned.

Declaration by Candidate

I have read and understood the **Notice to Candidate** (above). I have produced the attached work without assistance other than that which my teacher has explained is acceptable within the specification.

Signature

Date

This form *must* be completed by all candidates and *must* accompany work submitted for moderation.

MS4 is the examination unit of A2 Media Studies. This unit will develop from the work you have done at AS and contributes to a **synoptic assessment** bringing together all areas of the course. You will be required to demonstrate your understanding of the connections between different elements of the specification and to demonstrate your knowledge and understanding of the relationship between the media texts you study, the audiences that consume and respond to them and the industries which produce and distribute them. In your lessons you will explore a range of industries and the texts that are produced by those industries.

Content – what will I study?

In your lessons you will be required to study three different media industries from the list below:

- Television
- Radio
- Film
- Music
- Newspaper
- Magazine (including comics)
- Advertising
- Computer games.

For each industry you will focus on three main texts from the selected industry. There are rules to follow regarding the texts you are allowed to study:

- At least two of the chosen main texts must be contemporary (produced within the last 5 years).
- One of the texts must be British.

It is suggested that the texts that you study are contrasting texts so that you can demonstrate a broad understanding of your chosen industry. For example, if one of your chosen industries was Television and you studied three crime dramas, your ability to show your understanding of the television industry as a whole and its output may be severely limited.

What constitutes a text?

This varies according to the industry and the key aim of the specification is to ensure parity across all industries:

- Television – three main programmes. It may be that you will look at extracts from other texts as part of your preparation, but you need to have studied three main contrasting

Key Term

Synoptic assessment = Synoptic assessment encourages students to combine elements of their learning from different parts of a course and to show their accumulated knowledge and understanding of a topic or subject area. It helps to test a student's ability to apply the knowledge and understanding gained in one part of a course to increase their understanding in other areas. For example, the research and writing of the MS3 Research Investigation may help in your understanding of an MS4 text or industry.

texts and you must be able to analyse them in specific detail.

- Radio – like television, three main radio programmes, not a presenter or a station.

- Film – three main contrasting texts. You may also study related texts, for example the trailer and posters for the films, to allow you to answer all areas of the paper.

- Music – with this industry it is the **artist** that is the text. You will study the artist through the texts they produce. For example, if your chosen artist is Beyonce, then you will study a range of texts including CD covers, music videos, music magazines, etc.

- Newspaper – three main newspapers, although you may look at more initially to gain an understanding of the style of the publication. The expectation is that you will have studied all of each of the newspapers including, for example, the editorial and key features and not just the front pages.

- Magazine – three main magazines/comics that allow you to show your understanding of the breadth of this industry. As with newspapers, your analysis should not be just confined to the front covers and you should also be able to discuss other production areas, for example the magazine's website.

- Advertising – three main advertising **campaigns**, not just single adverts. Choose a campaign that has at least 3–4 advertisements as part of it, for example two print adverts and two television adverts. If the campaign has more than this, then focus on 3–4.

- Computer games – the focus must be three main contrasting games although you will, as with other industries, study related texts that will allow you to discuss marketing and promotional strategies.

Key Term

Grid = This appears on the front on the examination paper and must be completed after you have read the questions. It is there to ensure that you think about your choices and that you only use one industry for each question.

How will I be assessed?

The MS4 unit is assessed through a written examination of two and a half hours. The paper is divided into two sections: A and B. You must answer three questions, one from Section A and two from Section B. You must use a different industry for each question. You must discuss all of your three main texts in your response. There will be a **grid** to fill in on the front of the paper to identify your choices.

Section A: Text

You must choose one question out of two in this section and answer it using one of your industries and the three main texts you have prepared for that industry. The focus of this section is Text and that will incorporate:

- Genre: the generic codes and conventions related to your main texts. Consider whether your texts reinforce or subvert typical conventions.

- Narrative: the narrative structures and techniques appropriate to your three main texts.

- Representations: the main representations contained within your three main texts. These may be different for each text, or the same and may be: people, places or events/issues.

Exam Tip

You must spend some time at the beginning of the examination reading **all** of the questions carefully. Many students do not do this and therefore make the wrong decisions.

Section B: Industry and Audience

You must choose two questions from four in this section. You must not use the industry and texts you used for Section A. Although you may be more familiar with the 'text' and 'audience' elements of your main texts, you must prepare adequately for this section of the paper. You may be required to answer questions on the following areas related to your industry.

Industry

- Production – this should include links with digital technologies
- Distribution and exhibition (where relevant)
- Marketing and promotion
- Regulation issues
- Global Implications
- Relevant historical background and context – this should be brief and relevant.

Audience/Users

- Targeting
- Positioning
- Responses and interaction – this must include literal and theoretical responses
- Debates surrounding the relationship between the audience and the text.

What can I do to help myself?

- Revise the work you did at AS, it will help you when you come to study your A2 texts, the audience and the industry.
- Use past papers and practise choosing and **'unpicking' questions** and planning answers.
- Practise writing responses. It is important that you can demonstrate that you can construct a coherent response. Essay-writing skills are very important and must not be overlooked.
- Make sure that in your preparation and revision you have selected key examples from your texts for the different areas of the examination paper. You cannot write about all of the text, you must be selective.
- Ensure that you are prepared for all areas of the paper. For example, you could research the marketing and promotional examples for your main texts independently.
- Ensure that you have a broad understanding of the industry that goes beyond the primary analysis of your chosen texts.

Key Term

Unpicking questions = Many students make mistakes in their responses because they have not read the question carefully. Unpicking the question may involve underlining key words or phrases to ensure that your focus is appropriate.

Exam Tip

Remember to try to include an introduction and a conclusion in your response.

Exam Tip

Your aim in your response to the questions is to demonstrate your understanding of the industry, not just the texts. Your analysis of your main texts is the way in which you can illustrate your knowledge of the industry.

MS4

The Television Industry

Key Terms

Channel identity = That which makes the channel recognisable to audiences and different from any other channel. Presenters, stars, programme genres and specific programmes all help to contribute to a channel's identity.

Ethos = This is what the channel believes in and what it sees as its role. The ethos is usually set out in the channel's charter. Channel 4 outlines its ethos: *'Channel 4 is the UK's only publicly-owned, commercially-funded public service broadcaster, with a remit to be innovative, experimental and distinctive.'* www.channel4.com

Idents = This is the channel's 'ident**ification**'. The ident is a short visual image that works as a logo for the channel. It appears before the programme on channels like BBC1 and 2. BBC2 is famous for its animated '2' ident.

quickfire

⑪ Consider the impact of the different formats of television viewing on the industry.

Exam Tip

Try to develop a broad understanding of the television industry before embarking upon an analysis of your key text. This helps you to place the text within the industry.

Introduction

In studying this industry in preparation for the MS4 examination you will need to ensure that you have a broad and up-to-date understanding. Your main texts must allow you to demonstrate that understanding. Remember, it is helpful if your texts are varied and diverse; this way you will illustrate effectively your awareness of a range of issues related to the industry. The television industry is constantly changing, never more so than now as we are in the digital revolution. The link between the text, the audience and the industry is still closely related, but the way in which audiences access and respond to television texts has changed dramatically in recent years.

Channel identities

Each television **channel** has a distinct **identity** and appeals to different audiences. This is evident in the programmes they produce and the way in which they market themselves to those audiences. This identity has been built up over time and audiences have expectations of particular channels. The programmes produced and commissioned by the channel are often indicative of the channel's identity and **ethos**.

Task: researching channel identity

Choose a channel to research. This could relate directly to your main texts. Create a PowerPoint presentation about your chosen channel summing up the key points from your research and giving information about:

- The general profile of the channel
- The structure and organisation
- The ethos and identity
- Flagship programmes
- Scheduling decisions and techniques employed by the channel
- Marketing strategies, for example trailers, **idents**, etc.
- Include reference to the key texts where appropriate
- Up-to-date news related to the channel.

Scheduling

Scheduling is the decisions made by channels regarding where to place programmes in terms of the day and the time. The aim in constructing the schedule is to secure high ratings for the channel and for specific programmes.

It is the job of schedulers and planners to ensure the programmes are placed in such a way that they attract the greatest audience. However, scheduling is not as important as it was since the introduction of **time shifted viewing** in the 1980s. Audiences now watch programmes in different ways; they may record a programme on one channel and watch another channel, watch it on DVD or on a phone or tablet. Nevertheless, with the apparent return of **event television**, there are certain programmes that attract an audience who watch as it is broadcast.

Although it is diminishing due to technological advancements, there are still instances of **water-cooler television** programmes. Social media also play a part in generating excitement about certain programmes where an audience may tweet their responses before, during and after the programme. This may encourage audiences to watch the programme during the original programming slot and not at a later date where they will not be able to be a part of the discussion. Many programmes have created Facebook pages and Twitter feeds in order to build a fan base for their product. However, this can be a problem internationally where, for example, Britain may be one series behind an American programme like *CSI Miami*. Owing to the global nature of social media and the Internet, spoilers appear, which detract from the appeal of the programme.

The aim of television schedulers is to use a range of techniques to keep audiences watching that channel. These include:

- Broadcasting trailers and teasers for a programme during the day.

- Pre-echo – scheduling a less popular programme before a more popular one in the hope of catching viewers who may watch earlier.

- Hammocking – placing a new or less popular show on between two popular shows in the hope that the audience will watch through.

- Inheritance – putting a new or less popular show after a programme with high ratings in the hope that viewers will watch it and the programmes will therefore 'inherit' the audience.

- Stripping – broadcasting a programme at the same time every day/week. This ensures that audiences become familiar with the scheduling time and know when to watch. This technique is used for soap operas and news programmes, for example.

- Zoning – this is where programmes of a similar genre are broadcast one after the other on a particular channel. The assumption is that fans of the genre will stay with that channel. Five use this to broadcast their American crime programmes.

- Offensive scheduling – this is where a channel is confident that their programme will gain higher ratings then a programme on a rival channel so they broadcast it at the same time in order to lure the 'live' audience.

- Defensive scheduling – this is where a channel is aware that a programme on a rival channel will bring in high audience figures. They may decide to schedule a programme of minority appeal at this time.

Industry: regulation

The Communications Act of 2003 established Ofcom as the new UK regulator. Previously the role had been held by a range of different regulatory bodies. Accountable to Parliament, Ofcom are involved in advising and setting some of the more technical aspects of regulation, and implementing and enforcing the law. Ofcom is funded by fees from industry for regulating broadcasting and communications networks, and grant-in-aid from the government.

The role of Ofcom with regard to broadcasting in brief is:

- To ensure that a wide range of television services of high quality and wide appeal are available.

12 Why is social media important to television companies?

Task

Analyse a scheduling guide for one week. What examples of scheduling techniques can be found?

- To maintain **plurality** in the provision of broadcasting.
- To adequately protect audiences against offensive or harmful material.
- To protect audiences against unfairness or infringement of privacy.

Channels like the BBC, for example, are also self-regulatory. They work with producers to ensure that there will be no need for Ofcom to intervene except in extreme circumstances.

An audience member can complain to Ofcom regarding a particular programme that they may deem offensive or harmful, and audience pressure over certain programmes can often be a successful form of regulation. When Ofcom receives a complaint, it assesses it under the terms of The Broadcasting Code and decides what action to take. Ofcom produces a regular Broadcast Bulletin reporting on the complaints received and decisions taken.

Industry: issues and debates

- Can public service broadcasting survive?
- Should the licence fee be **top-sliced** to protect channels like, for example, Channel 4 that has a public service broadcasting remit?
- With advertisers moving to other platforms, in what other ways can commercial television be funded?
- Will the current financial crisis mean the death of innovative, creative television with high production values in favour of cheaper, easy to make, safe formats?
- What effect will the increased diversity of viewing experiences have upon financing and programming?

Industry: the BBC

The BBC is a **public service broadcaster**; along with other channels it is required to provide a range of programmes to satisfy all tastes. The BBC differs from other broadcasters in that it is funded by the licence fee, not by advertising and therefore, in theory, is a true public service broadcaster and as such has a greater responsibility to offer programmes that cater for diverse audiences. However, all channels must operate some elements of public service broadcasting, even those who do not levy a licence fee. This means, for example, they must be **impartial** in their coverage of news and current affairs and must include a proportion of news and educational programmes in their schedule. In the early days of television its role was seen by Lord Reith, the first Director General, to 'inform, educate and entertain'. Nowadays, the criticism is that channels are too governed by commercial interests making them most interested in producing popular programmes that attract wide audiences. This means that they can charge higher prices to advertisers whose revenue funds the commercial channels. Ironically, the BBC, despite its public service remit, must also be seen to produce programmes that attract large audiences to justify its existence.

The Broadcasting Research Unit lists the following as the characteristics of a public service broadcaster:

- Geographic universality – broadcasts are available nationwide.
- Caters for all interests and tastes – an example would be the BBC's digital channels and Channel 4.
- Caters for minority audiences.

- Produces impartial programming which is detached from agencies like advertisers and the government.

- One broadcasting system that is directly funded by the users.

- Has a concern for national identity and community – commissions programmes from within the country.

- Quality not quantity is the prime concern. This is becoming increasingly problematic in the current financial situation where at ITV and Channel 4 (a publisher-broadcaster) programmes have been cut and even the BBC has had to consider the programmes it can afford to fund. That said, the BBC still funds such programmes as *Africa*, which have a high budget due to their content and production values and can therefore be seen to justify the licence fee.

- Liberates programme makers and does not restrict them – public service broadcasters on the whole provide guidelines, not rules that govern programme makers.

In the modern world, the television industry, whether following commercial or public service interests, is very competitive. It is becoming an increasing challenge for a public service broadcaster to survive amongst commercial opponents, **audience segmentation** and the increased number of digital channels.

(14) Why is public service broadcasting important?

(15) How can you tell that the BBC is less governed by commercial interests?

Main text: *Strictly Come Dancing* (BBC1)

Strictly Come Dancing is a British television show featuring celebrities with professional dance partners competing in a range of dances. The title of the show has a link with the long-running series *Come Dancing* and alludes also to the film *Strictly Ballroom*. It is presented by Tess Daly and Bruce Forsyth.

Strictly Come Dancing: industry information

- The show has run on BBC1 since 2004. It has traditionally taken the Saturday early evening 'family' slot and attracts a broad audience.

- In 2009 it changed its scheduling time to go 'head to head' with *The X Factor*. This did not prove to be a successful scheduling move. In 2010 it operated **defensive scheduling** and was scheduled before *The X Factor* to maximise its audience. In November 2012 the show stretched its lead in the ratings war with *X Factor* by more than two million – its biggest for six years.

- *Strictly Come Dancing*, unlike *The X Factor*, has seen its ratings rise each year. On 3 November 2012 *Strictly* pulled in a 9.8 million average, which was 200,000 up on the previous week.

Key Term

Defensive scheduling = This is where a channel may not feel that their programme can gain higher ratings than a programme on a rival channel. They may decide to save the programme for a time when they can gain a larger audience, therefore adopting a defensive strategy. This is easier to do for BBC as the commercial channels tend to publish their schedules earlier so that advertisers can bid for slots in suitable programmes.

- There have also been seven standalone Christmas specials.

- In December 2012 *Strictly's* ratings had risen to 13.37 million and over 13 million for the Sunday results show. This was over 4 million higher than the third placed *Eastenders,* demonstrating its continued audience appeal.

- It is filmed in front of a studio audience and the music is provided by a live orchestra.

- The show is broadcast from a specially constructed set at the BBC. The set had a re-vamp in 2010 with the introduction of the 'Tess Tower' where Tess Daly interviews the competitors after their dance. However, in the first two series, shows were also filmed at the Tower Ballroom, Blackpool where the original *Come Dancing* series was filmed in the 1970s. Since then the show has returned to this ballroom for one of the episodes.

- During the series run there is a spin-off programme *It Takes Two* on BBC2. This programme runs every week night during the series and gives updates on rehearsals and offers interviews, behind the scenes filming and gossip. In 2011 the regular presenter Claudia Winkleman stepped down to be replaced by DJ Zoe Ball, a previous contestant and the presenter of the live tour.

Key Term

Flagship programme = This is a programme that is important to a channel as it has high ratings and is recognised by audiences as belonging to that channel. It may also signify the ethos of the channel.

Exam Tip

Some of this industry information is useful for an audience question; for example, ratings figures can support a discussion of literal audience responses.

Industry: marketing

Strictly Come Dancing, as we have established, is a **flagship programme** for the BBC. Each new series is anticipated by audiences, and the media 'hype' begins well in advance to whet the audience's appetite:

- Trailers for the new series exhibiting high production values usually appear well before the launch night. In 2012 they were broadcast before the announcements about which celebrity was partnering which professional dancer, introducing a 'teaser' effect for the audience with the slogan: 'The stars are ready. Are you?' There was also a trailer introducing the judges and showcasing their particular dancing talents emphasising their credibility and range of experience.

- There is also usually massive coverage in the press including the front page of listings magazines like *The Radio Times* and gossip magazines. In 2012 *The Radio Times* ran two different front covers in the same week, one featuring the women celebrities and one the men. Also in 2012, Lisa Riley commanded a lot of press coverage as the first female contestant to lift a male partner as did the representation of Olympic

Stills from Strictly Come Dancing, BBC1 (2012)

stars Victoria Pendleton and Louis Smith. There were also articles in newspapers – broadsheet and tabloid. This press coverage continues throughout the series as contestants break down, fall out and win the nation's hearts!

- The series also has its own website with news and comment including 'Tweets', a blog, a quiz, behind the scenes footage, and the opportunity to sign up for a newsletter. This encourages the audience to interact with the programme between episodes and to feel part of the *Strictly* family.

- There is also a range of merchandise available including the usual calendars and T-shirts as well as, new for 2012, a Dress Up and Dance game and a range of *Strictly* make up in conjunction with *Boots*.

- Between series there is a live tour that travels around the country featuring past celebrities from the programme. This sold 213,000 tickets in 2011.

quickfire

(16) **Why is it important to use a range of strategies to market established programmes like *Strictly Come Dancing*?**

Task

Find examples of the marketing strategies used by the series of *Strictly Come Dancing* you are studying.

Industry: global implications

Because of the formulaic structure of *Strictly Come Dancing*, it is easily exportable globally. The subject matter of dancing is also one that transfers easily between cultures – different countries can adhere to the format whilst also changing it to suit their audience. This may be done through the choice of celebrities or the dance focus.

Strictly Come Dancing is sold to 43 countries through the corporation's commercial arm, BBC Worldwide, making it one of the channel's most successful exports, earning the BBC tens of millions of pounds. *Dancing with the Stars* (DWTS), is the international format of *Strictly Come Dancing*. It's estimated that more than 250m people have watched a local version of the show and it is one of the first Western TV formats ever to be licensed in the People's Republic of China.

Dancing with the Stars: Thailand, MCL/Kantana (2012)

In the US, *DWTS* is now in its sixteenth series and is a ratings winner for ABC. The 2013 'stars' announced recently demonstrate a similar formula to the UK version; an NFL player, a singer, an Olympian, a comedian, a reality television star and a boxer. Judges Bruno Tonioli and Len Goodman also appear on the US version of the show.

France produced a second series of *Danse Avec Les Stars*, seen by over 5m viewers with a 25.2% market share for the final. In India, Jhalak Dikhla Jaa (the local version of

⑰ Why is *Strictly Come Dancing* popular with a global audience?

Task

Look at some clips from the format in other countries on YouTube. What formulaic features have been changed? How has the country adapted the format to suit its audience?

Key Terms

Hybrid genre = These are media texts that incorporate features of more than one genre, for example a romantic comedy.

Genre-specific lexis = This is where the media text includes language that an audience would associate with that particular genre.

Caricature = A comically exaggerated representation that makes the person appear 'larger than life'.

Repertoire of elements = These are the key features that distinguish one genre from another.

Dancing with the Stars) was commissioned by local entertainment channel Colors for two years and season four won the Best General Entertainment Programme at the Asian Television Awards.

Australia was the first country to adapt the show and other countries have recognisable formats. The latest country to buy the format is Thailand where the first showing of the programme was in 2012.

The BBC closely regulates the format once it is sold. When the format is bought by another country, a BBC producer goes to that country to ensure that the programme produced stays within the remit and maintains the spirit of *Strictly Come Dancing*. In 2011 the BBC took legal action against a controversial version of the programme aired on an Italian television channel.

In 2012 *Strictly Come Dancing* announced branded cruises with P&O, which will feature TV judge Craig Revel Horwood. In the US, a new *Dancing with the Stars* live show was developed and opened in Las Vegas in April 2012.

Text: genre

Strictly Come Dancing is an example of a **hybrid genre** incorporating aspects of reality TV and entertainment. It also includes codes and conventions relating to a competitive programme; for example, presenters, judges, contestants, voting, challenges and elimination rounds. The competitive element is emphasised regularly throughout the programme. The codes and conventions of the reality television genre are evident in the short documentary style films that preview the dancing couple each week. Here, hand-held cameras are used and the mode of address is direct. There is also **genre-specific lexis**; the judges and presenters comment on dance moves and steps, styles, etc. This use of language also serves to demonstrate their credibility and knowledge and justifies the decisions they make.

Characters

The 'characters' are recognisable and in some cases, established. The celebrity dancers are from a range of sport, entertainment and the media. They are chosen to ensure that they appeal to a broad audience. The judges are the 'experts' and in establishing their own styles they have almost become stereotypical **caricatures** with expected patterns of behaviour. This is played on by the programme's makers; for example, the grumpiness of Craig Revel Horwood and the paternal approach of Len Goodman. The presenters, Tess Daly and Bruce Forsyth, complement each other and their seemingly easy relationship attracts a range of audiences. Claudia Winkleman, replacing Bruce Forsyth in 2010, added a new dimension to the Sunday night results programme giving it a different style and appeal.

Setting and iconography

The **repertoire of elements** of the entertainment genre are evident in the iconography of ballroom dancing – the glitter ball, glamorous costumes linked to the style of the dance, a performance stage and a live audience. The setting is reminiscent of a 1950s dance hall and indeed, one of the episodes is usually filmed at the Tower Ballroom in Blackpool.

Other settings include the 'Tess Tower', a recent introduction to the programme; this is where the other contestants can look down upon the dance floor and where Tess Daly conducts her interviews while waiting for the judges' scores. It is a less formal environment and allows the audience to hear the analysis of performance from the dance couples. Another informal setting is the practice space seen on the short documentary films; this usually contains the iconography of a dance studio including a barre and mirrors.

Technical and audio codes

Owing to the hybridity of the genre, the technical and audio codes are many and varied, adapted to suit the programme's different styles. The technical codes also help to convey the narrative by, for example, showing the expressions on the faces of the judges and the contestants and by continually cutting to the studio audience to show audience members – these often include well-known celebrities. The camera constantly reminds the audience at home of the studio audience, thus making them feel part of the 'event'. When the judges give their scores the screen splits so that the audience can see the reaction shots of the contestants. The camera shots and editing employed in the dance sequences again ensure audience involvement as the dancing couple are tracked around the dance floor, or seen from above with an **'apparently impossible position'** shot. The long shots remind the audience of the genre taking in the set, the dance floor, the couples, the orchestra and singers and the studio audience.

In the short documentary sequences the aim of the technical codes is to establish an **observational documentary** style combining a **fly on the wall** filming technique with direct audience address. A hand-held camera is often used to help to create realism. The sequence often starts with an establishing shot, usually of the dance studio, to suggest that this is more informal, this is reinforced with the natural lighting and the often echoing sound. The editing of the sequence produces a carefully constructed narrative.

The audio codes employed include the music, which is played live, and also the audience responses. This may include cheers and clapping but does almost descend into pantomime when the audience boo the judges if they are unhappy with their comments. The recognisable theme tune heralds the start of the programme and is part of the programme's branding. The dialogue between the judges, and Bruce Forsyth's catchphrases encouraging audience involvement are also generic audio conventions of the programme that audiences expect to hear each week and have become iconic features of the programme.

Exam Tip

When discussing the genre of a text ensure that you cover the key elements of characters, setting and iconography, narrative and technical and audio codes. Remember to support your points with specific examples from the programme you have studied as your main text.

Key Terms

Apparently impossible position = This is where the camera gives the audience a view of the action from an unusual position. In this case, from above the dance floor. Audiences tend to accept this view if it enhances their enjoyment of the text.

Observational documentary = This is where the camera follows the subject around and 'observes' their behaviour and activities.

Fly on the wall = This technique of filming aims to be as unobtrusive as possible so seemingly producing a 'true' representation of reality. The camera is therefore as if it were a 'fly on the wall', watching events without being noticed.

quickfire

⑱ How do the technical and audio codes enhance the audience's enjoyment of the programme?

Text: narrative

Strictly Come Dancing establishes a formulaic narrative structure that does not change from week to week, or series to series. Audiences have an expectation of what will happen that is built up through familiarity with the format: Bruce Forsyth and Tess Daly come down the steps, have a little chat and a dance, Bruce makes jokes usually incorporating some of his favourite catch phrases, the judges are introduced, the contestants come down the steps and so the programme develops adhering to the established pattern.

However, the narrative features and **plot situations** do undergo changes; for example, 'The Dance Off' was scrapped in 2010 and the decision about who would leave the show was made purely on the phone votes from viewers. Then, after concerns that too much decision making lay in the hands of the audience it was reintroduced in 2012.

In 2010 a 'themed' programme appeared for Halloween – a new technique to keep audiences interested mid-way through the run. This was developed in 2011 and 2012 where a 'Broadway' theme was also used. In 2012 a new challenge was set whereby the contestants had to incorporate two dance styles in one routine. This also helped to reinforce the 'competition' genre of the programme and to maintain the attention and interest of the audience. Audiences like the recognisable but they also like small changes from year to year to maintain their interest.

Dancers in the 2012 Halloween special

There are also separate mini-narratives constructed through the footage of the contestants in rehearsal where the audience are encouraged to follow their highs and lows through the series. This reinforces the generic hybridity of the programme – this section is filmed in an observational documentary style encouraging the audience to think they are being given special access to the lives of the performers.

These narratives also manipulate the audience and place them in a **privileged spectator position**. They also **manipulate time and space** giving the audience a flashback of what happened the previous week and highlights from the week's rehearsals. Within this narrative the celebrities and the professional dancers adopt a direct mode of address and a confessional manner in order to further involve the audience. The short narratives will differ from couple to couple and the audience's emotions are manipulated as they laugh along and empathise with the participants. Within the overall structure of the programme, the documentary episodes vary in their construction. One designed to create empathy in the audience for a contestant having a particularly hard week will be followed by one with an upbeat storyline. They also serve to create enigmas for the audience as they anticipate their performance in the dance that is to follow.

Key Terms

Plot situations = Elements that are part of the narrative and that an audience will expect to see in a particular text; for example, the judges giving their feedback.

Privileged spectator position = Where the camera places the audience in a superior position within the narrative. The audience can then anticipate what will follow.

Manipulation of time and space = Where the narrative shapes the text through space and time. In this programme we are transported back in time to a week earlier and are then given 'snapshots' in time across a week in the lives of the dancing couples.

Exam Tip

Narrative may be a focus for a Section A question. Make sure that you can make a range of relevant points about your three main texts. Avoid making the same points three times.

Text: representation

This text is rich in terms of examples of representation. Whichever series you are studying there will be a range of representation areas for you to discuss.

Representation: age

The joint presenters Bruce Forsyth and Tess Daly are well chosen to appeal to an audience range. However, in previous series there has been controversy over the 'sacking' of Arlene Phillips amid rumours that it was because she was too old. This led to criticism of the BBC and allegations that the BBC discriminates against women in television because of their age. Harriet Harman, the then government's Minister for Women and Equality, called for her to be reinstated.

However, in each series, there are also usually positive examples of older contestants whose experience is commented on. This is often also followed up in the press and women's magazines. Some 'older' contestants, particularly women, are seen as aspirational for the older female audience, for example Lulu in 2011. In 2012 Fern Britton was seen to be a very positive role model for older women and was presented in the media generally as such. She was a good choice as she already appeared regularly in women's magazines and was a recognisable celebrity for the more mature woman. However, her alternative representation in the programme was as a 'cougar' who was interested in the younger men. This was the focus of the promotional trailer as seen in the image where Britton has her hands on the legs of the young men and was developed during the programme through the on screen relationship with her dancing partner, a much younger man. It is also the case, as in other media texts, that the representation of the 'older woman' is ambiguous, particularly in magazines and newspapers covering the programme. These texts, instead of celebrating the older woman, focus instead upon 'how good they are for their age' or their answer to staying young, or debates around the 'work' they have had done. Alternatively, the experience of the 'older man' is viewed more positively at times, particularly if they are a 'sporting legend'. However, older contestants have also been represented as figures of fun; for example, in the past, Ann Widdecombe and John Sergeant. Interestingly, audiences chose to vote these contestants in week after week because of their entertainment value.

Representation: gender

In every series of *Strictly Come Dancing* there is the usual range of glamorous females and sporty, good-looking men. However, there have, in the past, also been less stereotypically attractive and successful contestants like Johnny Ball and Lisa Riley and in each series the contestants usually cover a wide range of ages, shapes and sizes! This is in order for the programme to reach a broad audience. Interestingly, in terms of

Exam Tip

Remember not to just describe the representation or to define it in terms of positive or negative. You must show your understanding of how the representation is constructed and mediated and its effect upon the audience.

Exam Tip

In the opening paragraph of your answer establish what you understand by representation incorporating appropriate media terms.

(19) How is age represented in the series of *Strictly Come Dancing* you are analysing?

Key Term

Sexual objectification =
Refers to the practice of regarding a person as an object to be viewed only in terms of their sexual appeal and with no consideration of any other aspect of their character or personality.

QuickFire

⑳ How typical of *Strictly Come Dancing* are the representations of gender in the two images here?

Task

Consider the different representations of genre in your main *Strictly* text. How is that representation constructed through visual and technical codes?

representation of gender, in this programme the men as well as women are seen, at times, to be **sexually objectified** and are frequently represented in terms of their body image and attractiveness. In 2010, Gavin Henson, the rugby player was represented very much in terms of his body and even danced without a shirt. Louis Smith was represented in a similar way in 2012. The female audience are encouraged to engage with the male contestants in a voyeuristic way by the technical codes, editing and the comments of the judges and presenters. Bruce Forsyth often comments on the reactions of the females in the audience to a particular male contestant's physique or dance moves. The costumes in *Strictly* have been the subject of complaints from viewers where they have been seen to be too revealing for an early evening family show. Interestingly, in 2012, much was made of Victoria Pendleton's well toned physique, a focus normally reserved for male contestants.

Victoria Pendleton subverted the traditional representation in other ways, whilst most women who appear on the programme appear in the press because they have lost weight, Victoria Pendleton was sad to lose her muscle tone and weight gained through cycling. The Daily Mail reported:

'... asked if she feels more feminine now she has toned down the athletic physique that powered her to victory in the velodrome, she said: "No. That's not me."

"I have spent my whole life trying to get bigger, musclier thighs, and now they are just disappearing in front of my very eyes, daily. It is going to take some time to get used to it."'

www.thedailymail.co.uk. For the article go to tinyurl.com/knclypz

Audience

- *Strictly Come Dancing* is an established programme that targets a family audience and is part of the BBC's attempt to re-introduce 'event television'. It is zoned with other family programmes, for example *Dr Who* and *Merlin*, in the hope of sustaining the early evening audience.

- The programme encourages audience interactivity. They are able to vote for their favourite couple and so feel involved in the decisions about who stays and who goes. They can also be active through the red button, selecting what aspects of the programme to watch or listening to a commentary from a celebrity. There is some evidence that suggests that this active response extends to people taking dance classes as a result of their involvement in the programme.

The emotion of the Results Show

- They can also be involved in interactive activities via the website. Blogs, chat forums and emails are a good example of literal audience responses to the programme.

- The contestants are carefully chosen to appeal to a wide range of audiences, for example a soap star, an actor, a singer, a sports personality, etc. When they are introduced the celebrities are defined by their job or celebrity areas so that audiences can recognise and engage with them. Different audiences will have their favourites and want to follow their fortunes.

- Audiences are encouraged to become involved with the judges – they may like or hate them. They have an expectation of their responses and like to feel that the judges regularly behave in a particular way.

- The presenters are recognisable and will bring in their own fan base – this is especially true of Bruce Forsyth.

- This is a reality/entertainment/talent hybrid television show and as such contains many of the conventions of these genres and encourages the usual 'water-cooler' moments for audiences.

- The audience has expectations of the genre as now it is a well-established show. They like to have their expectations realised.

- The audience is positioned to become emotionally involved with the contestants through the 'fly on the wall' filming of rehearsals where they are shown to be upset, angry, struggling, etc. Narratives are constructed for the audiences to encourage this involvement.

- In terms of the **uses and gratifications theory**, *Strictly Come Dancing* offers entertainment and diversion though the romance and excitement of the dances and the involvement with the contestants. It also offers social interaction as it is 'of the moment' and discussed by audiences as it happens.

Key Term

Uses and gratifications theory = This theory suggests that active audiences seek out and use different media texts in order to satisfy a need and experience different pleasures.

21 What pleasures does *Strictly Come Dancing* offer audiences?

Summary: The Television Industry

APPEAL AND TARGETING

Scheduling time

Choice of celebs

Presenters

Themed episodes

Interactivity

USES AND GRATIFICATIONS

Escapism, surveillance

Water-cooler TV

Event TV

OTHER LITERAL RESPONSES

Ratings

Newspaper reviews

Magazine articles

Responses on the website/blogs

Stuart Hall response theorie
How can they be applied?

GENRE

HYBRID including codes and conventions of reality, documentary and game show

NARRATIVE

Formulaic structure

Linear with 'live' show

Use of flashbacks and manipulation of time and space

Individual narratives constructed around couples

Establishment of 'characters'

Technical codes

STRICTLY COME DANCING

GLOBAL APPEAL

Franchise sold to other countries

BBC control over the franchise

Global adaptations

IMPORTANCE FOR THE BBC

Scheduling decisions

Family viewing

Spin off programmes

Audience targeting and appeal

Competition with similar programmes

REPRESENTATION

Gender

Age

Ethnicity

Place

MARKETING

Cross platform:

Trailers including a teaser campaign

Press coverage

Appearances on radio, chat shows, etc.

Website

Merchandise

Live tour

MS4

The Film Industry

Introduction

A study of film for MS4 will, as with the other media industries, involve a detailed study of three **contrasting texts** focusing on the key areas of:

- Genre
- Narrative
- Representation.

You will also consider issues surrounding audiences:

- How audiences are targeted and positioned by the text
- How different audiences may respond to your chosen films
- The debates about the relationship between the audiences and the texts.

It is also essential that you develop an understanding of the industry that produced the text:

- How films are produced and distributed
- How your chosen films are marketed
- Regulation issues related to your films
- **Global implications**.

Films are defined and categorised by their genre, the stars, the production company and the production values. The production context of the film is also relevant and this will in turn attract different audiences and communicate different messages about the film itself. Studying examples of texts from different production contexts will allow you to demonstrate an understanding of the diverse nature of the film industry. For example, some films are mainstream, **high concept films** with a high budget, others may be classified as **'independent' films** which are less star-driven and can be seen to have lower production values.

What is meant by a high concept film?

This is a model for a film and is used to describe the concept of the Hollywood 'big budget' film. It originally consisted of a ten-point formula that ensured that the film conformed to the high concept model. The criteria of a high concept film included:

- Clearly defined characters, often recognisable in terms of stereotypes and archetypes.
- A simple narrative with universal themes. this can often be summarised in a single sentence or image.
- High production values evident in the cinematography, costumes, settings and special effects.
- Elements that are easy to market and promote, for example iconic repeatable images, a recognisable soundtrack and potential for merchandising.
- High profile stars often related to the film's genre.

Key Terms

Contrasting texts = Here this refers to films that allow you to demonstrate a broad knowledge of the industry. For example, different genres or diverse production concepts.

Global implications = The importance of the film in a worldwide context.

High concept film = This is a film that can be summed up in sentence or two. It is recognisable to audiences, easily marketable and high budget.

Independent film = This is a film made outside of the financial and artistic control of a large film company. A truly independent film should be privately conceived and funded. However, few films made are really 'independent'. This more commonly refers to a film that is made by a smaller film company on a low budget.

Exam Tip

Remember – the films you study are not isolated texts, they serve to demonstrate your awareness of the industry that creates them.

Key Terms

Media conglomerate =
A media conglomerate is a
company that owns other
companies across a range of media
platforms. This increases their
domination of the market and their
ability to distribute and exhibit
their product.

Exhibition = The means by
which a film is 'shown'; for example,
in multiplex or independent
cinemas, on television or on the
Internet.

Distribution = This includes the
organisation of the stages of the
film's release, production of DVDs
and Internet strategies.

Vertical integration =
Vertically integrated companies
own all or most of the chain of
production for the product. For
example, a film company that also
owns a chain of multiplex cinemas
to exhibit the film and merchandise
outlets.

Horizontal integration = This
is where the conglomerate is made
up of different companies that
produce and sell similar products.
For example, a film producer, a
TV company, a magazine and a
newspaper.

- 'Larger than life' protagonists.

- Visual appeal including lavish sets and expensive action scenes.

- Highly dramatic and hyperbolic plot situations.

All these elements are seen to be important in attracting a global audience to ensure the success of the product. High concept films are produced by the major film studios that are **media conglomerates** and therefore have the ability to back these films and rely on financial returns. Many major production companies also have the means for the promotion, **exhibition** and **distribution** of the films they make. In 2012, 90% of American media was owned by six companies including Disney, News Corporation and Time Warner. These companies operate a philosophy of synergy through the practice of **vertical** and **horizontal integration**.

What is synergy?

Synergy involves a range of media agencies coming together to help each other. As media conglomerates, they seek to own companies that are mutually beneficial. For example, Time Warner owns Warner Brothers, which make the films; HBO, a television company where products can be exhibited; and IPC that produces magazines where products can be advertised, featured and promoted; Turner Broadcasting and CNN news amongst others, thus allowing for the cross-promotion of media products without involving any other interests. Disney, America's largest media conglomerate according to revenue, owns Walt Disney Pictures making films, The Disney Channel exhibiting films and Disney Stores selling merchandise and promoting brand Disney. As stated earlier, the high concept film therefore fits the synergy model as it has easily promotable features that can be exhibited across a range of media platforms.

Deklofenak/Shutterstock.com

Task

Research the production
company and the production,
distribution and exhibition
strategies involved with the
release of your chosen film.

What is a British film?

One of the films that make up the three that you will study to illustrate your knowledge of the film industry, needs to be British. The notion of what constitutes a British film is complex and at times, confusing. The dominant definitions focus on institutional, industrial and cultural determinants. It is of advantage to the British government to have films officially classified as 'British' as this means there are tax implications that will earn them money. This also may attract overseas investment and also encourage the **indigenous** film industry. It also means that a British film achieves recognition in a global context.

The House of Commons Culture Media and Sport Committee Report of 2003 into the British film industry stated that, 'the nature of the British film industry is not what we would wish it to be. Ideally, we would prefer the main activity to be indigenous production of films about Britain, a substantial proportion of which break out to achieve success in the global market.' They suggested that the British film industry does three things:

- Provides services for the major Hollywood studios.

- Makes indigenous films that are shot in the UK.

- Makes films that are co-produced but not shot in the UK. This includes films like, for example, the Bond films.

- Under the Films Act, for a film to be certified British by the Secretary for Culture, Media and Sport it must meet the following tests:

  – The maker test – the film must be made by company that is registered, managed and controlled in the UK or EU.

  – The production cost test – 70% of the production cost must be spent on film-making in the UK.

  – The labour cost test – 70–75% of the labour cost must have been paid to residents of the UK.

  – Previously filmed material – no more than 10% of the film should contain images from a film made by a different maker.

  (publications.parliament.uk)

The BFI require that any film claiming to be British must pass a Cultural Test and adhere to the Golden Points Rule whereby points are awarded in a range of 'cultural' categories related to the production of the film. The film must score 16 out of a possible 31 points. For example, in the Cultural Content section, to score the full 16 points available:

- 75% of the film must take place in the UK.

- Three of the lead characters must be British (if the film has fewer than three characters, they must all be British).

- The film must be based on British subject matter.

- The film must depict a British story; for example, it could be about a British historical character.

- 75% of the original dialogue must be recorded in the English language or a regional language.

  (industry.bfi.org.uk)

Key Term

Indigenous = Originating and produced in a specific region or country, for example Britain.

quickfire

⑫ What services could the British film industry provide for a Hollywood studio?

Task

Consider how the film you are studying meets the criteria for a British film.

Main text: *Skyfall*

Skyfall is a high budget production with high production values. Audiences are familiar with the Bond series and the expectation is that there will be high profile stars, interesting and exotic locations and sets, evidence of a high budget (eight Audis were wrecked in the opening chase scene), complex action scenes, fast-paced editing and a flexi-narrative.

Skyfall: industry information

Key Term

Franchise = An entire series of the film including the original film and all those that follow.

- Directed by Sam Mendes.

- Production company: Metro-Goldwyn-Mayer/Albert Broccoli's Eon Productions/Sony Pictures Entertainment.

- Eon Productions is the UK-based production company which makes the Bond films. The 007 **franchise** is the longest running in cinema history having made 22 films since 1962. Danjaq LLC, part of Eon Productions, is the US company that, along with MGM, owns the Bond copyright.

- MGM is a multinational conglomerate that owns global production and distribution companies.

- Sony Pictures Entertainment is also a multinational media conglomerate. Its global operations include film and television production and distribution, home entertainment acquisition and distribution, new product and development and entertainment distribution in over 142 countries.

- *Skyfall* Release date: 26 October 2012.

- Estimated Cost: $200,000,000.

- Highest grossing Bond film: $980,000,000 Worldwide (Jan 2013).

- An estimated £29 million, one third of the film's overall budget, was raised by commercial deals including product placements.

- Awards: Nominated for five Oscars. Won a Golden Globe and an Oscar for the Best Original Song (Adele, *Skyfall*).

23 How will the companies involved in the film's production ensure the success of *Skyfall*?

24 What other examples of product placement feature in *Skyfall*? Why is this seen by some to be a controversial way of raising revenue for the film?

Text: genre

As stated earlier, Section A of the MS4 examination will require you to answer a question on genre, narrative or representation using one of your chosen industries and your three main texts. *Skyfall* comes under the category of: Action/Adventure/Crime/Thriller, according to publicity material. It could also be said that the Bond films themselves have established a genre of their own as audiences have clear expectations of the repertoire of elements that make up the film. This adds to the film's success as audiences get what they expect and usually a little more:

Characters

- A set of recognisable characters, some established, for example M and Bond, and some enigmatically different, for example the villain whose evil trait changes with each film.

- This film also challenges audience expectations with the reinvention of Q as a younger model more related to the modern cyber age. Audiences want the same but they also like something a bit different, just not too different!

Narrative

- This is usually linear in structure and predictable. *Skyfall* is a standalone film and does not have any obvious narrative tie-ins with the other Bond films featuring Daniel Craig. The opening scene of *Skyfall* clearly establishes the film in the action genre and provides the high-powered thrill element associated with the Bond franchise. Within the narrative there are also expected **plot situations** associated with this genre, for example a car chase. Surprising plot situations in this film include a lesser 'baddie' being eaten by a komodo dragon.

Key Term

Plot situations – These are, in film, key scenes that happen in the story that place the film within a particular genre. For example, a fight scene in an action film.

Setting and iconography

- The settings in *Skyfall* are both exotic and stereotypically British. The opening sequence, set in the bazaar in Istanbul, gives the opportunity for a chase in which stalls are overturned and motorbikes drive along roof tops – these scenes are reminiscent of other action films like *Indiana Jones* and the more contemporary *Bourne* series. Silva's hideout is the eerily deserted Hashima Island in Japan and serves as a fitting location for his base. However, much of the narrative takes place in London and features iconic landmarks constructing a representation of the city as the hub of the country. At the end of the film, Bond escapes with M to a stereotypically constructed remote Scottish house surrounded by mountains and containing intricate passages like the priest's hole that allows M to escape temporarily. Iconography has always played an important part in this genre and the Bond films are no exception. In the past the films have been full of unbelievable gadgets designed by Q, here the new Q gives Bond only a short pistol with embedded finger-print scanner and a tiny elementary radio tracker. Product placement aside we also see the Aston Martin which returns Bond to his roots.

Task

Look at this short YouTube film showing how the locations are chosen:

tinyurl.com/c2jruy4

What does it tell us about the production values of this film?

Technical and audio codes

- These are very important for establishing genre. Fast-paced editing and rapid cuts are conventional for the action genre. This is evident in the opening chase scene. Equally important are the construction of scenes building tension and using low key lighting. An example in *Skyfall* is the fight scene between Bond and Patrice in the Shanghai high-rise block. Non-diegetic dramatic music plays, the characters are silhouettes against the neon lights of the city. The shots move from long shots to a close-up of the two hands as Patrice is suspended over the lift shaft, then we get a point of view shot as he plummets down the lift shaft. The camera then interestingly cuts to the shot of Severine in the opposite block as she is framed between Bond's legs. A further audio code associated with the film is the regular refrain of the Bond theme tune to highlight the advent of action. Another convention of the action genre is the use of special effects demonstrating the high production values of the text.

QUICKFIRE

㉕ Give five elements of the opening scene of the film that place it in the action genre.

Exam Tip

When answering a question on genre, use narrative, characters, setting, iconography and technical/audio codes to help you to structure your response.

Text: narrative

Here you can use the information you learned about narrative structures and techniques at AS and refer to the revision section at the beginning of this book. The usual appeal of the narrative in action films and in particular Bond films is that it is refreshingly predictable. However, with *Skyfall*, the narrative, although seemingly **formulaic** and straightforward does also contain complexities that will challenge its audience. On the surface we have a Todorovian **linear** structure:

- The equilibrium is the action element at the start of the film – this is the expected start of this genre. We are plunged straight into the exotic, action-packed world of 007.

- The first disruption is unexpected as Bond is seemingly killed. The second and main disruption is the cyber crime executed by Silva who steals the details of all the British undercover agents. This introduces the conflict in the film. The narrative reflects the sociological context of the time.

- The quest to resolve the conflict takes place after the return of Bond to active service. His aim is to prevent Silva from killing any more agents and eliminate him.

- The confrontation/climax is constructed in true action genre style with high drama, special effects and a big budget!

- Equilibrium is restored in the end, but one without M. This heralds changes and a new start leaving enigmas for the film to come.

However, *Skyfall* is not so straightforward. It has a **flexi-narrative** structure which sharpens the story world. Although Bond and Silva may seem stereotypically Proppian in their roles as hero and villain, Bond is not a super-hero in this film, he is flawed. He is portrayed as ageing and one narrative strand follows his struggle to cope with this. The narrative is more complex than in earlier Bond films as the films featuring Daniel Craig have created a much more three-dimensional, human hero. Another strand deals with the demise of M and the pressure she is under and a further storyline is the culturally pertinent discussion of the role of the secret service in a modern Britain. These intertwine with the more conventional plot situations of the action genre producing a more challenging film.

Text: representation

Representations of men in *Skyfall*: Bond

Stills and publicity materials from Skyfall, director Sam Mendes, MGM/Eon/Sony Pictures (2012)

The role of Bond in the recent films has seen a new, more modern representation of **masculinity** created to match the expectations of a twenty-first century audience. This representation is an ambiguous one. The Bond in *Skyfall* goes some way to challenge the audience expectations of the heroic agent and undergoes an **arc of transformation** through the film. In the early scenes we see him in hiding, gambling and drinking. He is with a woman who is not even given a name. As the film develops he has to overcome his physical decline and prove himself. The range of close-up shots exposes his craggy features, tired expression and wrinkles. The audience is positioned to empathise with his situation as a more modern action hero with flaws. He is only reinstated with the help of M, who despite having turned her back on him, falsifies his test result, allowing him to return to active service. The audience share an intimate moment with him as he faces himself in the mirror and digs out shrapnel from his arm, like a real man! However, Bond's vulnerability is highlighted like never before: he has trouble shooting accurately, is reminded that he is ageing and he seems disenchanted with the political situation and MI5. He questions M's motives and decisions regarding the villain Silva and is seen to struggle with his responsibility on more than one occasion.

One of the most interesting aspects of Bond's representation in this film is his relationship with Silva. The scriptwriters interestingly included a scene where the sexual tension between the two characters is palpable. Silva unbuttons Bond's shirt and strokes his legs. Rather than seemingly uncomfortable with the action Bond states 'what makes you think this is my first time?' Silva is a different type of Bond villain in that he shares similarities with Bond himself: he was once a secret agent and a favourite of M. Towards the end of the film, seemingly to emphasise Bond's vulnerability, we learn more about his past as the action moves to his childhood home and we realise the significance of the film's name.

Key Terms

Masculinity = The perceived characteristics generally considered to define what it is to be a man. These can adapt according to sociological variations and cultural changes.

Arc of transformation = This is the emotional changes a character goes through in the process of the narrative. The events in the story mean that they will 'transform' by the end of the story.

Exam Tip

When you are answering a question on representation, remember to refer to specific scenes and to be ready to discuss how the representation is constructed and how the audience is positioned by that construction.

Representations of men in *Skyfall*: Silva

There have been many and varied Bond villains, and audiences have expectations of the uniqueness of this character. The villainy surrounding the Bond villain must also be applicable to the time, whether it be Cold War Russia or the imminence of nuclear war. We can apply Levi-Strauss' **binary opposites** theory to Bond and Silva in that they are very clearly hero and villain, but it is not as simple as that. In *Skyfall* we have a villain who has been part of the service, who shares similarities with Bond, who has been close to M and who now wants revenge. His weapon – his ability to hack into worldwide computer systems. His aim – to annihilate the British Secret Service, but most of all, M. This deviates from the usual need for Bond villains to take over the world, Silva has a much more personal score to settle. He feels betrayed by M, the betrayal becomes more pertinent when he refers to her as 'mother'. Bond villains are usually visually interesting, the blondness and general appearance of Silva is inexplicably disconcerting; he is physically imposing and the filming and editing often sees Bond at a disadvantage. In the scene where he has captured Bond, he approaches him from the end of the room; this is one take and creates tension. Bond is seated and appears vulnerable. In another scene Silva taunts Bond from above: 'not bad for a physical wreck', before showing him the extent of his power by crashing a train into the tunnel. His revelation of the injuries done to him by the cyanide pill places him in the category of the more horrific of Bond villains. However, what it also does, unlike some other films, is give him a motive for his actions. M had traded him for the lives of other agents and stands by her decision. The scene where she faces Silva in his transparent cage is constructed so that she looks vulnerable and he seems still in control. That control is emphasised when he manages to escape.

There is a homoerotic element to the relationship between Bond and Silva which makes their characters and interplay more interesting. Silva's explicit flirting with Bond is met with challenge rather than evasion thus, placing Bond firmly in the modern world. In the end it is Bond who personally kills Silva after a dramatic sequence where Silva is filmed in silhouette against the backdrop of Bond's childhood home.

Key Term

Binary opposites = This is where texts incorporate examples of opposite values; for example, good vs. evil, villain vs. hero. These can be apparent in the characters or the narrative themes.

Task

Choose two key scenes that you think best illustrate the way in which the representation of Silva is constructed in *Skyfall*. Select three main points you could use in a 'representation' essay.

Exam Tip

When discussing technical codes remember to analyse the purpose and the possible effect upon the audience.

quickfire

27 How does the character of Silva reinforce and challenge the typical representation of a Bond villain?

Key Figure

Claude Levi Strauss was a French anthropologist and ethnologist. He introduced the idea of binary opposites as a way of analysing meaning within narratives. He argued that all media texts are constructed around key opposites.

Representations in *Skyfall*: women

Bond films have a tradition of and a reputation for representing women in a negative way. Earlier films in the **franchise** epitomised women as sexual objects who could be 'used' by Bond as accessories and then discarded as he moved on to another 'model'. The names of the women, for example Pussy Galore, signified their role within the narrative. However, placed in a **sociological context**, the films tended to reflect what was acceptable in society at the time and evident in other media texts. The recent Bond films have had to address how they represent both Bond's masculinity and the representation of women in the narrative to adhere to the changing roles of women in society and in other texts and also what is seen to be acceptable by a modern audience. How far *Skyfall* has succeeded in presenting positive representations of women is a debatable and interesting question.

Representations of women in *Skyfall*: M

The representation of M in *Skyfall* is both complex and ambiguous. Within the brand she has been portrayed in previous films as a powerful female. She was first introduced into the Bond franchise to reflect the sociological changes in the real security services when Stella Rimington was made the Director General of MI5 in 1992. She is particularly interesting in that she is not defined by her beauty or body image, as women in Bond films have been in the past, but instead by her brain and ability to act and control situations. She can be bold and forthright with Bond as their relationship is not based on sexual attraction or ownership. It is also relevant that she is older and, in the earlier films in which she appears, this is seen as positive as she has experience. In *Skyfall*, however, the suggestion is that her lapses in judgement are linked to her advancing years and she is encouraged (by a younger man) to retire graciously.

Her arc of transformation in the film is from a determined force who at the start of the film orders Eve to 'take the shot' which ensues in the presumed death of Bond, to a vulnerable victim, emotionally scarred by events and forced out of the secret service 'shadows', relying on Bond to save her.

In the still from the film here, the visual and technical codes construct her representation as isolated and worried. The scenery and location are bleak, emphasising her predicament. This contrasts dramatically with the previous image which effectively represents her behind her desk, strong and in control. She is also seen to be culpable – the blame for the psychopathic acts of the villain Silva is laid at her door. Interestingly, Silva refers to M as 'mother' suggesting a once close relationship and reinforcing a sense of blame and responsibility. She is also seen to be 'hunted'; all that she thought was secure is now at risk. One scene in the film shows her alone at home, casually dressed but distressed by the direct messages she is receiving on her computer: 'reflect on your sins'. She has no way of preventing the death of the agents and she herself dies in a remote location in the arms of Bond. However, despite her end, M has been a largely positive representation of both age and gender in the films.

Representations of women in *Skyfall*: Severine

A more traditional female representation in *Skyfall* is Severine, played by Berenice Marlohe. This was acknowledged by the director Sam Mendes: 'If I could have invented a Bond girl, it would be Berenice. I wanted to find somebody with all of the classic components of a Bond girl: voluptuous, sexy, a woman and not a girl, mystery.' As with the other representations in the film, she is ambiguous. She is a victim and yet a survivor, having learned how to exist in the world in which she lives, which has abused and degraded her. She is beautiful and the technical codes in the film emphasise this. However, she is also trapped and afraid. In the scene where she meets Bond in the casino, the camera focuses on her shaking hands and she seems aware of her own fate. She is a possession who must play by the rules of the game. In terms of the plot, she functions much like a traditional Bond girl; Bond seduces her – he walks into her shower, no questions asked. He then uses her to get to the villain, Silva. She then becomes part of the competition between the two men, the camera cutting to show her bruised face and vulnerable position. She is represented as the weaker woman and her death signifies her role in the film – a pawn in the game between Bond and Silva.

Eve

Another example of female representation in *Skyfall* is Eve. She is a feisty field agent who initially seems to challenge the more traditional role of the 'Bond' girl. She is active, and the camera and editing, as in this shot, show her as forceful and in control. Her 'love scene' with Bond is not a one-sided seduction. However, from the opening scenes she is also seen to be fallible, it is her responsibility to save Bond who is fighting one of the villains on top of a moving train. She 'takes the shot' as commanded by M and instead shoots Bond. Naomi Harris was not comfortable with how this represented Eve in the narrative as it emphasised her weakness in a male dominated world: 'I was not happy about having to shoot him. I thought I really wanted to be a better shot than that.' Both she and M are therefore seen to be responsible for Bond's demise. However, Eve is also shown to be his equal. In the raid on parliament she helps him to save M and the technical codes reinforce her active role. Disappointingly and surprisingly, at the end of the film, she becomes the new Moneypenny, stating that field work is not for her. This is the traditional role for the passive female in the Bond franchise, whose role it is to worship Bond from behind a desk. It is to be hoped that the next film sees her bringing a more modern twist to this female role.

○ »»» quickfire

③⓪ What is the significance of calling this character 'Eve'?

Other representations: age

This is another interesting area for analysis in the film. We have already considered the generally positive representation of M as an older woman in a key governmental role. However, the effects of ageing upon physical ability and decision making are also important themes within the film. Despite her ability to be in control, M is also, at times, portrayed as vulnerable because of her age and the suggestion is that she retires. In the past the films have focused on her experience rather than her age. Bond's increasing age is emphasised at times during the film even though he asserts to Silva his hobby is 'resurrection'. We see close-ups of him looking tired and vulnerable, he is told that he can 'stay dead', implying that he is not up to the job. However, there is also new blood in *Skyfall* in the shape of the youthful Q. This is, in fact the first time Q has been younger than Bond.

○ »»» quickfire

③① Suggest three ways in which age is represented in the film.

Task

How is Q represented though visual, technical and audio codes?

'The Bond boffin becomes a trendy, cardigan-wearing techie in *Skyfall*... Most thrillingly for geeks, the modern Q can hold his own when verbally sparring with our action hero', says one newspaper article. In the past Q has been represented as an old 'boffin', eccentric and paternal, this new Q is another phase in the modernisation of representations in Bond. Interestingly, when he and Bond meet they are in the National Gallery, ironically in front of Turner's famous painting, *The Fighting Termeraire*, which depicts an old warship being towed off for scrap by a small tugboat. They are also sitting together, as equals and this relationship continues throughout the film – they get on. Q in *Skyfall* does not present Bond with an array of quirky gadgets as in previous films, although he does give him a gun that will only respond to his hand. His real skill is computers and being able to outwit the villain through technology!

Other representations: Britain and national identity

Although *Skyfall* has settings in exotic locations, the narrative and most of the action is set in Britain thus presenting the audience with a representation of Britain and **national identity**. MI6 offices, the National Gallery and other British locations feature heavily in the film and the theme is essentially the threat to British security. M has to fight through British red tape to attempt to avert disaster. We see iconic images of British landmarks, M has a British bulldog (a symbol of British strength and linked to Churchill) on her desk, which she bequeaths to Bond on her death. In the glimpses we see of Bond's obituary before his return, M has described him as an 'exemplar of British fortitude'. This still from the film features a shot we are familiar with in real life, coffins draped in Union Jacks signifying British deaths. Notice how small and insignificant M appears by the way the shot has been constructed. More than one shot in the film has Bond on the roof looking out over London and featuring iconic landmarks signifying tradition and heritage. The narrative focuses on Britain under threat of a different kind of terrorism and we watch with M as the MI6 building is blown up, emphasising the fact that she is not in control and is powerless to save the agents. In the fact that M is urged to bring the secret service 'out of the shadows' the plot echoes the modern discussions about national security.

Key Term

National identity = The representation of a country, in this case Britain, as a whole, encompassing its culture, traditions, language and politics. This includes the characteristics of the country that are clearly definable to other nations.

quickfire

(32) What other examples of national identity are there in *Skyfall*?

Audience

The focus for the questions in Section B of the examination paper will be Audience and Industry. Again, you need to incorporate your knowledge of audience learned on the AS course and from MS3. A discussion of audience can cover how the text appeals to the audience, the pleasures the text may offer the audience as well as how an audience may respond to and decode the text. Relevant examples of audience responses can be both **literal** and **theoretical**.

Who is the target audience? How are they targeted?

The audience range for this film is broad. Essentially, there is something for everyone including:

- Fans of the Bond films – the predictable storylines and plot situations are in keeping with audience expectations.

- Fans of the action genre – this is a high concept film with high production values displaying the codes and conventions of the genre.

- Fans of Daniel Craig – he may broaden the audience with regard to gender.

- A range of ages – the inclusion of the new, young Q may target a younger audience.

- Representations of strong women – this may target a female audience.

- The audience is also targeted by marketing and promotional strategies.

What is the appeal of the film? What pleasures does it offer audiences?

- Uses and gratifications theory – the film offers the audience escapism and social interaction opportunities.

- Sam Mendes is a high profile director and suggests a quality product.

- *Skyfall* is a high concept film, audiences know what to expect.

- There is a challenging narrative and strong characters. The subverting of some more traditional stereotypes may attract a new audience.

Audience responses

- Literal responses – reviews, blogs, messages on websites, box office figures, DVD purchases.

- Theoretical responses – Stuart Hall preferred/negotiated/oppositional.

- Responses can be diverse as audiences decode the text in different ways according to age, gender, etc.

Key Terms

Literal audiences = This refers to examples of responses from actual audiences that can be evidenced rather than the application of theoretical models; for example, statistics of box office numbers.

Theoretical responses = These are models that are the product of studies that suggest possible ways in which audiences may interact with texts.

QUICKFIRE

(33) Give an example of a literal and a theoretical way in which an audience may respond to *Skyfall*.

Exam Tip

Look for key words in the question to help you to focus your response. For example, attract, target, response. The question will never be: 'write all you know about audiences'.

Key Term

Cross-platform marketing
= In media terms this is a text that is distributed and exhibited across a range of media formats or platforms. This may include film, television, print, radio and the Internet.

(34) Give specific examples of *Skyfall*'s cross-platform marketing strategies.

Task

Look at the guidelines for the 12A certificate on the BBFC website: www.bbfc.co.uk. How does *Skyfall* conform to these guidelines?

Exam Tip

If you answer a 'regulation' question in the examination, be prepared to discuss how texts conform to the regulator's guidelines, as well as analysing the texts that have been controversial.

Industry: marketing

As with other high concept, blockbuster films, **cross-platform marketing** strategies are employed to raise audience awareness of the film's release. For *Skyfall* these included:

- The announcement that the film was to be made and selected pieces of information were 'leaked' about the villain, name of the film, etc. Teasers about the fate of M were discussed on the Internet.

- Posters and billboard advertisements which chose to highlight the Bond brand rather that showcase the director or stars. They were simple and included iconography associated with Bond, here it is the gun, the dinner suit and the 007 logo.

- Promotional tie-ins. These included the somewhat controversial appearance of Daniel Craig as Bond in a Heineken advert. VisitBritain Tourist Company launched a campaign in association with the film where you can 'Live Like James Bond'.

- Daniel Craig's appearance as Bond with The Queen in the Olympics' opening ceremony. This reminded a billion people globally of the franchise and *Skyfall,* the most recent film.

- Digital technologies, for example a website dedicated to the film.

- The launch and success of the Bond theme sung by Adele.

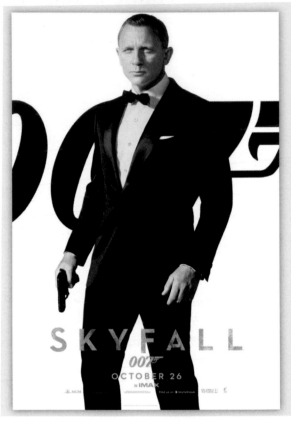

Regulation

The British Board of Film Classification was established in 1912 to classify films and has also been responsible for the classification of videos and DVDs since the Video Recording Act of 1984. All decisions are made using guidelines produced and regularly updated by the BBFC. The aim of classification is to protect children from harmful content and to give audiences the information they need to guide them before viewing the film. Two Examiners view the film to be classified and recommend a certification which is then ratified by a Senior Examiner. Where there is disagreement or cause for concern then legal advice may be taken. It is the case that some films are not deemed satisfactory in content to be given a classification at all. The aim of the film's producers is to ensure that their film is open to the widest audience to achieve box office success. The most controversial decision the BBFC has made in recent years is the introduction of the 12A certification which is seen by some critics to be the way in which some more violent and less appropriate films reach a broader and in this case, younger, audience.

Skyfall has a 12A certificate. The BBFC stated that it 'Contains moderate action violence and one use of strong language'. It passed without any cuts.

Summary: The Film Industry

APPEAL AND TARGETING

Target audience: broad appeal

How are they targeted?

Audience positioning

Responses: Stuart Hall - different responses

Pleasures: uses and gratifications – escapism and social interaction

Interactivity

Consider literal as well as theoretical audience responses. For example, reviews, box office figures, etc.

Sam Mendes – high profile director, audience expectations of quality product

GENRE

Consider the codes and conventions of action films and the sub-genre of James Bond films

NARRATIVE

Linear – Todorov

Predictable storyline and plot situations

High thrill elements – enigmas, plot twists, flexi-narrative

Recognisable characters with roles – villain, flawed hero (moves away from predictable Bond hero)

Interesting villain

SKYFALL

MARKETING

Range of posters featuring different characters and poses

Use of Bond logo – brand identity

Promotional tie-ins

Appearances by Daniel Craig

High concept, big budget film

Synergy elements

What makes it a British film?

007 franchise

Film company – multinational conglomerate

Production. exhibition, distribution

Websites – official, industry and fan base

Trailers

REPRESENTATION

Women – range of strong female characters. However, some continue to be victims and are sexually objectified through some of the technical codes

National identity – representation of Britain and the British

Men – Bond here is a more modern representation of masculinity

Age – introduction of the young 'geeky' Q
M is ambiguous – she is powerful but there are suggestions that she is too old and frail to maintain control

A GLOBAL TEXT?

Consider extent

Regulation – how is the film industry regulated?

The Magazine Industry

Introduction

Key Term

House style = This is what makes the magazine recognisable to its readers every issue. The house style is established through the choice of colour, the layout and design, the font style, the content and the general 'look' of the publication.

In studying the magazine industry in preparation for the MS4 examination you will need to ensure that you have a broad and up to date understanding. Your choice of key texts must allow you to demonstrate that understanding. Remember, it is helpful if your texts are varied and diverse; this way you will illustrate effectively your awareness of a range of issues related to the industry. For the magazine industry you must ensure that you have studied three different magazine titles. You must engage in a detailed study of one edition of a title, but it will also help your understanding to study aspects from other editions of the same title.

It is important that you are able to analyse your chosen magazines in detail using relevant technical terminology. You also need to understand how the magazines target, construct and appeal to their audience and how different audiences may respond.

© Alex Peak / Alamy

quickfire

㉟ Why are magazine front covers important in attracting readers?

For the purposes of the MS4 examination it is essential that the analysis is of the whole magazine not just the front cover. That said, the front cover is a good start as this is the 'shop window' of the magazine. Its purpose is to communicate the sub-genre of the magazine and what the reader will get if they buy it. In a competitive market it is important that the front cover attracts the eye of the consumer. Furthermore, it also has to establish the **house style** of the magazine so that audiences will recognise it and develop expectations of its content. The front cover may also communicate the ideology of the magazine and encode messages for an audience to decode. Analysing the front cover also allows you to apply the correct technical terminology related to magazines.

Analysing magazine front covers

The house style of different magazine sub-genres may be contrasting but all magazines use a similar repertoire of elements in their layout and design in order to appeal to their target audience:

- A recognisable masthead. This usually employs the same font from issue to issue and becomes an essential part of the branding of the magazine. This format will also transfer to web editions of the magazine. The font style used for the masthead will often suggest the sub-genre of the magazine, for example *Kerrang!* uses a bold, dramatic font suggesting the 'in your face' style of the magazine.

- A central image. This will be appropriate to the sub-genre of the publication. Lifestyle magazines, for example *Cosmopolitan*, may use an upmarket celebrity or glamorous model to provide aspiration for their readers, whilst *Good Housekeeping* usually uses an older celebrity who is 'good for their age' to appeal to their target audience. Often the mode of address will be direct so that the reader feels that the magazine is communicating with them and they feel part of its world.

- **Cover lines** reflecting the interests of the target audience. These are often instrumental in creating an audience. They tell the reader how they should live their lives and what they should see as important. This creation is often unrealistic and, although seen to be aspirational, may also result in readers feeling discontented with their lives. This is particularly the case with women's and men's lifestyle magazines.

- Sell lines. These aim to attract an audience by offering them something over and above the normal content of the magazine. This may be a free gift or chance to win concert tickets, for example.

- Language and mode of address. Magazines will adopt a relevant mode of address to target their audience. For example, magazines aimed at young people will employ chatty and informal language, often using personal pronouns. Some magazines will use **subject-specific lexis** to make them seem more exclusive and to appeal to a specific target audience, this will also alienate an audience who does not understand the terminology.

- The above elements that feature on the front cover will also establish the **discourse** of the magazine – this will be maintained throughout the whole magazine and is a central aspect of the magazine's ideology.

Inside the magazine

As stated earlier, unlike MS2, it is not acceptable to just study the front cover of a magazine. You are looking at the whole publication and its place within the industry. When analysing an entire edition of your chosen title you need to consider:

- The contents page. This should give you a quick resumé of the contents of the magazine and in its layout and design it will often be as complex as the front cover. It will include reference to the regular pages thus fulfilling audience expectations, as well as the 'specials' or 'exclusives'. Not all the pages will be included; the ones that appear will have been selected in order to appeal to the audience. The contents page will also establish the discourse and often the ideology of the publication and that in turn will suggest the target reader. This page will also reinforce the house style and brand identity of the magazine. The 'letter from the editor' often appears on this page, this will establish a more personal relationship with the audience by speaking directly to them and this will also reinforce the sub-genre of the magazine.

- The advertisements. These are partly responsible for funding the magazine and without them a magazine would be considerably more expensive. Don't ignore them – they

Key Terms

Cover lines = These suggest the content to the reader and often contain teasers and rhetorical questions. These relate to the genre of the magazine.

Subject-specific lexis = This is the specific language and vocabulary used to engage the audience. Subject-specific lexis used on the front cover of the magazine will make the reader feel part of the group who belong to the world of that magazine. For example, terminology used on the front covers of gaming magazines.

Discourse = The topics and language used by a media text. The discourse of lifestyle magazines tends to revolve around body image and narcissism.

quickfire

(36) How does the contents page of a magazine establish a house style and brand identity?

are a signifier of the sub-genre and the target audience. The advertisements would not appear if their producers were not sure of accessing the right audience. The magazine will usually produce a media pack, which will give potential advertisers information about the audience demographics, their interests and their lifestyle.

- Regular pages. These are pages that the audience will expect to see in each issue of the magazine. They are usually in the same place, for example the horoscopes at the back of a lifestyle magazine. They make up the magazine's structure or narrative. It may also be the case that there will be a particular contributor to the magazine that has their own regular column.

- **Features**. These will be particular to this issue of the magazine and may reflect the season, a celebrity of the moment, a pertinent issue for the reader or be an 'exclusive' for the magazine. They offer the reader something different and may be the reason why the audience will choose this magazine instead of another similar one.

Industry information

The magazine industry is vast and there are hundreds of different titles spanning many sub-genres. Unlike other industries, for example television, the magazine industry operates **narrow casting**. Magazine titles tend to target a specific, **niche audience**. For example, *Dogs Today*, which, as can be seen by the front cover, targets an audience with a very specific interest but employs similar codes and conventions to more high profile magazines. The highest circulation figures are for lifestyle magazines.

The top selling magazines are produced and owned by a few major global publishers that dominate the market. These include:

Conde Nast – its UK titles include: *Glamour, Vogue, GQ, House and Garden, Vanity Fair, Brides* and *Tatler.*

Bauer Media – this company launched its first magazine *The Angling Times* in 1953 and now owns over 300 magazine titles in 15 countries including: *Heat, Grazia, Closer, Match, Kerrang!* and *Empire.*

IPC Media – this company is part of the multi-national conglomerate Time Warner and publishes titles including: *Essentials, Look, Horse and Hound, Ideal Home, TV Times, Woman's Own* and *Marie Claire.*

Hearst Magazines UK – this is a subsidiary of The Hearst Corporation and includes Rodale, a US company specialising in health and well-being titles. It is the largest digital publisher in the UK. Their 20 magazine titles reach 1 in 3 UK women and 1 in 4 UK adults and include: *Men's Health, Red, Company, Cosmopolitan, Good Housekeeping, Inside Soap, Elle* and *Esquire.*

The industry in crisis?

The magazine industry, like other industries, has had to adapt to changing demands from consumers and with advances in digital technology, has had to make their products available on different platforms. A new generation of readers do not want print magazines, they want apps and interactivity. *'Most readers download digital editions of their magazines through Apple's App Store. The digital product has to be 95% similar to the print version of a magazine to classify as a digital edition under ABC rules.'* (guardian.co.uk.) These changes combined with the volatile market have resulted in several titles biting the dust in recent years. Magazines rely on the income from advertisers but advertisers want reassurance of a solid, loyal **readership**. With print sales falling magazine publishers have had to produce online versions of their publications for an audience who want to access the publication through tablets and iPhones. However, some titles have maintained their print success. For lifestyle magazines like *Cosmopolitan* and *Esquire*, digital editions account for only 10% of their **circulation** compared with *How It Works* where digital sales accounted for 22%. (guardian.co.uk)

Advantages of online magazines

- They are more portable and an app is lighter than a thick glossy magazine.

- They are interactive – users can access audio-visual content and there are more immediate opportunities to interact through blogs, etc.

- The navigation bar allows the user to more easily access the areas of the magazine that interest them and to bypass those that don't.

- They are cheaper, even paying for a download will save money, some of the glossy magazines cost over £4.00.

- They include links to related sites that are quick to use.

Appeal of print magazines

- Many readers like the tactile nature of magazines with the glossy pages and the sensory pleasures, for example perfume and make up samples in lifestyle magazines.

- Print magazines can be thumbed through, put down and then picked up again. They are a way of relaxing in the bath, in bed, etc.

- The size appeals to audiences who are less comfortable with the text and image size on smaller digital appliances. Many women's lifestyle magazines have produced a 'handbag size' version of the full-sized glossy in order to broaden the target market.

- The readership will be larger as the digital edition tends to be confined to one user.

- Print editions of the magazine can be saved by the reader and re-visited at a later date.

Key Terms

Readership = This number refers to how many people actually read the magazine. It is generally thought that two people in addition to the buyer of the magazine will pick it up and read it at some time.

Circulation = This refers to how many copies of the magazine are produced each week/month.

40 Why are print magazine sales falling?

41 What are the main advantages of online magazines for publishers and users?

Industry: regulation

How is the magazine industry regulated?

In terms of statutory regulation, there is no equivalent to Ofcom for print journalism. Magazines are therefore left to self-regulate. The Press Complaints Commission (PCC) is the self-regulatory body for the print journalism industry, created and funded by newspapers and magazines themselves. Its main function is to act and make decisions in the event of complaints about content in newspapers and magazines. The PCC also takes into consideration the activities of journalists as part of their information gathering. The PCC has a code of practice that must be adhered to by newspaper and magazine journalists. A journalist who breaks the code runs the risk of losing their job and publications may be asked to publically apologise for any wrongdoing. The main points of the code of practice cover:

- Accuracy – the press must not publish information that is inaccurate. When this happens an apology must be published.

- Privacy – it is unacceptable, according to the code, to photograph anyone in a private place without their consent. The private and family life, home, health and correspondence, including digital communications of individuals must be respected and any intrusion into this privacy must be justified by the publication.

- Harassment – journalists must not engage in intimidation, harassment or persistent pursuit of individuals.

- You can read more about issues regarding the PCC in the Newspaper Industry chapter.

How global is the magazine industry?

The magazine industry is global and in order to maximise their audience many titles are published in different languages suggesting that their discourses and content have universal appeal. As can be seen in these examples, the language may be different but the house style, mode of address and brand identity remain consistent. Hearst Rodale publishes *Men's Health* in 48 countries. *¡Hola!* magazine started life in 1944 and is now published in over 100 countries. Its sister magazine *Hello!* was launched in Britain in 2001.

Exam Tip

One of the questions on the MS4 paper may ask you about the effectiveness of your industry's regulatory bodies. Be prepared to discuss any of your texts that have fallen foul of the regulator but also be ready to explain how your texts have adhered to the regulator's code of conduct.

quickfire

42. Apart from the language, what changes may have to be made to the magazine issues in different countries? What aspects of the magazine can stay the same?

Analysing magazines

In approaching MS4 it is essential that your understanding and analytical skills have progressed from AS and that your perception of the industry is more complex and goes beyond a simple analysis of magazine pages.

Magazines construct an idea of their reader/audience, for example *Men's Health* man, *Cosmopolitan* woman. This is usually an unrealistic construction that has been mediated by the text. Magazines are media texts that disseminate ideas that are interpreted by audiences according to the constructed discourses. The discourse is that which defines and describes what is possible to be included in the magazine. This will be guided by what the audience have come to expect from the publication. This discourse is then communicated through the genre of the magazine, the mode of address, the representations included in the magazine, the images used and the language.

For example, the discourse of a magazine like *Men's Health* may be said to be:

- Quick-fix problem solving – everything is quantifiable and therefore seems achievable. The magazine suggests it has all the answers if you only follow their advice. For example, '10 easy ways to get a six pack!'

- **Male narcissism** and body image – the front cover image invariably features a single man, often topless, displaying his perfectly toned body. The image is usually in black and white so the body is more defined. The magazine cover is constructed to appeal to the aspirational male audience. The main focus is the 'six pack' or the abs. The related cover lines focus on how to achieve the perfect body – seen through the discourse of the magazine.

- The sensitivity of the new man – this magazine is in a different style from *Nuts* and *Zoo*, it reflects sociological changes in masculinity and attempts to address the anxieties of the modern man.

- Male superiority and manipulation – however, the magazine still, like its predecessors, asserts the superiority of men. Its discourse suggests that men can manipulate women through addressing their needs and desires and learn about these as a 'new man' would.

These discourses are reflected in the choice of content featured in the magazine. They also show how the magazine represents gender and issues relating to the audience. Through the discourse the aim of the magazines is to engender a sense of belonging – they make the discourse appear 'natural' and something that men will want to achieve. However, this may also have a negative impact upon how men view themselves and engender feelings of vulnerability if they do not fit the suggested 'norm'.

Key Term

Male narcissism = This literally means 'self-love' and its derivation is from the Greek god Narcissus who mistakenly fell in love with his own reflection! Here it suggests an obsession with body image and looking good.

Exam Tip

Ensure that you develop a broad understanding of your magazines and the more complex ideas and concepts related to them.

43 What are the discourses of your key magazine texts?

Main Text: *Men's Health Magazine*

Industry information

- The Magazine is published by Hearst-Rodale UK, a subsidiary of The Hearst Corporation and Rodale US.

- In 2009 *Men's Health* overtook *FHM* to become the UK's best selling men's magazine heralding an evolution in the type of magazine that appeals to a new generation of men.

- *Men's Health* is the best selling title in the men's market with a circulation of 215,380 per month and a readership of over 1,200,000.

- The Editor is Toby Wiseman, and Alun Williams is Group Publishing Director. *Men's Health* has an online edition www.men'shealth.co.uk and has been equally successful in digital edition sales with growth of over 60% year-on-year – a position reinforced by the recent launch of its enhanced magazine app onto Apple newsstand.

- It has strengthened its market-leading position by selling more copies of its March 2013 issue on the UK newsstand than the rest of the paid-for men's lifestyle titles combined.

- Industry data received from WHS wholesale (which excludes multipacks), recently, shows *Men's Health* registered a sale of 130,000 for this issue whilst the other titles within its market achieved a total combined March issue newsstand sale of 123,000.

- It is the first time since the popularity of *FHM* in the late 1990s that one magazine has had a higher newsstand sale than all of its competitors put together. (www.hearst.co.uk)

- Group Publishing Director, Alun Williams says, *'These figures demonstrate, now more than ever, that* Men's Health i*s the go-to brand for the intelligent male reader of the 21st century. To dominate the men's lifestyle market so emphatically demonstrates that even in challenging economic times,* Men's Health *is considered a must-have purchase.'* (www.hearst.co.uk)

- The June 2013 issue is to undergo a full new re-branding design incorporating new sections, fonts and templates.

Text: genre

The sub-genre of *Men's Health* magazine is lifestyle. Like other examples of this sub-genre it has a repertoire of elements that attempt to establish rules by which men can live their lives in order to become a *Men's Health* man. The genre conventions include:

- Characters – the men featured in the magazine share similar characteristics; they are toned and fit and are photographed working out, using fitness machinery or flexing their biceps. The women are in the minority and where they do appear they are dressed provocatively and are constructed as 'available'. However, they are also featured as strong and in control, for example, Sofia Vergara from *Modern Family* is featured in this issue of the magazine. Interestingly, although in the image used she is dressed in black lace and high heels, the focus of the feature is her healthy diet, thus seeming to justify using a provocative image of her body.

- Setting and iconography – gym equipment is a common prop suggesting the assumed preoccupation of the target audience. The images in the magazine are either set in a gym environment or are isolated images of men demonstrating fitness moves so that the focus is on the image itself without distractions. Fashionable exercise clothing also features prominently, the *Men's Health* man needs to look good in the gym!

- Technical codes. This will incorporate shot types, image manipulation, editing, lighting and camera angles. The front cover image will usually be a well-lit medium shot, for example, highlighting muscle definition to reinforce the magazine's sub-genre. There have been suggestions that the model's bodies are often airbrushed post production.

- Layout and design – there is a clear house style established through font styles and colour. The articles and features are eye-catching, easy to read and there is very little dense text. Many of the pages are image led with the inclusion of graphics and labels to maintain interest in the content. There is no expectation that the reader will spend time reading long sections of continuous prose – where it appears it is usually broken by sub-headings, coloured highlighting, etc.

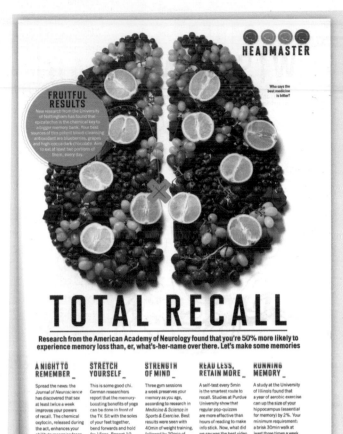

Text: narrative

The narrative of a magazine can be discussed in terms of the structure of the publication. The audience for the text will have an expectation of this structure and of what appears where. The narrative commences with the front cover, which tends to have a conventional house style and a brand identity recognised by the audience, this is then followed by the regular placing of other internal pages. The overall narrative theme in *Men's Health* is a man's journey to fitness and all the content reflects this. The narrative is also conveyed through:

- The language and mode of address of the text – this is instrumental in conveying the narrative. This magazine includes subject-specific lexis related to fitness; it even has a small section entitled 'gym speak' outlining new words and their meanings to be used in the gym! There is repeated use of **rhetorical questioning**: '*Can I Regain Instant Youth?*', '*Does Fasting Really Work?*' for example. This encourages the reader to place themselves within this narrative of self-improvement. Statistics are used to convince the reader that the suggested regimes to achieve the ideal lifestyle will work.

Exam Tip

Ensure that you can discuss the main focus of Sections A and B for each of your key magazine texts.

45 What is the repertoire of elements for the three magazines you have studied?

Key Term

Rhetorical questioning = A question asked for effect where no answer is expected. In magazines the focus of the question may encourage the reader to engage in self-reflection.

- The front cover functions as the start of the narrative and as such includes enigmas to encourage the reader to engage with the narrative and read on: '*The Ultimate DIY Sex Drug*', '*18 Performance Boosting Playlists*'. The narrative themes of fitness and lifestyle are also in evidence.

- The images develop the narrative through the way in which they are constructed. Readers are reminded throughout the magazine of the ideal they must aspire to.

- The captions and subheadings that accompany the images also define the narrative; they often use imperatives and the language of battle and aggression, metaphorically associating the fight to get fit with a war. The captions interpret the image for the reader and encode the preferred meaning to be decoded by the reader.

- The content – this is made up of regular pages that appear each month and are part of the magazine's narrative structure. These also contribute to the discourse and include: the contents page, which highlights what the magazine perceives are the most appealing articles and features; the '*Personal Trainer*' section, printed on less glossy paper to emphasise that this is 'serious'; the '*Core*' which each issue covers questions and issues of concern to the 'new man'; for example, '*Can Seduction be Taught?*' – this suggests that the *Men's Health* reader is willing to learn how to approach women even though the end goal is sex, not a relationship.

46 Why is it important that a magazine has a narrative structure?

Text: representation

The main representation area for *Men's Health* is clearly gender. As is discussed in other areas of this chapter, this magazine offers a representation of the modern, metrosexual man. Men's lifestyle magazines have risen in popularity matching the changing position of men in society. It is no longer seen as acceptable by some men to read publications like *Nuts* and *Zoo* and consequently their sales figures have fallen dramatically in recent years. The reason for the rise in popularity of *Men's Health* has been attributed to a 'crisis in masculinity' and as a backlash against feminism where men have felt the need to reassert their dominance in society.

As such, *Men's Health* offers a complex representation of masculinity. On the one hand, it is full of images of stereotypical, hyper real, extreme representations of men, conforming to the modern cultural stereotype. They invariably function alone, without the need of a woman and the magazine focuses on the concerns of the modern man aspiring for body perfection. The discourse of the magazine affirms the dominant position of the urban, heroic man in society. The negative aspect of this representation is an obsession with health and body image that promotes narcissistic tendencies and body anxiety. In this sense the magazine does offer a relatively narrow representation of the modern man.

Exam Tip

An important element of your examination response must be a consideration of the way in which the particular representation is constructed, anchored and mediated in the pages of the magazine.

An alternative view of the representation of men as discussed by David Gauntlett in his study '*Media, Gender and Identity*', is that this genre of magazine is a self-help guide for men who, in modern society, where their role is ambiguous, seem to have lost their way. He suggests that magazines such as this offer reassurance for men and develop their self-confidence. '*I have argued against the view that men's lifestyle magazines represent a re-assertion of old-fashioned masculine values, or a back-lash against feminism.... Instead their existence and popularity show men rather insecurely trying to find their place in the modern world, seeking help regarding how to behave in their relationships and advice on how to earn the attention, love and respect of women and the friendship of other men.*'

47 How are the representations of women constructed in *Men's Health*?

The representations seen in the magazine that support this argument are those of men seemingly wanting to learn about how to establish relationships, communicate and understand the opposite sex and to better themselves physically and emotionally.

Front cover

Analysing the front cover of your key magazine text is a good place to start.

- The masthead is bold and red – connotations of power and fervour. However, it is in lower case suggesting more sensitivity.

- There is a clear house style which is mainly established through the use of the primary colours of red, white and black and the conventional layout and design. This ensures that the magazine is easily recognisable on the shelf.

- The central image uses a film celebrity who is also known for his body. This offers a double aspiration for the audience. His mode of address is direct, encouraging the audience to emulate his physique. His 'assets' are on display, but he is wearing a T-shirt and is not bare chested. The cover line links to this emphasising the normality of aspiring to this body image: 'T-shirt arms by summer'.

- The language and mode of address contain imperatives that command the audience to take action regarding their own bodies. There are also references to war and battle reinforcing a **hegemonic male representation** of dominance.

- Quick fix problem solving is in evidence – '25 ways to put "old" on hold'. This also suggests the concern of the audience – ageing is seen to be a problem and something that the magazine unrealistically suggests can be delayed.

- The discourse and cover lines centre on male narcissism. The magazine constructs an image of modern **masculinity**. There are no references to women or relationships, only to 'sex'. One particular cover line seems to sum up the ideology of the magazine: 'Rock Star Lifestyle. Athlete's Body'.

- The slogan '100% Useful' reinforces the idea that the magazine will guide the reader in how to live their lives.

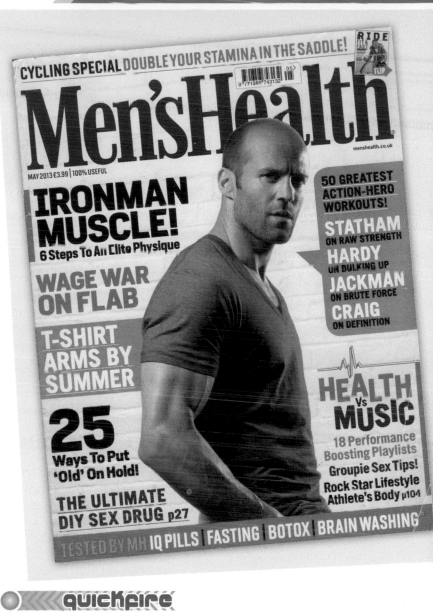

It is important that you also reinforce your initial observations from the front cover by analysing inside pages that you can use in your examination response. The advertisements within the magazine can give a good indication of the target audience. The magazine will provide potential advertisers with information about their readers/users, and the advertisers will be sure that they are targeting an audience for their products. Advertisements are essential for the magazine, without them the cost of the magazine would increase dramatically. The advertisements contained within this edition of *Men's Health* include:

- High end men's fragrances, for example *Victor and Rolf* and *Gucci Guilty*. These are **aspirational** products that will attract aspirers. The images linked to the products reflect the ideology of the magazine – the male in the *Victor and Rolf* advert is in black and white connoting sophistication. It has been manipulated post production with a focus on

Quickfire

(48) What are the positive and negative implications of the discourses contained within this magazine?

Key Terms

Hegemonic male representation = This derives from the theory of cultural hegemony by Antonio Gramsci. Simply put, it asserts that the dominant social position in society is taken by men and the subordinate one by women.

Masculinity = This is the state of 'being a man' and it can change to reflect changes in society. It is essentially what being a man means to a particular generation. This is reflected in media texts, for example men's lifestyle magazines.

his toned body and direct mode of address. The *Gucci* advert is in colour and features a man and the woman. The framing of the image suggests that the woman is attracted to the man, he is not looking at her but is engaging in a direct mode of address with the reader. This links with the notion of the dominant male who is in control. She is stereotypically beautiful, blonde and wearing red lipstick which carries connotations of the temptress. The name of the product itself suggests taking risks and being 'sinful'.

- Expensive watch brands including Omega and Breitling. These products are not subtle; they make a statement and say something about the wearer, again aspirational for the *Men's Health* reader. The celebrity endorser for Breitling is David Beckham, a **metrosexual man**. The copy language describes him as '*a legend forged by accomplishments'* giving the reader someone to emulate, a role model for modern masculinity.

- Cars – there is an advertisement for Audi Cars, but not a bottom of the range model, the R8 V10. This reinforces the stereotypical representation that men are interested in fast, expensive cars.

- Gadgets – the Sony Walkman that is waterproof with wraparound headphones for '*swimming, in the gym or running on the track'*. This reinforces the 'gym mentality' of the magazine. The construction of masculinity in the magazine expects that a gym regime is an essential part of the modern man's life. Another interesting gadget advertised is the Swiss Army Knife – a symbol of a man who can fend for himself in all conditions – another pressure for a man to live up to.

Feature pages

These are pages that are specific to that edition of the magazine. They will reflect the discourse of the magazine and address the issues pertinent to the target audience. This is also where women may appear within the magazine. In most of the magazine the focus is men and their interests. 'Rock Her World' is a feature in the issue studied focusing on how playing a woman the right music can '*amp up your sex life and grant you access to all areas'*. Through the use of statistics and assertions that 'real women' have been surveyed, the article attempts to convince the reader of its credibility.

The images are of tattooed women in typical rock clothing engaging in a direct mode of address with the reader. The women are photographed as men would like to view them thus conforming to Mulvey's **male gaze theory**. The language is overtly sexual in places employing the metaphor of music and consequent punning, '*find out how music flicks her switches and fast forward to the really good bit'* – it is all packaged in pseudo scientific analysis: '*a song she likes fires the part of her brain used for emotion'*, suggesting that the reader can understand female behaviour on a more complex level. There are several studies, statistics and university research projects mentioned in the article to help to validate the suggested male behaviour. To further attract a broad spectrum of male readers DJmagtech editor Michael Wilson reviews a range of gadgets and audio equipment with prices!

The article includes charts with graphics and a suggested playlist to ensure *Men's Health* man can please his chosen woman. Critics of the magazine have suggested that it really is not so far removed from the sexually explicit images and articles of *Nuts* and *Zoo*, it is just presented in a different, more politically correct way. This article and its reinforcement of the hegemonic man and the representation of women would go a long way to supporting that assertion.

Audience

Magazines and their online versions are rich texts to use when discussing audiences and users. This is mainly because they tend to have a clear and often niche target audience, but also because they are a media text that is instrumental in both constructing and categorising audiences.

Who is the audience for *Men's Health* magazine?

- Men who aspire to be the *Men's Health* man.

- The 'pick and mix' man who may read the magazine, but realistically knows he cannot achieve body perfection.

- The 'new man' who wants tips on how to survive in this role.

- Women who find the men attractive or who want to influence their own partner into a achieving a particular image.

- The statistical evidence suggests that the median age of the readership is 31 and that 66% are in the ABC1 **demographic category**.

Key Term

Demographic category = This is a group in which consumers are placed according to their age, sex, income, profession, etc. The categories range from A to E where categories A and B are the wealthiest and most influential members of society.

Key Term

Media pack = This is produced by the magazine publishers in order to inform advertisers of the magazine's target audience. It also includes information about advertising rates within the magazine.

quickfire

(50) Why would *Men's Health* want to inform advertisers that the majority of their audience belonged to the ABC1 demographic category?

Key Term

The Four Cs = This stands for Cross Cultural Consumer Characteristics and was a way of categorising consumers into groups through their motivational needs. The main groups were mainstreamers, aspirers, explorers, succeeders and reformers.

quickfire

(51) Which of the psychometric categories would be most likely to buy *Men's Health* and why?

How does *Men's Health* magazine construct an audience?

This is a complex idea of audience related to the ways in which magazines manipulate their readers and suggest to them how they live their lives. The images, language and mode of address, content and representations contained within the magazine suggest who the audience is and also who the magazine would like them to be! This is also reinforced by the **media pack** produced by the publication for potential advertisers. The aim of this pack is to 'sell' the audience to the right advertiser. Here the magazine's producers will give statistical and opinion-led information about their readers. However, it must be remembered, as illustrated in the possible audiences listed above, there is a difference between the magazine's construction of its audience and the actual reader. The *Men's Health* media pack claims:

'Men's Health *is the magazine for active, successful, intelligent men who want to make the most of their physical, professional and emotional lives. We give men the tools they need to make their lives better.'*

The media pack also includes detailed information about who the *Men's Health* reader is. For example, how much money they spend on skin care and shavers, thus contributing to the construction of their male audience that is then replicated in the magazine itself.

Social Status

ABC1	892,000	69%
AB	425,000	33%
C1	468,000	36%
C2	254,000	20%

AB 425,000 33%
C1 468,000 36%
C2 254,000 20%

MH HAS MORE AB READERS THAN GQ AND ESQUIRE

How does *Men's Health* magazine categorise its audience?

As stated earlier, one way in which *Men's Health* defines and categorises its audience is through demographics. This is reinforced in its media pack where the readership is defined in terms of luxury consumable goods including cars, watches and technology. This demographic is also reflected in the advertisements contained within the magazine and online. There is also an emphasis on age and gender offering more detailed information to the advertisers.

Psychometric profiling can also be used to categorise magazine audiences. This method defines audiences by their VALS – values, attitudes and lifestyle and was developed by Young and Rubicam, an advertising agency and became known as the **Four Cs**. They grouped recognisably stereotypical audiences together according to their needs which included: security, control, status, individuality, freedom, survival and escape.

What pleasures does *Men's Health* give an audience?

Here, the uses and gratifications model can be applied in considering what *Men's Health* offers an audience:

- It offers diversion and escapism from everyday life as the lifestyles included in the pages of the publication are often aspirational. The celebrity endorsement featured in the issues studied included Jason Statham and Mark Cavendish to appeal to a range of audiences.

- It gives information and can be said to educate an audience in, for example, nutrition and fitness. The lexis is often scientific and some of the articles are written by 'experts' to add superficial credibility.

- Some audiences may gain pleasure through personal identity, comparing their experiences with those of men featured in the magazine.

How might different audiences respond to *Men's Health*?

- The **pick and mix theory** suggests that audiences may select the aspects of the magazine that best suit them and their lifestyle and ignore others.

- Alternatively, there is some evidence to suggest that magazines like *Men's Health* are to blame for dissatisfaction with body image resulting in illness previously only seen in women, for example anorexia.

- Applying Stuart Hall's response theory, audiences may accept the preferred reading encoded by the creators of *Men's Health* and strive to attain a six pack. They may have a negotiated reading accepting some of the assertions of the magazine and ignoring others or be entirely opposed to the version of reality represented in the magazine.

Key Term

Pick and mix theory =
This was suggested by British sociologist and media theorist, David Gauntlett. He asserted the autonomy of the audience and challenged the notion that audiences are immediately affected by what they read. He maintains that audiences are more sophisticated than this and will select aspects of the media texts that best suit their needs and ignore the rest.

Task

Having established who the *Men's Health* reader is, consider how the magazine targets and appeals to this audience. Use specific examples from the issue you have studied.

Summary: The Magazine Industry

APPEAL AND TARGETING

Target audience: male and niche

How are they targeted?

Audience appeal?

Gauntlett – pick and mix audience

Responses: Stuart Hall – different responses

Pleasures: uses and gratifications – escapism and social interaction

Construction of the audience through the discourse, layout and design, etc.

Categorisation of audience – demographic and psychometric

GENRE

Consider the codes and conventions of the lifestyle sub-genre

Genre linked to discourse

How is the genre evident in the magazine style and content?

NARRATIVE

How does the structure and content reflect the narrative?

Regular pages

Features and articles

Placing of pages within the structure

Positioning of the reader within the narrative

REPRESENTATION

Men – 'masculinity in crisis'? Complexity of the representation

How is the representation of men constructed and mediated?

What are the different theoretical viewpoints – Gauntlett?

Representations of metrosexual modern man

Women – how are they represented?

MEN'S HEALTH

Publisher – what other titles do they own?

Readership and circulation

Issues regarding print versus online magazines – advantages and disadvantages

A GLOBAL TEXT?

Consider the extent

How do issues differ according to country?

Marketing and promotion of magazine

Magazine online version – consider what different experiences this offers the user

REGULATION

How is the magazine industry regulated?

How does the text adhere to the code of practice?

MARKETING

Cross-platform opportunities

Internet ads

Introduction

Brian A Jackson/Shutterstock.com

The newspaper industry is one of the longest running media formats and has undergone many changes in order to maintain sales and attract a readership in a society where audiences no longer automatically turn to the print media for their daily news.

When studying the newspaper industry in preparation for the MS4 examination you will need to ensure that you have a broad and up-to-date understanding. Your choice of main texts must allow you to demonstrate that understanding. Remember, it is helpful if your texts are varied and diverse; this way you will illustrate your awareness of a range of issues related to this industry effectively. For the newspaper industry you must ensure that you have studied three different newspaper titles. You must engage in a detailed study of one edition of a title, but it will also help your understanding to study aspects from other editions of the same title.

It is important that you are able to analyse your chosen newspapers in detail using relevant technical terminology. You also need to understand how the newspapers target, construct and appeal to their audience and how different audiences may respond to the text.

For the purposes of the MS4 examination it is essential that the analysis is of the whole newspaper for a specific day, not just the front page. That said, the front page is a good start as this is the 'shop window' of the newspaper and is important in catching the eye of the consumer – essential in a competitive market. Its purpose is also to communicate the ideology and the voice of the newspaper and what the reader will get if they buy it. Furthermore, it also has to establish the brand identity of the newspaper so that audiences will recognise it and develop expectations of its content. Analysing the front page also allows you to apply the correct technical terminology related to newspapers. However, it is also important that you consider how the text appears in other **media platforms**, for example the online version.

Key Term

Media platform = This is the range of different ways of communicating with an audience, for example newspapers, the Internet, and television.

quickfire

(52) Why are newspaper front pages important in attracting readers?

Key Terms

Tabloid = This actually refers to the dimensions of the newspaper, a tabloid is smaller and more compact in size. However, there are further connotations attached to the term and it also tends to refer to a newspaper whose content focuses on lighter news, for example celebrity gossip, sport and television.

Broadsheet = This term describes a larger newspaper that publishes more serious news, for example *The Daily Telegraph*, which has maintained its broadsheet format.

Gatekeepers = These are the people responsible for deciding the most appropriate stories to appear in the newspapers. They may be the owner, editor or senior journalists. They will only let the stories most appropriate for the ideology of the paper 'through the gate'.

News agenda = This is the list of stories that may appear in a particular paper. The items on the news agenda will reflect the style and ethos of the paper. The speculation over the date of the birth of Kate Middleton's baby was high on the news agenda of a tabloid paper.

Key Figures

Sir David Rowat Barclay and **Sir Frederick Hugh Barclay**, commonly referred to as the 'Barclay Brothers', are British businessmen. The identical twin brothers have very substantial business interests primarily in media, retail and property. *The Sunday Times* Rich List of 2013 estimated their wealth at £2.35 billion.

quickfire

(53) What observations can you make about the structure of newspaper ownership in the UK?

A range of different newspapers are published every day in the UK, these include national, local and Sunday editions. In the past, newspapers were mainly categorised by their size – **tabloids** and **broadsheets**. Although these terms are still used, they are no longer accurate, as newspapers over the years have experimented with different sizes and designs in order to bolster a diminishing readership and to address audience needs. Historically, tabloid newspapers constituted the popular press, and broadsheets were quality newspapers referring to the style of news they carried. Newspapers can now be divided into three groups: the quality newspapers, previously known as broadsheets, for example *The Guardian* and *The Independent*, the middle market tabloids made up of *The Daily Mail* and *The Express* and the tabloids, or 'red tops', for example *The Sun*.

Who owns the press?

It is important to be aware of newspaper ownership and its impact upon the production and distribution of your chosen texts. By far the biggest player in the newspaper and other media industries is News Corporation owned by Rupert Murdoch. His media empire includes *The Sun, The Times* and *The Sun on Sunday*. Other main newspapers are owned as follows:

- *The Independent, the i* and *The Independent on Sunday:* Alexander Lebedev's Independent Print Limited
- *The Guardian* and *The Observer* – Scott Trust Limited
- *The Daily Mirror, The Sunday Mirror and The People* – Trinity Mirror
- *Daily Express, Sunday Express, Daily Star, Daily Star on Sunday* – Richard Desmond's Northern & Shell
- *The Daily Telegraph* and *The Sunday Telegraph* – Press Holdings owned by The Barclay Brothers
- *The Daily Mail* and *The Mail on Sunday* – Lord Rothermere's Daily Mail and General Trust plc.

You must also bear in mind the hundreds of local papers that are produced around the country. Studying a local paper as one of your three main texts will give you an even broader perspective of the industry to use in the response to the examination question.

Who chooses the news and why?

News values are the criteria that will influence the decisions made by the owners, editors and journalists about which stories will appear in their newspaper. These decisions are made every day by **gatekeepers** who decide how the news is selected and constructed for the audience. This will reflect the **news agenda** for the paper. Although not all news values are relevant today, some of the criteria still used are:

- Threshold: the bigger the story the more likely it is to get onto the news agenda.
- Negativity: bad news is more exciting and interesting than good news.
- Unexpectedness: an event that is a shock or out of the ordinary, e.g. the New York hurricane. An event like this will push other news stories off the agenda and changes to the front page may be made at the last minute.
- Unambiguity: events that are easy to report and are not complex will be higher up the agenda of some newspapers. Modern wars are often difficult to report and are avoided by tabloid newspapers unless they involve personalities or can be graphically represented.
- Personalisation: news stories that have a human interest angle are more likely to appear

in some newspapers. Readers are interested in celebrities, and stories have more meaning if they are personalised.

- Proximity: the closer to home the story is, the more interested the reader. Tabloid and local newspapers tend to be more **ethnocentric** than quality newspapers.

- Elite nations/people: stories about important people and powerful nations, e.g. the USA, will be higher up the agenda.

- Continuity/currency: stories that are already in the news continue to run and are updated as new aspects to the story appear, e.g. the continuing financial problems and worldwide recession.

Key Term

Ethnocentric = This means that the newspaper will be more concerned to cover stories that are closely related to the reader and their concerns. Tabloid and local papers only tend to cover international news stories if they can relate them specifically to their readers.

quickfire

(54) What news values are evident on the front page of The Chronicle?

An industry in crisis?

Just like the magazine industry, the newspaper industry is facing a drop in circulation figures as the readership diminishes. This reflects sociological changes related to the ways in which readers want to access their news. With the advances in digital technology, news can be more immediate and a new generation of consumers who are used to receiving information in bite-sized chunks, are much less likely to want to pick up a newspaper. Just as, in the past, newspapers themselves have 'down sized' in order to address audience needs for a more compact version, they have also had to produce online versions of their papers to target a new audience. The digital revolution has also had an impact on how news is gathered. Frequently news channels use information from the general public rather than their own journalists as they now have the means to record images and send information immediately. This is particularly true when the story is unexpected, for example a riot. When the murder of the soldier occurred in the middle of the day in a busy street in Woolwich in 2013, the images were uploaded onto social networking sites almost immediately and news gatherers had to look to these platforms for their initial information.

Mirrorpix

Advantages of online news sites

- They are immediate and up to date. When something happens users can access the news and get regular updates.

- They offer more immediate interactive opportunities, for example there is access to audio-visual clips and opportunities to blog or email opinions. *The Daily Mail*, which has a high percentage of female readers, has had particular success with its online version of *Femail* with its diet of fashion and gossip.

- Apps for several newspapers are available for mobile phones and iPads.

Task

Look at the online version of the newspapers you are studying and consider how they differ from the print version.

quickfire

⑤⑤ What are the advantages of print newspapers for readers?

- There is an archive facility so that users can access back issues or features.
- The navigation tool allows users to quickly select the news and features that interest them.

Industry: regulation

How is the newspaper industry regulated?

The Press Complaints Commission (PCC) is the self-regulatory body for the print journalism industry, created and funded by newspapers and magazines themselves. Its main function is to act and make decisions in the event of complaints about content in newspapers and magazines. The PCC also takes into consideration the activities of journalists as part of their information gathering. The PCC has a code of practice that must be adhered to by newspaper and magazine journalists; a journalist who breaks the code runs the risk of losing their job and publications may be asked to publically apologise for any wrong doing. The main points of the code cover accuracy, privacy and harassment. It is also the responsibility of newspapers to regulate themselves and to make decisions about the accuracy of their stories and the means by which they obtained them. There have been several examples of newspapers being sued by, in particular, celebrities, over invasion of privacy or by the publication of **libellous** stories.

However, the PCC was severely criticised in the Leveson inquiry, which in 2012 investigated the culture, practice and ethics of the British press in the light of the phone hacking scandal and other issues related to intrusion of privacy by the press. The PCC was seen to be largely ineffectual in regulating the newspaper industry. Lord Leveson made recommendations for a new regulatory body to replace the PCC.

In the report he says:

'*The press needs to establish a new regulatory body, which is truly independent of industry leaders and of government and politicians. It must promote high standards of journalism and protect both the public interest and the rights of individuals. The chair and other members of the body must be independent and appointed by a fair and open process.*'

Key Term

Libel = Written communication of damaging false information.

Key Figures

Lord Justice Leveson is an English judge who chaired the public inquiry into the culture, practices and ethics of the British press, prompted by the *News of the World* phone hacking scandal.

www.bbc.co.uk

He also stated that there would be firmer sanctions including substantial fines for those newspapers that were deemed to have broken the law. Newspapers are concerned that this would be set up by royal charter and therefore the self-regulatory system would be governed by legislation.

The press industry is unhappy about these recommendations becoming a legal requirement.

The government has delayed implementing his suggested reforms to press regulation much to the anger of those involved in bringing about such reforms. Those against the reforms want newspapers to still have some independence regarding self-regulation in order to protect the freedom of the press.

Analysing newspaper front pages

Although it is not enough to just study newspaper front pages, it is a good place to start. The front cover will give information about the brand identity and ideology of the paper. The newspaper industry, like other media industries, is very competitive and what the newspaper's gatekeepers decide to put on its front page will be essential in attracting an audience. The main conventions of a newspaper front page include:

- The masthead. This is the name of the paper, which can signify the paper's ethos and ideology. For example, *The Independent* suggests forward thinking and a lack of bias. The typography of the masthead also communicates messages. *The Daily Telegraph* has maintained its traditional font style which has connotations of history and longevity. In contrast, *The Guardian*, in its rebrand, changed its font style to give a more modern feel to the paper.

- The plug/puff. This usually runs across the top of the front page and advertises what else is in the newspaper. The focus will often be on lighter aspects of the news or for quality newspapers may focus on the arts. The aim of the plug is to broaden the target audience.

- The headline. This will be in a larger font than the rest of the front page story, the aim being to attract an audience. Popular/tabloid newspapers have dramatic headlines using devices such as alliteration, hyperbole, colloquialisms and puns to target the audience. Quality newspapers are attracting readers who want more serious, detailed news and therefore their headlines tend to be more informative.

- The strapline. This is usually placed either above or below the main headline and provides more information or anchors the meaning of the central image.

- Subheadings. These are short headlines which break up the main text to make it easier to read. They appear throughout the paper but are mainly evident in popular, tabloid papers where they tend to be dramatic, for example 'tragedy', to encourage the audience to read on.

- The jump line. This follows the teaser headline on the front page and encourages the reader to buy the newspaper in order to read on. For example, 'turn to page 6'.

- The central image. For popular/tabloid newspapers the central image is essential in selling the paper. It may be often of a celebrity or be a dramatic image of an event. The image may be indistinct as it has been taken by a **paparazzi photographer**. This often emphasises the exclusivity of the story for the paper.

(56) What are the advantages and disadvantages of curbing the freedom of the press?

Task

Research the reasons for the Leveson Inquiry and sum up Lord Leveson's main findings.

Key Term

Paparazzi photographer = A freelance photographer who aggressively pursues celebrities and royalty to take pictures to sell to magazines and newspapers for the highest price.

Exam Tip

Referring to a newspaper front page will allow you to compare the differences between the texts you have chosen and to demonstrate your use of relevant media terminology.

©Mirrorpix

Inside the newspaper

As stated earlier, unlike MS2, it is not acceptable to just study the front page of the newspaper – this is not comparable with a student who has studied a whole film. You are looking at the whole publication and its place within the industry. The inside content will differ according to the newspapers you are studying. When analysing an entire edition of your chosen title you need to consider:

- The copy. This is the writing in the body of the newspaper. Quality newspapers are text led and their copy will be detailed and dense, even on the front page. It will also offer a more balanced viewpoint. The copy on the front page of a popular newspaper will be limited and bite-sized, encapsulating the main aspects of the lead story, it may also give the paper's viewpoint. The inside pages of a quality newspaper may still be text led but where photographs and images are used they will be of a high quality.

- The regular pages. These may include letters pages, horoscopes, cooking, international news, etc. Quality papers like *The Guardian* have a G2 supplement that has a different focus every day and the content is feature based rather than news. For example, the Friday G2 focuses on music and film reviews. The Page 3 girl is still a regular, if increasingly controversial, convention of *The Sun*.

- Letters pages. Here, the readers have their say; this can give you an insight into the readership of the paper. In quality papers the name and profession of the writer is published, which again signifies the target reader and their ideas and interests.

- The editorial. This is useful as it is where the newspaper gives its opinions about the stories it has run that day. This may give an insight into the **political bias** of the newspaper.

- **Features**. These make up a lot of the paper's content and will offer detailed analysis, information and research. The focus of the feature stories will reflect the interests and concerns of the target audience. For example, one of the feature stories in *The Independent* in June 2013 was 'The Real Kitchen Nightmares' and focused on the experiences of restaurant consultants.

- Sport. All newspapers have sports pages at the back. The actual sport featured, the amount of coverage and the headlines will be in keeping with the style of the paper.

Key Terms

Political bias = This is where a newspaper may show support for a political party through its choice of stories, style of coverage, cartoons, etc. It may be subtle and implicit or explicit as in the case of the tabloids on Election Day.

Feature = This is a story that is not tied to a news event. It may be more narrative in style and will be more detailed. It may be related to a human interest story or an issue of common concern to the readership.

©Mirrorpix

Main text: *The Independent* and *i*

Industry information

- *The Independent* was first launched on 7 October 1986 making it one of the youngest newspapers.

- It started its life as a broadsheet newspaper but in 2003, facing a decline in sales, it decided to launch a tabloid edition of the paper. This was initially just in the London area. This provoked a discussion around the changing ways in which readers 'used' their newspaper and was seen to be much more portable and easy to manage on the move. *The Times* followed suit and eventually both papers decided to produce only a tabloid version. The preferred name for this style of newspaper now is a 'quality compact' to differentiate from the popular **red top** tabloids, for example *The Sun* and *The Mirror*.

- Its original advertising slogan was *It is. Are You*, suggesting its 'independent' approach to the news.

- Its publishers are Independent Print owned by the Lebedev family who own *The Independent, The Independent on Sunday* and the *i*. They also hold a 75% share in *The London Evening Standard*.

- In June 2013 the **headline circulation** for *The Independent* was 75,089 whilst the paid for circulation was 56,437.

- *The Independent* has had several rebrands and continues to have a different style from other newspapers, often having a large image in the centre of the page or even tables of statistics or a graphic and very little copy beyond the headline and subheading.

- The online version of the newspaper was launched on 23 January 2008.

- In October 2010 the sister paper the *i* was launched. This sells for 20p and offers a more condensed menu of news and current affairs items. The target audience are lapsed newspaper readers: *'We are creating a newspaper for the 21st century that is designed for people who have a thirst for information and entertainment in the limited time that they have available.'*

  (www.guardian.co.uk)

- The *i* was one of the only newspapers to increase its circulation from April to May 2013, up 0.75% month on month, to 306,578 copies.

- The editor is Amol Rajan who was appointed in June 2013 and is the first non-white editorial head of a UK national newspaper; at 29 he is also young for the post. At the same time Olly Duff, another 29 year old and the executive editor of *The Independent*, was made editor of its 20p sister title, *i*. Lebedev said of the new appointments: *'Our businesses are at a critical stage and a bold approach is needed for our industry. Today I am continuing this approach by appointing as editors two highly talented young journalists. Their energy, creativity and resourcefulness will invigorate both* The Independent *and* i.'

  (www.guardian.co.uk)

 **quickfire**

㊗ What are the advantages of a newspaper like the *i*?

Text: genre

The Independent is a quality newspaper in a tabloid format. It offers serious daily news, current affairs and political news as well as entertainment including, sport, the arts and lifestyle. Politically it is to the left of centre and is viewed as a liberal paper. A repertoire of elements place it with other examples of newspaper from this genre:

- The layout and design is distinctive in *The Independent*. The headlines are informative and deal with serious issues. There is usually a main image that occupies most of the page; the aim of this is to catch the eye or to provoke a response. The plug/puff will give suggestions as to the wider content of the newspaper to appeal to a broader audience. The topics that appear here will be the arts, sport and lifestyle, for example.

- Each day has different sections and supplements, for example Tuesday motoring and Wednesday property. This is a genre convention of this style of newspaper.

- Technically, the expectation is that there will be high production values associated with this genre of paper. The standard of photography will be high; the use of paparazzi style photographs would be unusual. The graphics are also complex and are employed to illustrate features and stories where photography is inappropriate.

The *i* is interesting in that it is one of a kind; there is no other newspaper that markets itself in the same way. It is a concise, quality newspaper that offers a daily briefing delivering all the main news at a glance. The genre is reflected through:

- The 'busy' front page and the large branding of the masthead. The page is split up into sections and there is more content on the front page than would usually appear on a quality newspaper. The price is large and positioned in the top left as this is a selling strategy.

- The strap line that appears every day reminds the reader of the genre and its exclusivity, 'Britain's only concise quality newspaper'. 'Quality' is in red to add extra emphasis and to distinguish it from a publication like, for example, *The Metro*.

- The extensive use of colour. This emphasises the vibrancy of this newspaper and distinguishes it from others. This is also more likely to attract a younger target audience.

- There are still links to the sister paper to signify that it is part of the same brand. *The Independent* masthead appears in miniature underneath the *i* masthead. The production values, particularly with regard to the images used, are high.

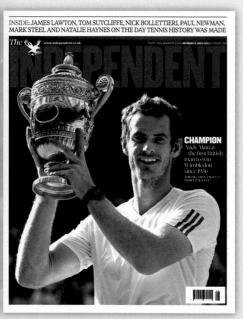

The Independent, 8.07.13

Text: narrative

The narrative of a newspaper can be discussed in terms of the structure of the publication. The audience for the text will have an expectation of this structure and of what appears where; this will have been built up over time. The narrative commences with the front page which tends to have a conventional house style and a brand identity which remains consistent for that newspaper and is recognised by the audience. This is then followed by the regular placing of other internal pages. The narrative is also conveyed through:

- Language and mode of address. The mode of address of *The Independent* is formal and colloquialisms and slang are rarely used. There is often use of subject-specific lexis related to a story or feature and an expectation that the reader will understand this. For example, 'call for amnesty on illegal immigrants'.

- Content. This newspaper is less concerned with gossip stories related to the rich and famous and more concerned with news and current affairs. The lighter aspects of the paper will focus on lifestyle and the arts. Often the newspaper will have an ongoing narrative related to a particular story and will include follow-up reports.

- The front page is instrumental in establishing the overall narrative of the paper. Through its front page stories it will set out the agenda of the newspaper and what the reader can expect. It will also use narrative devices such as enigmas, these are evident in the headlines and subheadings and encourage the reader to buy the newspaper to find out the rest of the story.

- The images in the newspaper also have a role in developing the narrative. They give the audience a visual depiction of the story and can capture a moment in time effectively. This is particularly true with regard to news stories where the reader has not experienced the event first hand and has to rely on the newspaper report for their information. The caption that accompanies the image anchors it and mediates the image and therefore the story for the audience. This constructing of the narrative can manipulate the reader's response to the story. Images in newspapers can be very dramatic and can tell the story much more effectively than words.

Text: representation

Newspapers are rich texts to analyse with regard to a range of areas of representation. On the front page and inside you should be able to find examples that allow you to discuss the following representations:

- Events. This is what newspapers are about, the representation of news events. According to the paper and their readers these events may be portrayed differently. The representation of an event may also reflect the ideology of the newspaper. This may be more explicit according to the event, for example a general election.

- Issues. The features pages of quality newspapers like *The Independent* and *i* will frequently discuss and analyse issues that are pertinent to their readers. These may include wars, terrorism or political issues. In the example of the newspapers for 28 June 2013 both newspapers led with issue-based stories. *The Independent's* main story was a new technique to allow the fertilisation of an egg with the DNA of three people. This was represented in a balanced way in this paper but was also celebrated as a scientific breakthrough. The *i* led with a story about the shortage of classrooms in primary schools, an issue relevant to its readers. In another issue of this paper, the issue of Aids was represented by a special edition of the paper edited by Elton John.

- Age. Quality newspapers will tend to include more positive images of older people, particularly as due to the type of news they cover, these will tend to be featured as an authority nationally and internationally.

- Gender. It is often the case, because of the focus on world and national news, that the stories will be dominated by representation of men. However, several of the columnists and contributors are women and in the issue studied there was a page given over to an article entitled 'Why can't women in public life be treated more like a man?'

The *i*, 1.12.10

Analysing front pages

The Independent

- The masthead is in a strong, large, blocked font with connotations of stability and reliability. The use of the colour red signifies power and is dramatic and eye catching. This suggestion of power is further emphasised by the logo of the bird of prey delivering the paper.

- The central image of a fertilised egg cell is large and thought provoking and is typical of the style of this newspaper in that it is also enigmatic and takes up most of the page. It is unusual not to personalise the story, further suggesting the concentration on serious, ground-breaking stories.

- The headline and subheading anchor the image and explain its relevance. Although not essentially dramatic, the headline is portentous. The use of the word 'our' makes the story relevant to the reader.

Exam Tip

When discussing areas of representation in your chosen newspaper text remember to analyse how the representation is constructed through aspects like language, mode of address, use of images, for example.

The Independent, 28.6.13   *The i, 28.6.13*

- Enigma is also used: 'babies with three parents...'

- The copy associated with the main story is relatively dense for a front cover and uses technical and specific lexis: *'legislation to allow the use of mitochondrial replacement could be passed by Parliament at the end of next year...'*. The expectation is that the reader will understand or want to find out more about this story, signifying the target audience and their concerns.

- The plug/puff focuses on food and drink. The expectation is that the reader will recognise Gordon Ramsay and understand the intertextual headline. The other plug items refer to 'punch' and ' the 10 best rosé wines' suggesting the middle-class target audience.

- The secondary stories remain with serious news items including Leveson and the funeral of James Gandolfini, the star of *The Sopranos*. The subheading 'Back to Homs' assumes that readers will know that this is about the Syrian conflict.

Key Terms

Splash = The story that is given the most prominence on the front page of a newspaper.

Sister paper = One that is published by the same company and has links to other papers in the brand.

The *i*

The front cover of this newspaper is for the same day.

- The layout and design is very different suggesting the contrast in purpose and audience of this publication compared with the main paper. *The i* front cover is packed with snippets of stories; the 'genetic inheritance' story is just one of them and has not been chosen as the **splash**. Colour is used widely to present the paper as interesting and dynamic.

- The masthead is positioned to the left in a column, the use of a lower case letter links to the **sister paper** but also suggests its more compact format. The masthead and logo of *The Independent* also feature in miniature to establish the positive links with this paper.

- The slogan reinforces the paper's purpose, *'Britain's first and only concise quality newspaper'*. The word 'quality' is highlighted to distinguish it from other papers.

- The price is prominent as this is a selling technique. At 20p it is a very cheap newspaper.

- The focus on 'quality' is further reinforced by the range of stories. The topics of these stories include shale gas and illegal immigrants.

- The lead is about the crisis in primary schools, the main aspects of the story are bullet pointed for easy reading. The central image anchors the story by featuring keen middle-class schoolchildren. Interestingly, they have their backs to us, consequently the reader is positioned as part of the class and encouraged to empathise with their predicament.

- Sport is featured in a plug at the bottom covering a range of sports in order to attract a wider audience and differentiate it from the football-focused tabloids.

- The social networking sites are featured on the front page to encourage audience interactivity.

Inner pages: The News Matrix

The *i*, 26.10.10

- This gives 'The day at a glance' and offers digested news that is easy to read. The double page spread contains a range of bite-sized newspaper articles covering news and general interest. There is national and international news including the standard of living, the suspects in the Boston bombing and statistics about the amount of cyclists killed.

- The layout and design suggests a younger reader who does not have the time to read the news in detail but who wants to keep up to date with events and will therefore be attracted by the concise format.

- There are clear informative headings, for example 'Internet trolls are bored, not malicious' and a subheading highlighting the topic, for example 'Cyber Bullying'.

- This includes the 'Letter from the Editor'. This, however, is very personal and does comment on the news of the day. In it Oliver Duff tells an anecdotal story about

Task

Analyse the News Matrix pages for the edition you are studying. What similarities are there to this example?

quickfire

⑥③ How does The News Matrix page appeal to the target audience?

Exam Tip

Ensure that you have an overview of the whole paper and can discuss the inner pages as well as the front page in your examination response.

---

proposing to his girlfriend which involves the audience and humanises him, subverting the stereotypical representation of a newspaper editor.

- There are also light-hearted items with graphic images related to EU myths about supposed rules. These are humorous but there is an expectation that the reader will understand the references.

- There is a 'Page 3 Profile' of Henry VIII, which is informative whilst also wryly suggesting that if he had lived today he would have been a psychopath. This lightens the article and reflects the younger reader.

- This 'matrix' format is replicated for the business and sport section. The aim is to guide the reader quickly through the key issues with colourful subheadings which act as markers.

- At the top of each page there is an index that looks like a website navigation bar to allow ease of movement through the paper to the sections that are of most interest. This suggests that the reader may be more of a 'pick and mix' reader who will turn to the pages of most interest rather than reading the paper from start to finish.

Audience

Newspapers in the print and digital versions are media texts that are instrumental in attracting, constructing and categorising audiences. The website www.newsworks.org.uk gives you up-to-date readership figures.

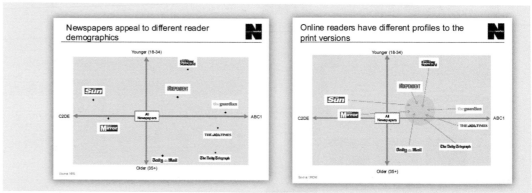

Who is the audience for *The Independent*?

- The average daily readership for the year up to March 2013 was 412,000. Twice as many men as women read the paper.

- The demographic audience profile is: 48% AB adults, 73% ABC1 adults and 93% ABC1C2 Adults.

- The age bracket with the highest amount of readers is 25–34 followed by 35–44. The readership profile is:

Young, urban professionals who regularly purchase goods and services online. They may not have children yet and therefore have a higher **disposable income**. They are interested in the combination of news and other aspects offered by the paper. They are interested in technology – *The Independent* has recently integrated **Blippar** into its daily editorial to allow readers to access multimedia platforms including videos and additional photographs related to a particular story.

- In February 2013 *The Independent*'s online newspaper had a huge growth with its daily average browsers up 95.3% year on year.

Key Terms

Disposable income = This is the amount of money available to a person after they have paid taxes, bills, etc. It is their money to spend as they wish.

Blippar = Blippar is the first image-recognition phone app aimed at bringing to life media texts like newspapers and magazines with augmented reality experiences and instantaneous content. The company launched in the UK in the summer of 2011 and will be expanding globally throughout 2013.

Who is the audience for *i*?

- Those who want a new kind of paper to match their busy lifestyles. The readers are younger, less concerned with reading detailed news stories, but want to keep up to date with current affairs and be entertained by lifestyle stories and features. The element of humour will also attract this audience.

- The average readership for the year was 579,000; 92% of the readers were from the ABC1C2 demographic; 57% of the readers are men and 43% women.

- The editor of *i* described it as 'colourful, concise and intelligent' and added that his role was as a 'guide through the information overload'.

How might different audiences respond to *The Independent*?

- The pick and mix theory suggests that audiences may select the aspects of the newspaper that best suit them and their lifestyle and ignore others.

- Applying Stuart Hall's response theory, audiences may accept the preferred reading encoded by the creators of *The Independent,* if they are loyal readers who believe in the ethos of the paper, then this is more likely to be the case. They may have a negotiated reading, accepting some of the assertions of the newspaper and ignoring others, or be entirely opposed to the newspaper as they do not share its ideology or political leanings.

- Critics of the paper have accused it of being a 'viewspaper' and not a serious newspaper with an unbiased, balanced stance on issues of the day.

How do *The Independent* and *i* construct their readers?

This is a complex idea of audience related to the ways in which newspapers communicate ideas about who they think their readers are. The images, language and mode of address, content and representations contained within the newspaper suggest the reader profile and what they want information about, but also who the newspaper would like them to be! The ideology of the newspaper will be clearly discernible through its content and style and there is an assumption on the part of the newspaper that the readers share the same ideology and that is why they buy the newspaper. In the past *The Independent* has taken a strong line on main issues of the day: it was against the Iraq war and criticised the UK and USA's policy on combating terrorism in the wake of the 11th September attacks. The paper has also taken strong positions on environmental issues, campaigned against the introduction of ID cards, and campaigned against the restriction of mass immigration to the UK. In voicing its viewpoint about these issues the newspaper suggests that the reader will feel equally strongly and that is why they continue to buy the paper. This is also reinforced by information produced by the publication for potential advertisers. The aim of this is to 'sell' the audience to the right advertiser. Here the newspaper's agents will give statistical and opinion-led information about their readers. However, it must be remembered, that there may be a difference between the newspaper's construction of its audience and the actual reader.

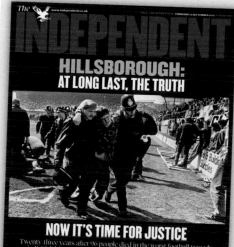

Summary: The Newspaper Industry

APPEAL AND TARGETING

Target audience: middle class, politically aware, left of centre

How are they targeted?

Audience appeal?

Gauntlett – pick and mix audience

Responses: Stuart Hall – different responses

Pleasures: uses and gratifications – social interaction, information

Construction of the audience through the content, ideology, mode of address, layout and design, etc.

Categorisation of audience – demographics

GENRE

Consider the codes and conventions of the quality newspaper

Genre linked to content and style

How is the genre evident in the magazine style and content?

NARRATIVE

How does the structure and content reflect the narrative?

Front page

Choice of images

Language and mode of address

Regular pages

Features and articles

Placing of pages within the structure

Positioning of the reader within the narrative

REPRESENTATION

Events, issues, gender, ethnicity, regional and national identity

How is the representation constructed and mediated?

What are the different theoretical viewpoints – Gauntlett?

THE INDEPENDENT

AUDIENCE

TEXT

INDUSTRY

Publisher – what other titles do they own?

Readership and circulation

Issues regarding print versus online newspapers – advantages and disadvantages

Newspaper online version – consider what different experiences this offers the user/reader

What other platforms are available, e.g. Blippar

REGULATION

How is the newspaper industry regulated?

How does the text adhere to the code of practice?

What are the current issues surrounding the regulation of this industry?

MS4

The Advertising Industry

Introduction

In studying the advertising industry for MS4, you must ensure that you develop an in-depth understanding of this industry that you are able to demonstrate through the choice of your three main texts. To facilitate this, as with all the industries you will study, these texts should be three different **advertising campaigns**, not three single advertisements. This would not be comparable to the complexity and length of texts studied in other industries. Each campaign should comprise 5–6 advertisements that could be a combination of print and audio-visual. You must aim to discuss 3–4 of these advertisements in your examination response.

Advertising is one of the most powerful media industries and is additionally interesting in that it is also an integral part of all the other industries you will study. All media texts need to market and promote themselves in order to communicate with audiences and achieve success. The aim of all texts is to create a **brand identity** that becomes recognisable to an audience. The advertising industry, like other industries, has adapted in order to reflect sociological change and consumer demands. The industry has had to examine how it can best access a modern audience. As audiences have changed aspects of their behaviour, for example their television viewing habits, advertisers have been forced to consider new platforms, for example mobile phones, to reach audiences.

Advertising comes in a variety of forms and is used for a variety of purposes and it is helpful if your choice of texts reflects this. For example:

- The producers of consumable products like clothing and beauty products persuade us to buy things we want but don't necessarily need.

- Charities want to raise audience awareness and encourage donations. They can use different and harder hitting strategies as their aim is to shock their audience into action. This may be through disturbing or emotive images.

- Event organisers want to promote the particular event and to encourage the buying of tickets to fund this event. Their campaigns may be cross platform.

Key Terms

Advertising campaign = This is a co-ordinated series of linked advertisements with a clear recognisable theme. It will be broadcast across a range of different platforms.

Brand identity = This is the association the audience make with the brand, for example Chanel or Nike. This is built up over time and reinforced by the advertising campaigns and their placement. For example, Chanel produces campaigns with high production values which appear in expensive, glamorous magazines. Part of their brand identity is their choice of 'spokesperson', for example Brad Pitt and Keira Knightley.

quickfire

68 What different formats do advertisers use to communicate with audiences?

The power of advertising: advertising strategies

The main aim of advertisers, whatever their 'product', is to persuade their audience; this is why advertising is often called 'the art of persuasion'. Advertisements are usually created and produced by **advertising agencies** whose job it is to conduct market research (which may be sub-contracted to another external agency) and come up with the creative ideas. The makers of the product will sometimes change agencies if they feel that their product needs a re-vamp or to target a new audience. In 2006 Cadbury Schweppes recruited the advertising agency, Fallon London, to revive their failing brand. The advertising campaign that followed, featuring a gorilla playing the drums and children with dancing eyebrows, was hugely successful. The Gorilla advert received 500,000 views on YouTube in the first week as a result of **viral marketing** and was instrumental in reversing the brand's decline. Some campaigns do not use agencies and are produced **in house**, this may be the case for high profile, financially secure brands, although they may recruit agencies to aid them

Task

Think of other examples of types of advertising and their purpose? Consider where the advertisements would appear and in what form?

(69) What makes a successful advertisement?

in, for example, digital promotion.

Other strategies used by advertisers include:

- Hard sell – this is aggressive, 'in your face advertising'. Hard sell television adverts are usually short and loud. They give the audience clear information about the product, its price if relevant and what it does.

- Soft sell – these advertisements sell the audience a lifestyle, the product is often not the main focus of the advert and may only appear at the end as an **iconic representation**. These adverts are often narrative based.

- Celebrity endorsement – using an iconic celebrity to tell the audience how good the product is or persuading them to donate money. Consider the use of celebrities in telethons like Comic Relief. Other types of endorsement can use ordinary people, as audiences are often more convinced if they see someone more like themselves using the product or service.

- Language and mode of address – the advert may use hyperbolic, emotive or persuasive language to sell the product or service. Catchy slogans or jingles can be an important element of an advertising campaign.

- Demonstrative action – seeing the product in use, for example a cleaning product, can persuade an audience of its efficacy.

- Ideology and messages – some adverts convey messages about what effect the product may have upon the audience.

Industry: regulation

The Advertising Standards Authority

*'The Advertising Standards Authority is the UK's independent **regulator** of advertising across all media. We apply the Advertising Codes, which are written by the Committees of Advertising Practice. Our work includes acting on complaints and proactively checking the media to take action against misleading, harmful or offensive advertisements.'*

(www.asa.org.uk)

The ASA was established in 1962, its aim is to ensure that all advertisements produced and broadcast in the UK are legal, honest, decent and truthful. They make and publish decisions about advertisements every week responding to complaints from the public. They monitor adverts regularly concentrating on high profile sectors, for example health, beauty and alcohol, which are seen to be more likely to breach the ASA's code of conduct. Advertising plays a huge role in our society and advertisements now appear across many platforms. Advertisements on the Internet are subject to the same rules as those in other media forms; it is the job of the ASA to monitor all advertising. They produce an annual report detailing the decisions that have been made. Not all of the complaints made are upheld by the ASA. In 2011 the ASA received 31,458 complaints about 22,397 adverts.

Advertisements containing and broadcast to children come under particular scrutiny so that young people are protected and are not exposed to adverts that may be harmful or misleading. One of the main concerns of parents is regarding adverts that are placed early in the evening during children's television and may be inappropriate and advertisements that appear on billboards near schools for the same reasons.

ASA ruling: Chanel Coco Mademoiselle

The recent Chanel Coco Mademoiselle advert featuring Keira Knightley (this advertising campaign will be the main focus in this section of the book), came under an ASA ruling in March 2013. The section of the advert that caused the complaint was the undressing of the model by the photographer and the obvious sexual tension between the two people. This was seen to be inappropriate as it was scheduled during a children's film.

'The complainant, who saw the ad during the film *Ice Age 2*, challenged whether the ad was suitable to be broadcast during a film that was likely to appeal to children, because she believed it was overtly sexual.'

ASA assessment: *'We considered the ad was suitable for older children, but that the sexually suggestive material was unsuitable for young children. We therefore concluded that the ad was inappropriately scheduled and an ex-kids restriction should have been applied to prevent the ad from being broadcast in or around children's programming.'*

The ASA ruled that the advert must not be broadcast during programmes that would appeal to children.

quickfire

⑦⓪ Why is it important to have a regulator like the ASA for advertising?

Task

Visit the ASA website: www.asa.org.uk. Look at the ruling for Chanel Coco Mademoiselle. How did Chanel respond to the complaint? What key points were made?

Main text: Chanel Coco Mademoiselle campaign

This campaign is a multi-layered advertising and promotional campaign comprising a series of print advertisements, two television adverts, interactive digital performance adverts and a high profile online promotion of the campaign itself. For this reason, it is a rich example to study as a main text for MS4.

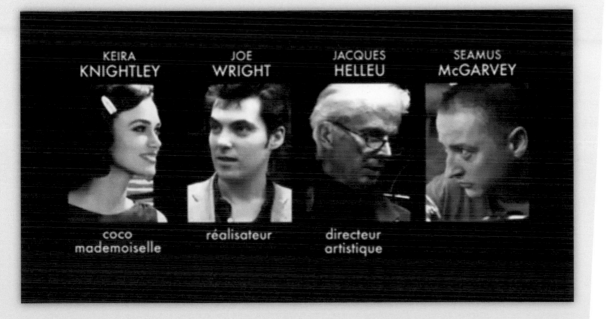

Still from 'Coco Mademoiselle Behind the Scenes – The Jewelry', Chanel

Chanel Coco Mademoiselle: industry information

- There have been two linked campaigns, both using Keira Knightley as the **spokesperson** for the brand. These were created and produced in house by Chanel. In 2007 there were three/four print advertisements and a television advert and in 2011 there were two print adverts and an extended television advert. In 2007 and 2011, there were also other promotional films broadcast before and during the campaign.

- Both television advertisements were directed by Joe Wright, who also directed Keira Knightley in *Pride and Prejudice* and *Atonement*, thus reinforcing Chanel's desire for high production, cinematic advertisements reflecting the sophistication of the brand.

- This is further reinforced by the fact the Chanel also used cinematographer Seamus McGarvey.

- Karl Lagerfeld, Chanel's fashion designer, also helped to create the campaign, which has close links with Coco Chanel herself and was filmed in her apartment in Paris.

- The 2007 print campaigns were photographed by Dominique Isserman, the 2011 campaign was shot by Mario Testino. The print advertisements are directly linked to the audio-visual adverts and you can view footage of the shoots on YouTube.

- To create a brand identity and to establish links between the two campaigns, Joss Stone recorded the soundtrack for both adverts: *L.O.V.E.* by Nat King Cole in 2007 and *It's a Man's World* in 2011. This also reflects Chanel's aim to appeal to a younger audience with this fragrance.

- Although the creative work was handled in house, for the 2007 campaign an interactive agency, Vansken Group was employed to generate **buzz marketing** prior to the launch of the main campaign.

Industry: marketing

In this age of competitive marketing, advertising campaigns themselves are promoted to audiences before and during the campaign launch. This is especially true of high budget and high profile campaigns like Chanel Coco Mademoiselle. These more sophisticated brands had been more reticent to use new media platforms, preferring instead more tried and tested formats, but Chanel's most recent campaign effectively employs the Internet and digital media to sell the brand. The aim of the campaign in 2007 and 2011 was to create a global buzz. The following marketing devices were employed to raise audience awareness.

For the 2007 advertisements:

- Online advertising on specific websites and **search-engine marketing** on Google and Yahoo.

- The creation of a special website mademoiselle-forever.com where users could watch video clips and have a virtual tour of Coco Chanel's apartment.

- Chanel actively recruited influential bloggers from more than fifteen countries to help to generate the 'buzz', giving them previews of the making of the advert and inviting a select few to Paris to receive a tour of Coco Chanel's apartment and a preview of the new adverts.

- Accessing digital media was seen to be important according to Maureen Chiquet, global chief executive of Chanel: *'We all know our next generation of consumers is consuming information in this way ... we can't afford not to be there.'*

Key Terms

Advertising spokesperson = In advertising terms, this is someone who is employed to promote, speak about and be 'the face of' a brand. They are usually high profile celebrities who will have audience appeal, for example Keira Knightley and Brad Pitt for Chanel.

Buzz marketing = This can also be termed more simply 'buzz' and is the term used for word of mouth marketing. It is the interaction of consumers which creates a positive association, excitement, or anticipation about a product or service.

Key Figure

Mario Testino – he is a well-respected and high profile Peruvian fashion photographer famous for his work with Vogue and Vanity Fair and his photographs of Kate Moss and royalty. His style is described as 'luxury realism'.

Key Term

Search-engine marketing = A form of Internet marketing that seeks to promote websites by increasing their visibility in search engine result pages.

- Although the advertisements were created in house by Chanel, they recruited a digital advertising agency, Vansken, to help with the global marketing of the campaign. They produced a street marketing campaign in Paris, New York, Hong Kong and Tokyo with projections on shop fronts of images from the adverts and quotes. The windows offered interactive opportunities for passers-by. These can be seen at: tinyurl.com/cd25osb.

- Chanel also created a series of short films featuring Keira Knightley about the making of the advertisements and focusing on specific elements; for example, the jewellery, the dress, the actress, etc. These can be viewed on YouTube (tinyurl.com/buanjyy, tinyurl.com/cc57ba6).

quicKfire

71 What evidence is there to suggest that Chanel Coco Mademoiselle is a global brand?

Still from 'Coco Mademoiselle Campaign', Chanel, Joe Wright

Still from 'Coco Mademoiselle behind the scenes – The Look', Chanel

For the 2011 adverts, there was:

- A similar word of mouth promotion via social networking and fan sites, for example lachanelfile.com.

- A **teaser advert** was released featuring Keira Knightley in the iconic cat suit, standing next to the Ducati motorbike in the courtyard of a sophisticated Parisian building.

- The Chanel website included a series of short interviews with Keira Knightley discussing the perfume and the advert.

- The site also includes short films about the making of the audio-visual advert and the photoshoot for the print advertisements. These marketing devices very clearly position Keira Knightley as the 'spokesperson' for the brand.

Exam Tip

If you choose to answer an MS4 examination question on marketing using the advertising industry, remember that you need to discuss the marketing of the campaign, not of the product itself.

Key Term

Teaser advert = This is when part of the advert for a new campaign is released before the main campaign, for example a short clip from the audio-visual advert. The aim is to use enigmas, here the motorbike and the setting, to catch the interest of the audience.

⑦② Why would a marketing campaign need to advertise itself?

Task

Look at the short films on the Chanel website. What do they contribute to the campaign?

- In the USA Chanel placed their adverts on Hulu, an upmarket online service for streaming videos. Its monthly users are predominantly wealthy 18–35 year olds, the target audience for the fragrance.

Credit: Chanel.com

Text: genre

In studying this campaign you will need to consider the generic conventions of print and audio-visual advertisements as well as considering the genre of the perfume advertisement itself. Perfume advertisements for high profile brands like Chanel have a recognisable repertoire of elements, they are high budget productions; this is signified through the endorser, the setting and iconography and the technical codes. This is also reinforced through the length of the production – the 2011 Chanel Coco Mademoiselle television advert is over three minutes. Perfume adverts usually use soft sell techniques, the aim is to sell the target audience a lifestyle and hope that they will buy the fragrance as they, through the product, aspire to attain some of the sophistication, beauty and romance contained within the advert.

Characters

The focus of all the advertisements, both print and moving image, is the character created by Keira Knightley. This creation is interesting and multi-layered and contains enigmas for the audience. In the 2007 advertisement she has many links to the young Coco Chanel and in both she plays a strong independent woman who is happy to be alone. The enigma is related to who she is; the short marketing films present her as the actress, the advertisement as a fictional creation, a modern day Coco Chanel who was known for her strength of character and independent spirit. The female character is the feature of both adverts and the man plays a much lesser role, but does contribute to the glamour and romance of the narrative.

Setting and iconography

True to the genre, we expect a glamorous, romantic setting that offers aspirational promises for the audience. In the more recent Chanel advert the setting is a very deserted Paris through which Keira Knightley rides on a Ducati motorbike, passing iconic Parisian buildings. She is dressed in a beige cat suit which, although covering her fully, is also tight fitting. The whole advert is saturated in this neutral colour scheme. The other setting is Coco Chanel's actual apartment featuring the staircase pictured here. It is set up as a photo shoot. The rooms are beautiful and luxurious and the rows of gowns remind the audience of the long established fashion house that produces this and other fragrances.

QuickFire

73 What are the main codes and conventions of a perfume advertisement?

QuickFire

74 What reasons may Chanel have for setting the advertisement in Coco Chanel's apartment?

Key Figure

Coco Chanel (1883–1971)

Gabrielle 'Coco' Bonheur Chanel was a French fashion designer and founder of the Chanel brand. She was the only fashion designer to appear on *Time* magazine's list of the 100 most influential people of the 20th century.

© Everett Collection Historical / Alamy

Technical and audio codes

The aim of all perfume advertisements is to create a luxurious, glamorous world into which the audience can escape and which they will then associate with the product. This is usually constructed through the technical and audio codes and the editing. The links with the product are subtle and inferred. The technical codes and conventions may include a close-up shot of the perfume bottle at the beginning and the end, establishing shots of the setting to reinforce a sense of luxury and sensuality and close-ups of the beautiful people in the narrative. In addition, the aim of the Chanel Coco Mademoiselle advertising campaign is to involve the audience with the characters and the narrative. The female character is 'shown ' to the audience first. The relationship between her and the audience is established with the direct mode of address employed in the opening shot. Here there is a shot featuring the perfume bottle, and the audience is positioned as the mirror as she applies the fragrance. The connotation being that this action code will determine the narrative that is to follow. The advert ends with her placing a bottle inside her cat suit, thus reinforcing this idea. Audio is also important in perfume adverts; the choice of song or music gives clues to the style of the fragrance and has links to the narrative.

Still from 'Coco Mademoiselle: The Film', Chanel, directed by Joe Wright (2007).

Key Terms

Intertextual = This is where one media text makes reference to aspects of another text within it. For example, reconstructing a short scene from a film in a television advertisement. The secondary text chosen will usually appeal to the target audience.

Enigma code = This is where the camera does not give the audience all of the information and leaves them with unanswered questions.

(75) How are narrative techniques used to construct the narrative in these advertisements?

Text: narrative

Not all perfume advertisements construct a narrative; some rely on a montage of loosely linked, evocative images to convey a message about the product. However, Chanel has a tradition of producing adverts that are also mini films with a clear storyline. The 2004 advertisement for Chanel No 5 featuring Nicole Kidman had **intertextual** references to Kidman's film *Moulin Rouge* and at £18 million was, at the time, the world's most expensive advertisement. Both the 2007 and 2011 Coco Mademoiselle adverts construct a narrative around a central strong, independent, female character played by Keira Knightley. The character she plays also has links to a modern-day Coco Chanel, this is further emphasised by the use of Coco Chanel's apartment as a setting. The narrative in both is linear and **enigma** and action **codes** are clearly established. The fascinating enigma of the 2007 narrative is created around who the character is and where she has come from.

The narrative resolution for both characters, having 'seduced' a man, is to leave, as they arrived, on their own and content to be so. In the 2007 advert, the female character runs off laughing down a Parisian street, in 2011, she leaves on her motorbike. There are intertextual plot situations in the 2011 advert; the shot of the curtains billowing at an open window has been used in film for many years to suggest that a character has left or vanished by a rather unconventional means. However, the construction of the storyline of the 2011 campaign is more complex in that there is a double narrative; Keira Knightley is being photographed as herself, 'the face of Chanel', this narrative is reinforced by the short films that accompany the campaign and look at the photo shoot itself. The second narrative involves her as a modern-day, rebellious Coco Chanel and as such, is a more fictional construction.

Key Term

Aspirational (brand/ product) = This means that the product is marketed to an audience who would like to own it but it is too expensive for them to buy. It can also refer to the lifestyle that is presented in the advert – the audience would like it to be the way they live their lives if they could.

Text: representation

Representations of gender in Chanel Coco Mademoiselle advertisement 2011: women

Perfume advertisements have traditionally offered similar representations of women: beautiful, flawless and **aspirational**. They are the advertising genre that is most criticised for constructing and presenting an unrealistic image of women and one that it is almost impossible to achieve. These images of perfection are used to make the product seem more attractive, combine that with a slender, beautiful celebrity and suggest that her attractiveness to men is linked to her perfume and the lifestyle element creates a whole world to aspire to.

Mario Testino for Chanel (2011)

In the 2011 Chanel Coco Mademoiselle campaign Keira Knightley is that woman and here we have, like Lara Croft before her, an ambiguous representation of gender. Keira Knightley is a postmodern representation of femininity. She is represented through the technical and audio codes as a strong, independent woman who is central to the narrative and very obviously in control. However, she is also sexually objectified and is constructed to be looked at. This representation is created through the technical codes and the editing. The colours and lighting are muted and sensuous, the first shot we have of the female character is in bed. We see her mounting a motorbike, iconography usually associated with a man and suggesting her power and control. This is reinforced when she races away from the other men on motorbikes at the traffic lights. However, we are positioned behind her and the camera focuses on her bottom and her high-heeled shoes offering a more stereotypical sexual objectification of the female. This dual representation continues throughout the advertisement, her code of clothing and gesture as she enters the shoot setting exudes power and control, the camera tracking her movements.

However, alongside this, the sexual tension between her and the photographer is constructed through close-ups and point of view shots. We are positioned as him, viewing her upside down through the camera lens and then looking directly into her face. These close-ups of her lips and face are very sensual combined with the soft focus lighting and soundtrack. Here, the woman resorts to more stereotypical behaviour of the temptress as she leads him and the audience along. The audience is positioned to be as surprised as he is by her vanishing act. Her final, enigmatic glance at him from her motorbike reaffirms her position in control of her actions and life. In the interviews that accompanied the launch of the campaign Knightley refers to the character as a 'Chanel Superwoman'.

The choice of music track reinforces the strong role of the woman in the advert. It is Joss Stone's version of *It's A Man's World,* the fact that it is sung by a woman adds an irony that is significant within the narrative – she is clearly in control in this man's world as the final lines of the song indicate. Joss Stone is associated with the Coco Chanel brand as she also sang the song for the 2007 advert.

The print advertisements that accompany this campaign echo the themes that are established in the audio-visual advert. The colour of the actual perfume and the clothing are muted and natural. The mode of address is direct and there is a sexual, smouldering feel to the code of expression as Keira Knightley holds the bottle to her lips. Here we also have the iconic representation of the product placed centrally, a generic convention of perfume adverts and she is the only one who features in the print adverts, emphasising her importance as the central spokesperson for the brand. The font style on the print advertisements highlight the young, rebellious nature of this fragrance, it is unstereotypically Chanel and is the brand's attempt to further appeal to a younger female demographic.

Representations of gender in Chanel Coco Mademoiselle advertisement 2011: men

We have already stated that the woman is the central focus of the campaign, but the way in which the male character is constructed is also interesting. The other male characters (men on motorbikes) appear only briefly to further accentuate the power and control of the female. The photographer has a greater role to play, he is stereotypically attractive and therefore will appeal to a female audience. As in the 2007 campaign, he is used to suggest the power of the fragrance in seducing the opposite sex. He is also part of the romance that will attract an audience who aspire to this lifestyle and narrative scenario. To some extent he does have some control over the situation and the technical codes position the audience as him at times. He is initially presented to us as in charge of the space; however, in the shot where the clothes rail moves up and they walk towards the audience, she is in the front and he, behind. The lack of dialogue reinforces the sexual tension but we are reminded by the song lyrics that 'a woman makes a better man'. He obeys without question her commands to send the others away and to lock the door. The shots of him preparing the room, shutting the curtains, etc., are edited together with close-ups of her eyes and lips. The long shot of him running to the open window shows his desperation and confusion, as does the final shot we have of him looking down at her from the balcony before she rides away.

Still from *'Coco Mademoiselle: The Film'*, Chanel, directed by Joe Wright

Audience

Targeting the right audience is essential for the producers of advertisements regardless of whether they want to sell a product, promote an event or raise awareness of an issue. Advertising agencies engage in market research and build databases as part of their preparation for a new advertising campaign in order to ensure that they appeal to the right audience. They are also one of the industries that work particularly hard to place audiences into categories in order to create a more direct appeal.

One of the ways in which audiences for advertising are categorised is through demographics. A **demographic audience profile** categorises an audience according to their class, occupation and income. For other media industries this method is now seen to be outdated, but it is still relevant to advertising and the magazine industry as it clearly illustrates which types of people have the highest consumable income. Audiences are categorised in groups from A to E, where A and B are the highest earners in society or the ones with the greatest **consumable income**. Retired people, for example, may not earn money but may have an income they can and are willing to spend on luxury items. Chanel is at the top end of the perfume market and would be seeking to appeal to those audiences at the peak of the demographic profile.

Key Terms

Demographic audience profiling = Using data about age, sex, income, occupation and other factors to target a specific audience more effectively.

Consumable income = This is the money left when bills, etc., are paid, which can be spent on items like luxury goods and non-essentials. The people with high consumable incomes can be targeted by advertisers.

A different type of profiling used to determine audiences is the psychometric audience profile, where audiences are categorised according to their VALs (values, attitudes and lifestyles). This is clearly very relevant to the advertising industry and this method was first developed by Young and Rubicam, a New York based advertising agency. They considered how Cross-Cultural Consumer Characteristics can group audiences through their motivational needs. With regard to Chanel Coco Mademoiselle, the main audience categories would most likely be 'Aspirers' and 'Succeeders'.

Audience theories

Other audience response/effect theories are applicable to the advertising industry and specifically to a study of the Chanel campaign. With the digital age and the advent of viral marketing as a new and effective way to access audiences and to create a marketing 'buzz', then the two-step flow theory can be applied. Here, an audience may be informed about the campaign or the product through a third party or by **word of mouth**. This is often the case when the style or the novelty of the advert itself creates interest. This was effective when Chanel released teasers to Chanel and Keira Knightley fan sites prior to the launch of the actual campaign creating anticipation. If the audience values the opinion leader then they will respond well to the text and to the product. It could be said that Keira Knightley herself, as a spokesperson for the brand and a high profile celebrity, acts as an **opinion leader**. The audience associate her with the brand and therefore may be more likely to purchase the product.

The uses and gratifications theory suggests that audiences are active and will seek out different media texts that offer specific needs and pleasures. For example, some advertising campaigns will educate audiences and give them information, some are so different and interesting, for example the Cadbury's Gorilla campaign and 3 Mobile's moon walking pony, that they encourage social interaction. As many advertisements now are high budget and almost cinematic in their production values, they offer audiences escapism and entertainment, hence the assertion by some that the adverts are more interesting than the actual programme!

Who is the audience for the Chanel Coco Mademoiselle advertising campaign?

- A younger demographic.

- Aspirers who are aware of the Chanel brand but who may also have associated the other fragrances with an older woman.

- Fans of Keira Knightley who are persuaded by her endorsement of the product.

- Those who are attracted by the ideology of luxury, freedom and romance encoded in the adverts.

- Those who are positioned by the advertisements to feel aspirational about the lifestyle created by the campaign.

quickfire

⑦⑧ Why would the Chanel Coco Mademoiselle advertising campaign appeal to Aspirers and Succeeders?

Exam Tip

Revisit the work you did on audiences at AS to help to prepare you for this section of the MS4 paper.

Key Terms

Word of mouth advertising = This is where someone recommends a product or service they have used to someone else.

Opinion leader = Those people in society who may affect the way in which others interpret a particular media text. With regard to advertising, this may be a celebrity or other endorser recommending a product.

quickfire

⑦⑨ How is the audience for Chanel Coco Mademoiselle targeted by the campaign?

Exam Tip

Remember that not all audience models, frameworks or theories are relevant to all media texts. Some have a very specific application, for example Young and Rubicam for advertising.

Key Term

Stuart Hall's audience response theory = Stuart Hall is a cultural theorist who researched how audiences respond to media texts. He suggested that producers encode texts, and audiences may take on the preferred meaning, have a negotiated response where they accept some aspects of the text and disagree with others, or have an oppositional response where they reject the ideology of the text.

(80) What may affect the way in which an audience may respond to a text?

Exam Tip

Be aware of the different ways in which an MS4 question about audience may be worded. Be prepared to unpick the question looking for the key word that may help you, for example attract, target, and respond.

How may an audience respond to the advertising campaign?

Consider how **Stuart Hall's theories** regarding **audience responses** may be applied here:

- The audience may accept the preferred reading encoded by the makers of the text and aspire to the lifestyle constructed in the advert. This will tend to be the case for women. They will therefore buy the product to access some of the world that is presented to them.

- They may have a negotiated reading of the text, accepting that the world is constructed but aware that the Chanel brand suggests sophistication and has connotations attached to the wearer.

- An audience may not agree with the ideology contained within the advert and so have an oppositional response to the text. This may be related to the culture, age, gender or other factors pertaining to the audience.

- Men may have an oppositional response and may be positioned by the narrative to feel sympathy for the man in the advert who appears to be used and rejected by the female character.

- Parents had an oppositional response to the content of the television advertisement and its placement in the schedule. Their literal, active response was to complain to the ASA.

Other responses may include:

- A literal and active response would be the actual buying of the perfume. The agency or company producing the product will monitor this actual response closely to assess whether the campaign has been a success.

- Men may buy the perfume for their partners because of their attraction to Keira Knightley.

Another literal audience response was the discussion of the campaign:

- On fan sites like Lachanelfile.com. Here direct response was available through the site and blogs, etc.

- One particular blogger, Daisynation, takes you through a step-by-step process to look like Keira Knightley does in the advert. She admits: 'You know my respect for and, let's face it, lustful abandon when it comes to all things Chanel – well I love their perfume adverts, too. Shocked? I didn't think so, I love the Chanel Coco Mademoiselle commercial with Keira Knightley.'

© Conrado/Shutterstock.com

Summary: The Advertising Industry

APPEAL AND TARGETING

Target audience: young female aspirers 25–35 demographic. How are they targeted?

Audience positioning

Responses: Stuart Hall

Pleasures: uses and gratifications

Young and Rubicam: Four Cs / VALs

Demographic profiling

GENRE

Consider both print and television advert conventions and the generic conventions of perfume adverts

NARRATIVE

Consider for each advert, but then look at campaign development and at narrative extensions to the campaigns; for example, the story behind Keira Knightley/Coco Chanel as it develops through the campaign

Enormous fan-base for product, Chanel and advertising campaign. Big word of mouth promotion via social network sites – blogs and Facebook especially

Consider literal as well as theoretical audience responses

REPRESENTATION

Gender – ambiguity of female character, she is a strong independent woman; central to narrative, attitudes, etc.

Empowering for target audience

However, she is also sexually objectified through some of the technical codes

Men – lesser roles

Place – Paris, apartment, etc.

CHANEL: COCO MADEMOISELLE

Used in-house Chanel creative team and Vansken Group – digital ad agency

Also bloggers

Websites – official, industry and fan base, e.g. Lachanelphile.com

MARKETING

Big pre-advert launch campaigns. Teasers, press releases, stills – all created a marketing buzz

Release of mini movies featuring Keira Knightley as brand spokesperson

Consider director, photographers, cinematographer, artistic influences

GLOBAL CAMPAIGN

Consider extent

Regulation – how was the campaign affected?

Keira Knightly spokesperson and celebrity endorser– how important is the person to the campaign?

Music – Joss Stone

Consider branding, impact and audience appeal

Introduction

In studying the music industry for MS4, you must ensure that you develop an in-depth understanding of this industry and that you are able to demonstrate this through the choice of your three main texts. For the music industry the text will be the music artist(s), you will therefore focus on three main music performers/groups and their output in order to highlight key points about the industry itself. A study of how the artist(s) and their work are promoted, distributed and exhibited through music companies, CDs, music videos and other marketing devices will allow you to analyse their place within the music industry.

The music industry is one of the longest running media industries, its role is to produce and control how music is distributed to an audience. The music industry is made up of companies and individuals whose aim it is to make a profit out of music and who employ **synergy** and **convergence**. The music industry, like some of the other industries you will have studied, has changed dramatically to keep pace with the changing ways in which music is produced, distributed and exhibited and the diverse and changing means by which modern audiences access and consume music. The year 2013 saw the closure of many HMV stores; this is a good illustration of the fact that some consumers of music have abandoned more traditional methods of 'owning 'music in favour of digital methods.

A brief history of the music industry

- It is one of the longest running industries – recorded music was one of the first mass-produced formats.

- The industry has seen many changes since then; the biggest have been related to advances in digital technology.

- The 1980s saw the technical innovations of the CD, the video cassette, cable and satellite broadcasting and the music video.

- MTV was launched, this was the first channel to be dedicated to music and as such revolutionised the way in which music and performers could be marketed.

- Portable devices, for example the Sony Walkman, began to be produced. These devices broadened the ways in which consumers could access and listen to music.

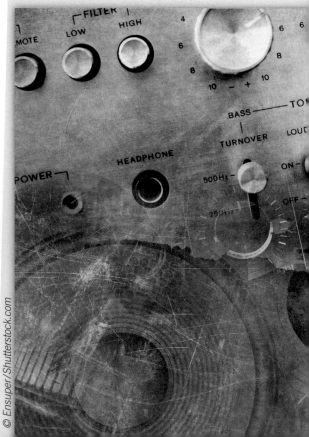

© Ensuper / Shutterstock.com

Key Terms

Synergy = This is the interaction and co-operation of two or more media organisations in order to produce mutually beneficial outcomes. For example, the combination of the artist and the recording company.

Convergence = This is the coming together of previously separate media industries. This is often the result of advances in technology whereby one device contains a range of different features. The mobile phone, for example, allows the user to download and listen to music, view videos, tweet artists, etc. All this can be done through one portable device.

quickfire

(81) How have advances in technology helped the distribution of music?

- This developed further in the 1990s with the arrival of the MP3 player, this allowed music to be distributed digitally across computer networks allowing the copying of CDs, the transferring of files and downloading. Now the floodgates were well and truly open!

The structure of the music industry

The music industry, unlike some other industries, is not integrated. The major recording companies are distributors, not exhibitors. The exhibition part of the industry is undertaken by television, radio, retail outlets and music download sites. At the time of writing, the three major record companies are:

- Universal Music Group incorporating EMI Group

- Sony/BMG

- Warner Music Group.

However, these 'majors' are multinational conglomerates whose size and ownership of other media companies makes them very powerful in the music industry. Each music company owns a range of different **record labels**.

© Pavel L Photo and Video/Shutterstock.com

Another element of the music industry is made up of **independent record labels**. These are very important within the industry as many artists start in the business by signing to a small independent label before moving to a major music company. These smaller independent music companies offer a range of services to new, up and coming bands, for example organising gigs and ensuring that they get exposure. Fierce Panda is an independent record label credited with the early releases of now big artists, for example Coldplay, Keane, Supergrass and Placebo, before they moved on to bigger labels. Independent labels do not have all the advantages of the larger companies, mainly because of their size. They do not handle their own distribution and are more reliant on the more traditional ways of selling new music. The demise of HMV in 2013 was therefore a blow to many independent music producers like World Music Network. HMV accounted for 50% of its CD sales and the loss of a high street music retailer was worrying for small companies like this who are responsible for a range of different artists but do not have the means to engage in digital distribution:

'We knew CDs were under attack from digital sales', said Neil Record of World Music Network, who is worried about reaching his customers with HMV disappearing from the high street, *'It was inevitable, but we didn't expect it this soon.'*

© Marekusz/Shutterstock.com

How has digital technology changed the music industry?

- It has encouraged convergence within the industry. The industry links easily with other digital media platforms.

- The Internet gives the user the ability to easily access a range of music to suit their listening preferences.

- It has changed the culture of music ownership. In the past it was seen to be important to have a physical representation of the artist in the form of a vinyl record, an audio cassette or a CD. Indeed, there was an art form related to album sleeves and to some extent CD inserts that has been lost.

- The development of digital technology has allowed users to download and listen to music across a range of formats.

- Unlike a retail outlet, a download store has no restrictions on the amount of stock it can hold. The range of different music that can be accessed is vast, users can easily gain access to back catalogues of individual artists and therefore broaden their listening experience. As the 2013 DMR report stated:

'... *download stores continue to see steadily growing sales and are spreading globally. They represent around 70 per cent of global digital revenues. Major technology players – Amazon, Apple, Google, and Microsoft – have joined the market or upgraded their services. Download sales increased by 12 per cent in 2012, to 4.3 billion units globally. There were 2.3 billion single track downloads worldwide, an increase of 8 per cent and 207 million digital albums sold, up 17 per cent on 2011.*'

Extract from IFPI Digital Music Report 2013, *ifpi.org*.

- Carly Rae Jepson's single *Call Me Maybe* topped the digital singles chart in 2012 with 12.5 million sales. Digital technology aided the marketing as Justin Bieber promoted it to his 30 million Twitter followers and uploaded a parody of the music video on YouTube which gained more than 50 million views globally. (www. pro-music.org.)

- Seven of the ten most followed people on Twitter are music artists and nine out of ten of the 'most liked' people on Facebook are musicians.

- Some download stores, for example Apple iTunes, have had a huge impact on the industry. Apple have engaged in vertical integration as the iPod has outstripped its competitors and taken on the role of a necessary fashion statement, the owners of iPods then have to use iTunes as their download site thus securing a partial monopoly for the Apple brand.

- As Frances Moore, the Chief Executive of IFPI, stated in their annual report: '*music has not only adapted to the Internet – it is at the very heart of its development. Music is driving technology, helping sell devices, fuelling economic growth with a ripple effect far beyond the limits of the recorded music market. It is helping drive online search and social networking, as well as demand for fast broadband connections. Music is creating economic value at virtually every level of life. It is an engine of the digital ecosystem.*'

Extract from IFPI Digital Music Report 2013, *ifpi.org.*

- The music they produce is the '**Intellectual property**' of the artist(s). They can receive payment for the sale of a CD or for a legal download, which gives them the finance to make more music. Intellectual piracy in the form of illegal downloading of music, although seen to be of benefit for the user, has been detrimental to the music industry.

- For artists, the Internet gives an alternative means by which they can sell their music to audiences and make contact with fans. This allows them to establish a fan base and makes the relationship with the consumer more personal.

(83) What are the advantages of digital technologies for music performers?

Exam Tip

Be prepared to respond to an examination question on the impact of digital technologies for your chosen industry. You will need to give specific examples.

Key Term

Intellectual property = This is a legal concept which refers to creations of the mind for which the owner's rights are recognised. These rights cover such intangible assets as music, literary and artistic works; discoveries and inventions; and words, phrases, symbols, and designs.

How global is the music industry?

The music industry has been more able to develop globally due to the simplicity of the technology needed to make and distribute music. The major recording companies are usually keen to encourage the music of **indigenous cultures** and have bought smaller music labels in different countries to diversify their music range. For example, Sony/BMG owns labels in over 30 countries. Music artists offering a range of music genres are already established in countries around the world and have impacted upon the world music scene. In this industry audiences are much more accepting of different musical styles and genres and language is not perceived as a barrier.

Digital technology has facilitated the distribution of music globally. The largest digital services (2013) include iTunes, Spotify and Deezer. In 2011 they were established in 20 countries; by 2012 this had risen to over 100.

Social networks have also helped to promote music, '*67% of social network users in 20 countries discuss music and movies ahead of community issues, sports and politics. Social networks have developed vast user bases, with 66% of global Internet users accessing them.*'

Extract from IFPI Digital Music Report 2013, *ifpi.org.*

Key Term

Indigenous cultures = These are the cultural habits and pastimes, for example musical styles, that originate in and are characteristic of a particular region or country.

Global Music Connection
ESSENZIAL SOUND SPECIAL
extreme electro metal remix

quickfire

84 How global is the music industry?

Main text: Ed Sheeran

Background information

© epa european pressphoto agency b.v. / Alamy

- Ed Sheeran moved from Suffolk to London in 2008 playing gigs in small venues.

- In 2009, still unsigned to a record label, he played 300 gigs and produced six self-released EPs, some collaborating with other artists.

- In 2010 he went to Los Angeles and played in **open mic venues** across the city where he was spotted by Jamie Foxx who gave him the use of his recording studio.

- After also coming to the notice of Elton John, he then signed to Asylum Records. His debut single was *The A Team* which was released as a digital download in 2011. It entered the UK Singles Chart at number three, selling over 58,000 copies in the first week. It rapidly became a top ten hit globally.

- The single *Lego House* followed, and then *Drunk*, his fourth consecutive top ten single in the UK.

- Sheeran's debut album + was released in September 2011. It became the second best selling debut album and the ninth biggest-selling album of 2011 in the UK, selling 791,000 copies.

- He co-wrote the song *Moments* for the boy band One Direction. He also contributed to the band's second number one hit *Little Things.*

- In 2012, he won two BRIT Awards for Best British Male and British Breakthrough. *The A Team* won the Ivor Novello Award for Best Song Musically and Lyrically.

- In 2012 Sheeran began to receive critical acclaim in the United States. He made a guest appearance on Taylor Swift's album *Red* and is to spend much of 2013 touring as the opening act for her Red Tour. There was much media speculation about a possible romance between the two. '*I think Taylor's just opening up a lot of doors and it's up to me to make sure that I get through them.*'

  www.mtv.com

- He has a loyal fan base which sits a little uncomfortably at times with his indie image. They are called Sheeranators, are mostly female and have helped in his rise to success. They do, however, behave remarkably similarly to the fans of the more 'pop' bands, for example One Direction and Olly Murs, although they do tend to be slightly older. He has voiced his own concern about the perception of his fans: '*A lot of people seem to think I'm a kind of British Justin Bieber and it's only girls that are into me, but it's really a 50/50 thing.*'

  www.guardian.co.uk

Key Term

Open mic venue = These are live shows for the performance arts, for example poetry reading, comedy and music. Anyone can turn up on the night, book a slot and then perform without payment.

Exam Tip

Ensure that you have three key texts (artists) that allow you to be able to discuss different aspects of the music industry. Consider which artists may be a good contrast to Ed Sheeran.

© KHAP/Splash News/Corbis

Industry: marketing

As in all media industries, it is very important that the product, in this case, the music performer, is marketed effectively to an audience. Without successful marketing and promotion a performer cannot sell their music and make a profit for themselves and their record label/company. However, it is a vicious circle, as major record labels are usually reticent to take on an unknown, unproven artist, hence the importance of the independent labels in kick-starting the musical career of many artists. Ed Sheeran has achieved global success with a brand of music and a style that would normally remain in the quieter corners of the music business. However, he and his team have used a range of promotional strategies to ensure that he became known and then maintained his image in the music world:

- One of Ed Sheeran's main marketing devices in the early days of his career was the Internet through YouTube and by word of mouth marketing via social networking sites. This facilitated the growth of his fan base.

- Despite the success that Sheeran and his producer Jake Gosling had without being signed to a record company, they needed industry input to develop. They had recorded EPs independently and achieved success in the iTunes charts and on SBTV video with *You Need Me*. They also managed to get onto the playlist of Radio 1 and 1 Extra. However, signing to Asylum/Atlantic Records, part of the Warner Music Group, allowed them to broaden their appeal and gave them access to other marketing opportunities that were more difficult to attain without the support of a record label. Gosling says: *'You still need labels. You've got to remember they've got marketing teams, press teams, **radio pluggers**, accounts departments and when you get bigger you need help with that stuff.'* www.guardian.co.uk

- Ed Sheeran has shunned the more constructed, commercial marketing outlets adopted by many artists anxious to stay in the public eye; for example, an appearance as a guest on *The X Factor*. Part of his success may be down to the disillusionment of music fans with the manufactured pop produced by such programmes.

- Ed Sheeran does have a recognisable image, one that could not be said to be constructed. However, as Richard Dyer suggested in his research into stars, Ed Sheeran does use media texts, for example CD covers and music videos, to present an image and to market himself to his fans. As Dyer also asserted about stars generally, he does have a 'unique selling point', something about him that is different to other artists. For Sheeran this could be said to be his hair, ginger and tousled and his generally casual appearance, usually jeans and a T-shirt. This has become part of his marketable brand identity and many fans see it as a refreshing change from the manufactured images of his contemporaries.

Key Terms

Royalties = This is the fee paid to the owner of the music, which allows another person to play, perform or record that music. The organisation of payment of royalties has been made more complex with the advancements in digital technology.

Mechanical copyright = This gives the artist sole right of reproduction of their recorded work. 'Mechanical' refers to the physical or digital copy of the recorded song. The term dates back to when records were produced mechanically.

Key Figure

Napster was conceived as an independent peer-to-peer file-sharing service. The service operated between June 1999 and July 2001. Its technology allowed people to easily share their MP3 files with other users and to freely download music. Although the original service was shut down by court order, the Napster brand survived after it was purchased by another company.

Industry: regulation

The regulation of the music industry is much more complex than that of other industries, mainly related to how music is distributed and exhibited. The industry is largely self-regulatory and controlling the industry involves a range of different people. This regulation has also been made more complicated due to advances in technology and the diverse range of ways in which consumers buy, access and listen to music.

Main points

- The recording company/record label is initially responsible for and can regulate what it produces. One way in which it does this is by placing a 'Parental Advisory' sticker on CD covers. This practice began in the USA by the Recording Industry Association of America to highlight where lyrics contained explicit phrases or sexual references. They acted under pressure from the Parents Music Resource Centre established by four women including Tipper Gore, wife of the then American senator, who were concerned about children's access to unsuitable music. They became known as 'Tipper Stickers'. This practice was then adopted by other countries. There are, however, no guidelines and it is up to the record company to decide when these stickers are needed.

- Copyright law – in the past this was the way in which artists had control over their intellectual property. Whenever records were sold **royalties** were paid. All this changed with the advent of the MP3 player which heralded the arrival of illegal downloading of music. This was infringement of copyright, but it was impossible to monitor. There was then a further development – Napster appeared on the scene, this was the first file-sharing software and meant a huge loss of revenue for the music industry. In 2009, 95% of music was downloaded illegally. In 2013 an estimated $12.5 billion dollars was lost to the music industry due to piracy.

- To protect the music industry and in an attempt to regulate it, there now exist legal downloading sites where some music can be downloaded for free and some is paid for. Some sites have a subscription. These sites include iTunes, Spotify and Amazon.

- Another group: Performance Rights for Music (PRS), exists to ensure that artists receive royalties when their music is performed. It also protects the **mechanical copyright** and represents the rights of record companies and artists, however the music is reproduced and distributed.

Text: genre

There are several different music genres and it will aid your ability to show knowledge of the complexity and breadth of the music industry if your key texts (artists) come from more than one genre. The genre of the artist is established through a range of elements including themes of songs, song lyrics, codes of clothing, iconography, etc. Fans of the genre will sometimes copy one of the visual aspects that make them easily recognisable as fans of that genre, some more extreme than others, for example Marilyn Manson's contact lenses.

Ed Sheeran is generally accepted as being from the **indie** genre. This genre evolved from the style of music produced and promoted by independent record labels and so became a music genre.

Codes and conventions of the indie genre

- Indie bands were seen to be more autonomous and less concerned about commercial success.

- The genre does encompass a range of musical styles that are linked together by their ethos and generally comprise those that may not appeal to mainstream audiences.

- Indie music is less manufactured than mainstream music and instead focuses on the talent of the performer. The music videos of indie musicians often showcase their talent, i.e. their ability to sing naturally and play an instrument. There is a sense that they are playing for themselves as well as for their audience and that they have 'something to say'.

- Iconography tends to be the setting of music videos, which is often urban and gritty, and the clothing, which is casual.

- The lyrics associated with the indie music genre tell stories related to real-life experiences. The narrative is raw and unglamorous and often focuses on emotions. In indie music videos that are not performance videos, the artist is often not the focus – this is the lyrics and the telling of the story.

Key Terms

Indie = This is a term used to refer to artists that are not linked to a major record label and are therefore seen to be more 'independent'.

Underground = This is made up of a range of musical genres that operate outside of the commercial, mainstream music scene. These music genres tend to be more creative in their expression and promote individuality rather than a formulaic style.

© Christian Bertrand/Shutterstock.com

⑧⑥ How does Ed Sheeran conform to the conventions of the indie genre?

Indie music was originally distinctive in that it was **underground**, outside of the conventional music scene. However, some of Ed Sheeran's songs do have elements of more conventional pop music leading him to be termed indie/pop, a hybrid music genre. Sheeran has called himself 'acoustic soul'. He has also collaborated with musicians from other genres including rap and hip-hop.

However it is termed, it is clear that he wants to be recognised as something different from the constructed, manufactured mainstream 'popular' music genre.

The themes and lyrics of his songs are realistic, hard-hitting and resonate with young people in today's society. As such they fit into the indie genre which takes itself more seriously. They are at times both autobiographical and emotional and contain a strong narrative. He usually performs alone with an acoustic guitar and a spotlight. His very successful first single, *The A Team*, is about a young homeless woman with a drug addiction. In another single, *Small Bump,* he sings in the first person about a close friend who had a miscarriage.

© Christian Bertrand/Shutterstock.com

Study the CD cover for the + album and the EP *You Need Me*. These two texts reflect the codes and conventions of the indie genre. The + CD cover features a close-up shot of the artist; the mode of address is serious and direct. This suggests that he is serious about his music; it is all about the music, not him. It is simple and unstylised, selling the image of him as an artist true to his music and not selling a constructed idea of himself. It is very minimalist; he has chosen to use a symbol not the word and this gives the audience few clues to what they will get when they buy the CD. The symbol is not central, instead it is positioned at the bottom right, the audience are being asked to work out the meaning. The central colour is orange, significant as this is part of his iconic image – his ginger hair. However, it is also a warm colour. The image is grainy and indistinct as if it had been drawn, the colour muted, a convention of the indie genre. The font style too is simple, it is like a typewriter and just states his name, there is nothing to distract from his face.

The *You Need Me* EP cover is made up of a montage of hand-drawn images many of which have associations with music. It suggests an independent, creative artist who is also interesting. The images also relate to his everyday life and to the lyrics of his songs, again reinforcing that his music is related to ordinary experience, a convention of the genre. The branding of the orange and black colour scheme is reflected here and becomes recognisable to audiences.

87 How do Ed Sheeran's other songs reflect the codes and conventions of the indie genre.

Text: narrative and representation

As the text, for the music industry, is the artist, then narrative and representation can be considered through the texts produced by and featuring that artist. One of the main ways in which an artist promotes themselves and interprets their song lyrics and themes for the audience, is through the music video. Music videos have a range of presentational styles including performance video, narrative reconstruction or a mixture of the two. They can include the artist or feature actors who interpret the narrative of the song. Ed Sheeran's music videos tend to use a narrative style and often feature him only in a cameo role, although there are also videos of him playing the song in concert as a separate promotional tool.

In one of his most successful videos *Lego House,* the actor Rupert Grint is the main protagonist. His similarity to Sheeran is central to the narrative which manipulates audience expectations. Ironically, at the time he was more famous than Ed Sheeran. He is represented as Sheeran using visual codes, for example clothing, hair, iconography including an acoustic guitar and pieces of Lego relating to the lyrics. The urban setting, iconography and muted colours reflect the indie genre. They also serve to reinforce the character's isolation. Grint assumes the persona of Sheeran as the star, appearing on stage and waving to crowds. We even see him in the act of song writing, again emphasising the creativity of the indie musician. The use of close-ups of the character's face as he sings to us, a convention of the music video, establishes an intimacy with the audience.

Stills from 'Lego House', Ed Sheeran, written by Ed Sheeran and Jake Gosling, Warner Music Group, directed by Emil Nava.

Lego House is ostensibly a love song, but in this video the narrative presents a different kind of love – that of a fan for the star and as the narrative unfolds the reality of the fan's obsession dawns on the audience and becomes more disconcerting as the lyrics take on a new meaning; '*And of all these things I've done I think I love you better now*'. We see him on the tour bus and hanging an iconic image of Sheeran on his wall. The video follows a linear narrative structure and the character undergoes an **arc of transformation** as we see him begin to disintegrate. The audience witness the fan's breakdown matched by the lyrics: '*out of sight, out of mind*' and he is taken off stage as the shots represent him as a stalker. He is confronted by his idol, the only appearance of Ed Sheeran in the video, as the lift doors close on him. The narrative considers notions of stardom and of living in a celebrity culture and gives a new perspective on the love song that aims to challenge audience perceptions.

Text: representation

Reference has already been made about the way in which Ed Sheeran is represented in media texts. The artist is not always in control of their representation or the image of them that a particular text may create. Some texts, for example CD covers, allow them some sort of autonomy and control over the way in which they are presented. Other texts, for example newspapers and gossip magazines, offer the artist very little say regarding the way their image is presented. Some artists, for example Lady Gaga, work hard to construct and maintain a particular image. The two texts below construct a representation of Ed Sheeran:

Key Term

Arc of transformation = This is when the character changes from the beginning to the end of the narrative.

 **quickfire**

(88) What other narrative techniques are used in this music video?

Task

Consider how narrative and representation are constructed in another of Ed Sheeran's videos. What are the similarities and differences?

The magazine is aimed at a niche audience of music lovers and reflects the genre of Sheeran's music.

The image is central and his **mode of address** is direct, engaging with the audience. His expression is enigmatic, encouraging the reader to buy the magazine and read the interview.

His **casual code** of clothing is recognisable and links him to the indie genre. His tousled ginger hair has become an iconic way to represent him.

The **iconography** of the guitar establishes his role as a serious musician with a talent. The fact that he is hugging it to him suggests its importance to him.

quickfire

89) How would the way in which the representation of Ed Sheeran is constructed on this front cover attract the target audience?

The **anchorage** reinforces his representation as a musician and highlights his success. The suggestion is that he is to be even more admired because of his 'acoustic' guitar

The **font style** is hand drawn and shaded, this creates intertextual links with the style of his CD and EP covers. It also reinforces his indie roots, which are less concerned with false representations and are more down to earth and realistic, like the font style.

Exam Tip

Ensure that you consider a range of different texts to allow you discuss the diverse ways in which your chosen artist may be represented in the media.

This is a more detailed in-depth interview with the artist which appeared in *Q* magazine. *Q*'s audience is 15–24-year-old mainly affluent males from the ABC1 demographic.

The headline for this article in *Q* magazine is a direct quote and challenges the stereotype of what it means to be 'ginger'. It is an imperative and is assertive. It also reminds the audience of his iconic, recognisable feature.

Q Magazine / Bauer Media

The sub-heading represents him as a *'honey-voiced songwriting phenomenon who's breaking hearts'*, reinforcing his talent and his appeal. This mediates his representation and anchors the image.

The code of clothing is again relaxed; this is part of his iconic image, as is the code of gesture. His mode of address is indirect, reinforcing the 'cool' image.

He is positioned against a London backdrop with his guitar as further iconography. The photograph is constructed to reinforce his image and to make links to his busking days on the London streets. This is reinforced by the cover line placed in the flag *'Ed Sheeran has given up on busking to look at skirt instead'*. This will appeal to the *Q* reader and is not necessarily in keeping with his image.

His representation is further developed in the article: *'Polite, articulate and a little shy'* and *'crucially though, he remains self-conscious enough not to be entirely comfortable with the demands of modern publicity.'* This reinforces his representation as a serious musician who is not a construction of the music industry and is therefore less at home with commercial success.

90 How do these texts reinforce the genre of Ed Sheeran's music?

Task

Find another text that offers a different representation of Ed Sheeran.

Audience

Who is the target audience? How does Ed Sheeran appeal to them?

- Fans of the indie genre. This will include those who support an artist who is ostensibly against the more commercial aspect of the music industry.

- Loyal fans of Ed Sheeran – this fan base will have been established over time.

- Although his fans are from both genders, an unexpected fan base is older teenage girls who follow the artist. They give him the sort of reception usually associated with more commercial 'stars'. They call themselves The Sheeranators. Sheeran suggests that this is because *'I look like their brother's mate'*.

- Younger people who have been aware of the artist through the Internet.

- The appeal to this audience is the themes and ideas behind his music that attempts to relate to young people and their experiences. His image is very accessible to discerning young people who are looking for something a bit different, authentic and away from the mainstream. Sheeran himself acknowledges the relationship with his fans in an article for *The Guardian*: *'I dress like them, I'm not in a wig and a load of glitter, I speak like them, use the same slang words, watch the same TV programmes ....'*

(91) How does Ed Sheeran appeal to his audience?

© Splash News/Corbis

Audience responses

- A literal response is the amount of people who have bought Ed Sheeran's music across a range of platforms.

- Fan sites also show a literal response.

- The Sheeranators are very loyal – when Alexis Petridis of *The Guardian* reviewed Sheeran's album and only gave it three stars, he was bombarded with abusive messages on Twitter and Sheeran had to step in to calm things down.

- When the + album was launched it received several lukewarm reviews including one from NME which termed him the 'New Boring'. Nevertheless, this did not seem to hinder the success of the album. Upon release, + reached the top of the UK Album Chart with first-week sales exceeding 102,000 copies. The album has now sold over 1 million copies.

- Theoretical – uses and gratifications. The song themes and lyrics may allow an audience to identify personally with him. Involvement with a 'star' can also offer escapism to the audience.

Task

Look at a fan site for Ed Sheeran. What does it tell you about the fans?

Exam Tip

Be ready to discuss a range of possible audiences and responses in your examination answer.

Summary: The Music Industry

APPEAL AND TARGETING

Specific audience – indie music fans

Gender – different appeal

Targeted – music distribution and access.
Interesting he has only released one CD

GENRE

Indie conventions:

Casual clothing

Lyrics – realistic and related to
young experience

Singer/songwriter

Acoustic guitar suggesting
serious musician

Minimalist, artistic CD cover

NARRATIVE

Music videos are narrative driven

They are related to experience

Use of Rupert Grint and other
actors distances performer

Use of narrative devices

Lyrics tell short stories about
modern lives – themes relate to
audience

Stuart Hall response theories.
How can they be applied?

OTHER LITERAL RESPONSES

Record and download sales

Newspaper reviews/magazine articles

Responses on the website/blogs

USES AND GRATIFICATIONS

Personal identity

Social interaction

ED SHEERAN

Structure of industry –
recording companies.

Impact of digital technology

REPRESENTATION

Consider how Ed Sheeran is represented in
different media texts for different audiences

Who is in control of the representation?

Guitar Magazine – serious musician

GQ – target audience?

CD/EP – rep as Indie musician

MARKETING and PROMOTION

Cross platform:

Press coverage

Appearances on radio, chat shows, etc.

Appearance at The Brit Awards

Website

Merchandise

Live tour

Tour supporting Taylor Swift

Creation of image that is easily
recognisable and distinctive

GLOBAL APPEAL

Global success of artist

Global accessibility of music

The Radio Industry

Key Terms

Profile = For radio stations this refers to how they are defined to their target audience. This includes their aims and their ethos.

Cross-platform marketing = This is where one format is advertised on another media platform. For example, BBC1 will broadcast promotional advertisements for its radio stations.

Format = This refers to the way in which the media text is constructed and presented to the audience.

Introduction

In studying this industry in preparation for the MS4 examination you will need to ensure that you have a broad and up-to-date understanding. Your main texts must allow you to demonstrate that understanding. Remember, it is helpful if your texts are varied and diverse; this way you will illustrate your awareness of a range of issues related to the industry effectively. The radio industry is one of the oldest and most traditional media industries; it has seen many changes, never more so than now in the digital revolution. The link between the text, the audience and the industry is still closely related, but the way in which audiences access and respond to radio texts has changed dramatically in recent years.

Station profiles

Each radio station, whether commercial or the BBC, has a distinct **profile** and identity and appeals to a different audience. This is evident in the programmes they produce, the presenters and the way in which they market themselves to those audiences. Each station also has a logo, which is a visual signifier of the station and is used in **cross-platform marketing**. This identity has been built up over time and audiences have expectations of particular stations and their output. The programmes produced and commissioned by the station are often indicative of the station's identity and ethos. Radio differs from television in that it is available in a range of different **formats**:

- BBC Radio. The BBC is a public service broadcaster and as such it is funded by the licence fee and does not air commercials. BBC Radio is both national and regional, there are over 40 local/regional stations attracting more than 9 million listeners each week. However, these numbers have been steadily falling due to the competition from commercial broadcasters.

There are over 300 commercial radio stations in the UK. These are:

- National commercial radio. There are three of these stations broadcasting at the time of writing: Classic FM, Talksport and Absolute Radio.

- National brands. These are regional stations that have been collected into networks, sharing some programmes and **syndicated output**. They are:

  - Global Radio – Heart, Galaxy, Gold and Xfm

  - Bauer Media Group – Kiss and Magic

  - Guardian Media Group – Real Radio

- Independent local radio. These are regional commercial stations. They are specific to a certain area of the country and are not part of a network group.

- Community radio. This is a different format from public service and commercial stations. Community stations serve their local areas and produce content of interest to local people. The station is non-profit making and is usually funded by the local community.

- Hospital radio. There are hundreds of hospital radio stations based in hospitals and staffed by volunteers broadcasting in the UK. Many radio presenters started out in hospital or community radio.

Key Term

Syndicated output = This is where radio stations make and sell a programme to other stations, or buy a programme that may be available to other radio stations.

Task: Researching a station profile

Choose a radio station to research. This could relate directly to your main texts or just allow you to broaden your knowledge of the medium. Create a PowerPoint presentation about your chosen station summing up the key points from your research and giving information about:

- The general profile of the station

- The structure and organisation

- The ethos and identity

- Flagship programmes

- Scheduling decisions and techniques employed by the station

- Marketing strategies, for example trailers, logos, etc.

- Include reference to the main texts where appropriate

- Up-to-date news related to the station.

Task

Research the radio station formats that are available in your local area.

Key Figures

The **Bauer Media Group** is a multi-national conglomerate that operates in 16 countries. It owns a range of global magazine titles and part of its organisation is Bauer Radio.

In an age where we are dominated by visual images, many will question how radio has managed to survive and indeed, develop. The medium of radio has a range of different appeals as it consists of:

- **The blind medium** – it only involves the sense of hearing with no visual images. In this sense the medium can be seen to have advantages in that it allows the audience to use their imagination.

- **The companion medium** – the radio format provides a strong sense of personal communication for the audience. It also offers interactive opportunities – audiences can text and email programmes and get a 'mention' or a 'shout out' on the radio programme. Some programmes have phone-ins where the listeners can air their views or select music to be played.

- **The intimate medium** – radio is very personal. It encourages intimacy by the use of the direct mode of address.

- **The undemanding medium** – it allows the audience to do other things while listening. A criticism of television in the early days was that it didn't 'go round corners' as, with radio, a listener does not need to devote their time entirely to the text.

Different stations will also have diverse styles and their programming will reflect the target audience. This will in turn influence and reinforce the profile of the station. Audiences build up a knowledge based on experience of what each station will offer. Stations tend to be divided stylistically and in terms of content between those that are speech based and those that are music led. Speech-based stations and their individual programmes tend to target an older audience demographic. The generic codes and conventions of speech-based radio programmes are:

- A presenter – although this can also be the case for music-led formats, the presenter in speech-led programmes acts as an anchor to guide, for example, the discussion between various guests, or as a judge in a quiz programme, for example Sandy Toksvig in Radio 4's *The News Quiz*.

- Discussions – a group of people sitting around discussing a range of topics. This genre of programme is often a key part of Radio 4's schedule.

- Phone-ins – these are effective, cheap ways of involving the listener. They are encouraged to take part in the programme and offer their point of view. For example, Jeremy Vine's lunchtime programme on Radio 2.

- Contributors – news magazine programmes like *Today* and *PM* on Radio 4 invite guests who tend to be experts or knowledgeable in the topic under discussion. The 8.10 am slot on the *Today* programme is renowned for being reserved for eminent contributors like, for example, the Prime Minister.

Evan Davis on the Today programme

- Drama – Radio 4 has a regular feature of *The Afternoon Play*. Other dramas include the long-running radio soap *The Archers*.

- Documentaries – these may be related to news items or current affairs, or be music themed, for example the life of a particular pop star or musician. *The Essay* on Radio

Exam Tip

Choosing a speech-led radio programme as one of your three texts alongside a music-led example will allow you to analyse different radio formats.

3 late in the day's schedule is a programme where different writers discuss their experiences and aspects of life that interest them.

- Outside broadcasts – reporters, presenters and mobile studios bring stories and features from different national and global locations. The flexibility of the radio medium means that it does not have to rely on visual images and therefore the reports can be more immediate. The focus is on the human voice and sound effects.

Nick Grimshaw from Radio 1's Breakfast Show

Scheduling

Just like television, each radio station has a schedule and programmes are **stripped** across the schedule. The regular programmes for each station are broadcast at the same time each day. The scheduling of a particular programme will have been researched in order to maximise the target audience. The radio, more so than television, divides up its day related to what the audience may be doing. Radio 1 and 2 both have breakfast shows which bring in a large section of audience who are getting ready for, or travelling to, work. These are largely music led but also incorporate chat, sport, traffic and regular slots specific to the programme. For example, Chris Evans's Radio 2 *Breakfast Show* includes a feature called 'Top Tenuous' where listeners text or email in their most 'tenuous' links to a celebrity chosen by Evans and his team. These regular features build up expectations in the audience and give a structure to the programme. These breakfast shows are important to the station as they hook the audience early and establish their loyalty to the programme. In May 2013 listener figures suggested that the Radio 1 breakfast show was struggling.

> 'Nick Grimshaw's Radio 1 breakfast show has lost nearly a million listeners since he took over from Chris Moyles. Not only have the Northern DJ's audience figures dropped dramatically, but they are the lowest the station has recorded from that time slot in 10 years. And to add insult to injury Nick, 28, also has four million less [sic] listeners than Radio 2's breakfast show with Chris Evans – the biggest ever gap recorded between the two station slots.'

www.dailymail.co.uk

Key Term

Stripped = This is a technique used in radio and television whereby a certain programme is broadcast at the same time every day. In radio this attracts an audience who associate a particular programme with their daily routine, for example driving home from work.

Task

Analyse the schedule for a particular radio station. Can you give examples of stripping and where programmes are broadcast to attract a specific target audience?

Key Terms

Audio streaming = This is where listeners can click on a link to play the radio programme instantly. This has increased the global reach of BBC Radio as listeners abroad can tune in to hear the live programme.

DAB radio = This is Digital Audio Broadcasting and it allows the listener greater choice and makes the selection of radio stations easier. The digital sound quality is better and free from the interference common with analogue transmission.

Key Figure

Professor Andrew Crisell

He is a lecturer in the history of the mass media at Sunderland University and is an expert in radio. He has written several books about the changing face of radio as a communication medium.

Industry: regulation

The BBC as a public service broadcaster is regulated by the BBC Trust and Ofcom. (See the section on the Television Industry for more information on Ofcom.) Like television, BBC Radio has a public service remit to inform, educate and entertain. This is evident in its range of stations catering for diverse audiences and interests including the classical output of Radio 3, Radio 1Xtra, which plays contemporary Hip Hop and RnB and is aimed at 15–24-year-olds, and the BBC Asian Network to cater for the British Asian community. Commercial and community radio stations have to apply for their licences from Ofcom and have to abide by their rules and regulations regarding output.

Industry: new technology

Recent technological advances have had an impact upon radio in terms of how programmes are broadcast and how listeners receive those programmes. These technological developments have allowed radio to develop and increase in popularity, despite critics heralding the end of the radio format. Although radio is a blind medium, many radio stations now have webcams in their studios allowing listeners to view the presenters and guests in a radio show. Radio programmes also often produce a podcast of the best bits of a particular week or collate the week's highlights for a regular feature; for example Simon Mayo's Confessions on Radio 2, where listeners send in their secret stories and the team on the programme decide if they should be forgiven. This is put together in a weekly podcast. Podcasts can be downloaded on a range of platforms and make listening to the radio more flexible.

Most radio stations allow listeners to access the output on the Internet through an **audio streaming** facility; this has broadened the global audience. A major development has been **DAB Radio**. This has created more wavelengths allowing a greater number of stations. It has also increased the quality of the output, ensuring less interference. This digital platform will gradually replace analogue transmission.

Main text: BBC Radio 2 *Steve Wright in the Afternoon*

Industry information

- This is BBC Radio 2's afternoon show hosted by presenter Steve Wright. It is also known as *The Big Show*. It is scheduled from 2 to 5 pm every weekday afternoon.

- The show is one of the most successful and popular on Radio 2 and has become established as a brand with a formula recognised and expected by audiences.

- The show started in the 1980s on Radio 1 and ran on that station until the early 1990s. It was then revived and broadcast on Radio 2 in 1999 where it has run ever since.

- Steve Wright is a popular broadcaster and also presents Sunday Love Songs on Sunday mornings on Radio 2. He was also the voice over presenter of TOTP2 until 2009.

- The show is said to be the first to use the **zoo format** on radio, this started with 'the posse' when Steve Wright was at Radio 1. This programme won several awards in the 90s including best DJ. This format is now a central part of the structure of the Radio 2 programme. The present co-presenters are Tim Smith and Janey Lee Grace; however, there are other regular 'characters' including The Old Woman and Barry from Watford who contribute to specific programmes.

- Part of the house style of the programme is the inclusion of regular features including the Factoids, Non-stop Oldies and horoscopes. Some of these appear in the programme daily, others on the same day each week.

- The programme 'brand' is so distinctive that when Steve Wright is absent the stand in hosts, for example Jo Whiley and Chris Tarrant, do not attempt to replicate the formula and the programme is very different and does not include any of the usual features.

Industry: the BBC

As stated earlier in this section, the BBC is a public service broadcaster with a remit to inform, educate and entertain. You can read more information about the BBC in the chapter on the Television Industry. Like television, radio has to produce programmes that attract and appeal to a broad audience. BBC Radio is funded by the licence fee so there are no advertisements other than those for other BBC Television and Radio programmes and events organised by the BBC, for example Proms in the Park. As with BBC Television, the funding arrangement allows the stations some aspect of freedom to produce programmes that may target less mainstream audiences. All radio stations are obliged to broadcast regular news bulletins, these often will reflect the style of the station and the target audience. For example, the condensed, pacey delivery of Radio 1's *Newsbeat* which covers issues relating to its younger demographic, or the more traditional mode of address of the *Today* programme on Radio 4. However, it is also important that all stations prove their popularity as it is a competitive market.

In 2013, Chris Evans and BBC Radio 2 both recorded their highest ever audience figures, with the station now reaching over 15 million listeners. *The Breakfast Show* with Chris Evans now has 9.8 million listeners up from 9.2 million in 2012.

Task

Watch the advert promoting BBC Radio. http://www.youtube.com/watch?v=PKp9dJiVYVU

How does this attract the target audience and market the stations?

Exam Tip

Choosing radio programmes from different stations and different genres will allow you to demonstrate your broad understanding of the medium in an examination answer.

Key Term

Factoid = For this show the term has come to mean pieces of true but insignificant and sometimes strange, bits of information. Originally, the term meant information that was presented as fact but without the evidence to support it.

Helen Boaden, Director of BBC Radio, said:

'Radio kicks off 2013 with a robust set of figures for the industry as a whole and I'm delighted that BBC Radio still attracts more than 35 million people every week. Radio 2 goes from strength to strength, setting new records across the board.'

www.radiotoday.co.uk

Industry: marketing

BBC Radio engages in the following marketing strategies to promote its stations and programmes:

- Cross-platform marketing. Other radio stations and BBC Television will promote radio stations and events related to BBC Radio, for example T in the Park.

- Billboard and magazine advertisements for stations and presenters.

- Each station has its own website within the umbrella website for BBC Radio. These allow listeners to access live audio streaming and to listen to archive programmes. They also provide interactive opportunities for an audience.

- BBC Radio produces promotional films focusing on a particular part of its output, for example its presenters or news coverage.

Text: genre

The Big Show with Steve Wright is a speech and music daytime magazine programme. As such, it shares a repertoire of elements with other similar programmes, but is also distinctive and this brand identity is part of its appeal. Its generic codes and conventions include:

- Characters. These are well established and contribute to the zoo format style of the show. The programme is presenter led; Steve Wright is a seasoned broadcaster who has a recognisable radio voice. The other main contributors are Janey Lee Grace and Tim Smith who are both broadcasters in their own right. They have distinct characteristics that define them, and audiences have come to expect how they will react. They also relate to the older Radio 2 audience. Janey Lee Grace is a mother, vegetarian and is environmentally concerned. She is often teased good naturedly about this. Tim will often conduct interviews with guests and is teased about his obsession with golf.

- Other 'characters' will appear sporadically and are included for a humour and are part of the distinctive nature of the programme. These include an Elvis impersonator for the Ask Elvis element of the programme, the Old Woman and Barry from Watford.

- Guests. Each day there will be 2–3 guests who are chosen from a range of cultural areas including the arts, current affairs and sport. In one week in July 2013 the guests included Bee Gee Barry Gibb and Chris O'Dowd from *Bridesmaids*. Some guests are regulars on the show and as such are greeted as old friends and have a rapport with the team. The guests will be interviewed in the studio or are pre-recorded at an outside location.

- The magazine style format of the show means that as well as music there are other features including: news, traffic updates, **factoids**, sound bites from celebrities, interviews and astrology.

- Language and mode of address. This is informal and chatty, welcoming the audience into the intimate radio medium. This also establishes a sense of community. The team, particularly Wright and Tim Smith are known for mispronouncing certain words and for making up words.

- Audio codes. As the medium is radio, audio obviously plays an important part. These codes include jingles that are created specifically for the show and feature music stars or impersonators. The introductory music is loud, dramatic and involves enthusiastic clapping establishing the sense that an event is about to happen. This clapping sound effect is also used at the beginning and end of interviews with guests. There is also distinctive, dramatic music signifying the end of the programme.

quickfire

(94) How is this programme typical of its genre?

Text: narrative

Steve Wright in the Afternoon has, over time, established a formulaic narrative structure that remains consistent from show to show. This structure gives the illusion of being unscripted, but is in fact tightly constructed. The narrative is time driven and certain aspects of the programme appear at the same time every day or on specific days. For example:

- The news is broadcast on the hour. This read by a news reader to establish a distance from the more light-hearted main programme.

- There is traffic information at regular time slots. This is read by 'Sally Traffic' who is a recognisable voice in the afternoon on Radio 2. She does more than just present the traffic news; she is invited into the narrative and is asked her opinion on topics under discussion by the team.

- From 3–3.30 pm each day there are the Non-stop Oldies where a listener selects their favourite tracks. This feature often has a narrative attached to it depending on the reasons why the tracks have been chosen.

- The factoids are another integral part of the show that helps to establish its brand identity and its structure. The factoids are read out by the team. They are also linked to a Twitter feed and a book has been made about them.

- At different times during the week there will be other key features, for example astrology and dream interpretation.

The narrative structure of the show is divided into segments punctuated by jingles made specifically for the show. Audio codes also signify when particular aspects of the show are about to start.

The team also contribute to the narrative structure in the way in which they behave and interact with each other, the audience is familiar with them and has expectations of their role. Steve Wright as the presenter is the anchor of the show and his specific role is to lead the listener through the narrative of the day, he initially sets out the programme's schedule, he also introduces the main features and instigates the discussion with the team though his use of questions. When there are guests he supplies information about them to keep the listener informed.

Task

Listen to your chosen radio programme and consider how the narrative is constructed.

Chris O'Dowd chats to Steve Wright
DURATION: 05:00

Text: representation

Gender

Gender is generally represented in a positive way in the programme. The 'team' contains men and women. Janey Lee Grace is a well established older female presenter whose opinions are regularly aired on the show. She is also a positive role model in that she is a mother of young children and holds strong views about health issues and the environment. She has also had her own music career and has written a best-selling book, *Imperfectly Natural Woman,* this would appeal to the female target audience. Radio 2 has other similar positive role models including Jo Whiley and Zoe Ball. Jo Whiley is one of the regular stand-ins for Steve Wright, reinforcing her credibility with the audience.

The men on the show are represented as approachable and human. This is established through the use of the 'radio voice' and the language and mode of address used. Steve Wright frequently addresses listeners as if he were speaking to them personally as a friend therefore establishing a relationship with the audience.

The guests are drawn from both genders and because it is the medium of radio the audience listen rather than judge a person on how they look, therefore the representation is more considered and related to what the celebrity can do and not their appearance.

Janey Lee Grace

Guests on Steve Wright in the Afternoon

Age

As the target audience profile for Radio 2 generally is 35+, the presenters will tend to reflect this in their age. However, there are areas of the station's programming that clearly have a younger age group as their target, Chris Evans for example. There has also been a criticism of the station that they have a stereotypical view of this age group constructed through the choice of music played which tends to be soft rock. All of the regular team on *The Big Show* are 50+ and as such are a positive representation of age in this medium. In other areas of broadcasting there have been issues with ageism that has not been so apparent on radio. Is it because they can't be seen?

quickfire

⑨⑤ Which social groups do you think are under-represented by Radio 2?

Task

Listen to a week of your chosen radio programme and analyse the representations of gender contained within the programme. How do they reflect the target audience?

Exam Tip

When discussing representation in radio programmes consider how the representation is constructed and how this relates to the target audience.

Audience

Who is the Radio 2 audience?

According to the BBC, *'The remit of Radio 2 is to be a distinctive mixed music and speech service, targeted at a broad audience, appealing to all age groups over 35. It should offer entertaining popular music programmes and speech-based content including news, current affairs, documentaries, religion, arts, comedy, readings and social action output.'*

- 90% of the population tune into radio every week.

- On average a listener tunes into 12.9 hours of radio per week.

- 50% of the population tune into digital radio.

- 23 million adults have access to a DAB radio.

- 20% listen on their mobile phone.

- Recent figures from Rajar (Radio Joint Audience Research) in 2013 suggest that the Radio 2 audience continues to rise with over 15 million listeners.

- Listeners are also making use of iPlayer to listen to the radio, in January 2013 *Steve Wright in The Afternoon* was in the top 20 programmes with 71,000 **requests** for one episode.

(www.rajar.co.uk)

How does *Steve Wright in the Afternoon* attract and appeal to its audience?

- The choice of guests. These are drawn from a range of cultural areas. In one week in July 2013 the guests included actor Simon Pegg, chef Rick Stein, comedian Marcus Brigstock, actor Michael Palin and musician Nile Rodgers.

- The playlist. The range of music and artists featured on the programme reflects the age and the musical preferences of the target audience.

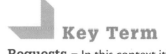

Key Term

Requests = In this context it is when an audience 'clicks' in order to stream or download a programme.

Key Figures

RAJAR stands for Radio Joint Audience Research and is the official body in charge of measuring radio audiences in the UK. It is jointly owned by the BBC and the RadioCentre on behalf of the commercial sector.

Task

How does the playlist of your chosen music-led programme reflect the genre and target audience?

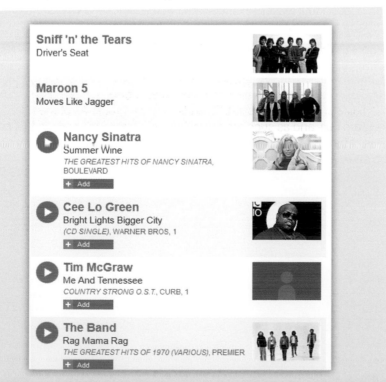

- The structure of the programme. The magazine format ensures that audiences are given a diverse menu of music, gossip, chat and regular features to keep them interested.

- The presenter. There is the appeal of the star persona of Steve Wright. He is an established radio icon and will bring with him a fan base.

- The team. Aspects of their personalities and the way in which they interact with each other allow the audience to relate to them and their topics of conversation which can be very ordinary and mundane.

- The programme is stripped and scheduled effectively to target an audience who may be at work or at home.

- The audience is positioned as part of the community of the programme through the informality of the mode of address of the presenter and the team. They may feel a sense of personal identity with one of the team that encourages them to listen.

- The accessibility of the programme across media platforms. The programme can be downloaded as a podcast; it can be listened to as a **simulcast** on the Internet or streamed at a later date.

quickfire

96 What does the choice of guests tell you about the target audience for the show?

Key Term

Simulcast = This is the streaming of live radio programmes from the website at the same time as they are broadcast on the radio.

quickfire

97 How might you apply the uses and gratifications theory to this programme?

How may an audience respond to the programme?

- This may be a literal response. The programme gives a range of interactive opportunities for the listener. These include texting in for a 'shout out' on the programme; this is often from people at work who make a funny comment about their work colleagues. This reinforces the concept of the radio as a medium that can be accessed whilst the audience is doing something else. There is almost an unwritten rule that to get your text read out you must say that you 'love the show'. The listener can send in ideas for their Non-stop Oldies to be played in this section of the programme. They can phone-in to appear in the astrology section of the programme where they ask the astrologer for advice.

- The assumption is that listeners will have actively tuned into the show and therefore accept the preferred reading of the show's creators. However, there is evidence on blogs and forums that not everyone out there likes the show or its presenter. This suggests there is an oppositional response to the show. Some like Steve Wright but are unhappy with the choice of stand-ins when he is away.

- The format of the magazine programme suits the 'pick and mix' audience. Not all listeners from the target group will tune into the programmes from beginning to end. Whenever they do listen, due to the style of the programme, there will be something to interest them.

Task

Look at the forum on digitalspy. co.uk. What literal listener responses are there to the programme?

Summary: The Radio Industry

APPEAL AND TARGETING

Target audience: older, have moved with Steve Wright from Radio1

How are they targeted?

Audience appeal?

Gauntlett – pick and mix audience

Responses: Stuart Hall – different responses

Pleasures: uses and gratifications – social interaction, information

Construction of the audience through the content, ideology, mode of address, layout and design, etc.

Categorisation of audience – demographics, channel profile, Rajar data

Station profiles indicating listener and categorising the audience

GENRE

Different mediums for stations

Commercial/BBC

Consider the codes and conventions of the magazine radio format

Genre linked to content and style

How is the genre evident in the programme's style and content?

NARRATIVE

How does the structure and content reflect the narrative?

Language and mode of address

Regular items

Time-driven narrative

Character-driven narrative

Positioning of the reader within the narrative

RADIO 2 STEVE WRIGHT IN THE AFTERNOON

TECHNOLOGICAL ADVANCES

DAB transmission

Podcasts

Audio streaming

Simulcasts

Effect on industry?

Increase of global reach

REPRESENTATION

Gender and age

Which social groups are under-represented?

How is the representation constructed and mediated?

REGULATION

How is the radio industry regulated?

How does the text adhere to the code of practice?

What are the current issues surrounding the regulation of this industry?

The website for Radio 2 and for the specific programme – consider what different experiences this offers the user/reader?

What other platforms are available to access the programme?

Introduction

In studying this industry in preparation for the MS4 examination you will need to ensure that you have a broad and up-to-date understanding. Your main texts must allow you to demonstrate that understanding. Remember, it is helpful if your texts are varied and diverse; this way you will effectively illustrate your awareness of a range of issues related to the industry. Your examples can be selected from different platforms and formats; this will allow you to broaden your discussion of the industry.

The computer games industry is relatively new in comparison to other media industries, but it has seen a rapid growth in recent years. Its profits have rivalled those of major films, and sales of consoles are still expanding. Games can be played on a range of different consoles offering diverse gaming experiences including the XBox360, Playstation3 and the Wii. These also enable the user to engage in multi-player interactivity that broadens the gaming experience. According to recent ESA data:

©jcjgphotography/Shutterstock.com

'No other sector has experienced the same explosive growth as the computer and video game industry. Our creative publishers and talented workforce continue to accelerate advancement and pioneer new products that push boundaries and unlock entertainment experiences. These innovations in turn drive enhanced player connectivity, fuel demand for products, and encourage the progression of an expanding and diversified consumer base.'

Michael D. Gallagher, President and CEO, Entertainment Software Association (www.theesa.com)

In recent years the profile of gamers has changed and it is no longer the case that a gamer is a lone teenage boy in his bedroom, gamers are now of all ages and demographics and of both genders.

The playing of computer games is now also taken more seriously as a media industry and computer games are accepted as media texts valid for study in the same way as films and television programmes. Indeed, some games are very complex in their construction and the demands made on the gamer compared with other media texts.

'I consider video games a form of design that is amazingly important today and that is going to become even more important in the future, because it is a way we interact with machines and screens.'

Paola Antonelli, Senior curator of the Museum of Modern Art's department of architecture and design (www.theesa.com)

Key Figures

The ESA
The Entertainment Software Association is a US-based company exclusively dedicated to serving the business and public affairs needs of companies that publish computer and video games for video game consoles, personal computers, and the Internet.

Task

Research the top computer games and the top films and compare their sales. What conclusion can you draw about the gaming industry?

Industry facts

The ESA engages in regular research into the computer gaming industry in the USA. It found that in 2013:

- 58% of Americans play video games.

- Consumers spent $20.77 billion on video games, hardware, and accessories in 2012.

- Purchases of digital content, including games, add-on content, mobile apps, subscriptions, and social networking games, accounted for 40% of game sales in 2012.

- The average game player is 30 years old and has been playing games for 13 years.

- The average age of the most frequent game purchaser is 35 years old.

- 45% of all game players are women. In fact, women over the age of 18 represent a significantly greater portion of the game-playing population (31%) than boys age 17 or younger (19%).

- 51% of US households own a dedicated game console, and those that do own an average of two.

- 36% of gamers play games on their smartphone, and 25% play games on their wireless device.

- Parents are present when games are purchased or rented 89% of the time.

In the UK, gaming is equally popular. In 2012 two physical games sold over 1 million units, according to UKIE and GfK Chart-Track data. These were *Call of Duty: Black Ops II* and *FIFA 13*, which were comfortably the No.1 and No.2 sellers last year. In 2013 the chart was dominated by *The Last of Us*, a zombie survival game for the Playstation3. In its opening weekend it sold more than 1.3 million copies and made more money than the new *Superman* film. It has been critically acclaimed for its narrative, its themes that are seen to be more mature and emotional than those usually dealt with in this genre and the economical soundtrack. This game is sound evidence that the computer games industry is developing in response to the demands of an audience who want to be both surprised and challenged.

©chaoss/Shutterstock.com

(98) Are any of the statistics from the ESA surprising?

Still from The Last of Us, *Sony Computer Entertainment*

Analysing computer games

As stated previously, computer games differ from other media texts in a range of ways:

- They give the user experiences not available in other media texts. Many games offer a multi-playing online experience not replicated in any other media platform. In the **MMORPG** format a large number of players can be involved in the virtual world of the game at one time.

- These huge multi-player games are also unique in that they have **persistent worlds** which add to the realism of the experience.

- Smaller versions are online multi-player games where there are usually fewer players and a non-persistent world. This interactive experience crosses genres, for example *FIFA 13* and *Call of Duty* are examples of **CRPG**, but clearly the roles for the gamers are different.

- Computer games are role-playing games and the aim is usually for the players together to complete a mission. Along the way they will need to work together and to overcome challenges to reach a common goal.

Still from Call of Duty
Activision Publishing

Key Terms

MMORPG = Massively multi-player online role-playing game.

Persistent worlds = These are a feature of MMORPG games. It means that the game world continues even when the gamer is not part of it. In this way the virtual world replicates real life.

CRPG = Computer role-playing game.

Key Figure

Jesper Juul

He is a ludologist – a computer games researcher and a visiting assistant arts professor at the New York University Game Center. He has written extensively on the subject of computer games. Some of his ideas can be found on his website: www.jesperjuul.net

quickfire

99 Why might links to other media texts help in the marketing of a computer game?

- Within the game the player may have to succeed at certain tasks in order to proceed to the next level. The tasks generally become more complex and challenging as the player advances through the game. Certain challenges may have to be repeated several times before success. *The Guardian* journalist Stuart Heritage, in an article on the challenges of mastering computer games, writes about his lack of skill when playing *The Last of Us*:

'...spending 25 minutes in every single room I enter, uselessly shining a torch at a vending machine in the blind hope that it will somehow lead me to an exit .... getting killed in the same way by the same zombie 60 times in a row.'

www.theguardian.com. For the article go to tinyurl.com/ktk63km

- Computer games are also different because they are intertextual, that is, they use the codes and conventions of other texts within their structure. For example, they may be derived from a novel, comic or existing audio-visual text; this clearly also helps in the marketing of the product. They may incorporate graphics, cinematic filming or recognisable audio codes from other texts within their structure.

- Different games position the players in different ways, for example single player, multi-player, distanced controller or specific character role-play. The play can be first person or third person.

- One of the main distinguishing features of the MMORPG is the use of the **avatar**. This is a key element of this type of game and allows the gamer choices about how they will represent themselves in the game.

- Computer games are available on a range of different platforms which, in turn, will affect the user experience. The Xbox 360 and the Playstation3, and the new Xbox One and Playstation4, allow the gamer to speak directly to the other gamers thus enhancing the credibility of the virtual world experience.

- The big debate in the computer games industry is whether games have narratives. In simple terms, a **narratologist** will assert that games have clear narratives that are similar to those in other texts, for example films and television programmes. An analyst of **ludology** will maintain that as games are simulations, they are therefore essentially different from other media texts in that the player 'plays the game' and therefore has a control over the structure that is not available to the viewer of a film or television programme. It is therefore difficult to place computer games in a traditional narrative structure because the narrative is fluid, not fixed and open to a personal interpretation.

Industry: regulation

The regulation of computer games is a sensitive issue and there are regular reports regarding the suitability of the content of computer games and the easy accessibility to this content by young people. The wider media usually wastes no time apportioning blame for the violent behaviour and lack of sociability of young people to the gaming industry. Certain games, for example *Grand Theft Auto* and *Call of Duty*, have caused concern over their content and its potential effect on the gamer. This, combined with research showing that children much younger than the age restriction were playing games, has caused concern with parents and the government.

The computer games industry is controlled and regulated by the BBFC. Their role is to regulate and classify games and they work alongside the PEGI system to give a game a rating and additional information about the content of the game that will help consumers, particularly parents, to decide upon the suitability of the game. The system is supported by the major console manufacturers, including Sony, Microsoft and Nintendo, as well as by publishers and developers of interactive games throughout Europe. Consumers can contact PEGI if they want to complain about the rating of a game. PEGI also supported the 'Safe Internet Day' in 2013. In July 2012 PEGI became the single video games age ratings system, under which it was made illegal for a retailer to sell a game with a PEGI age rating of 12, 16 or 18 to someone below that age.

However, recent research by **UKIE** had some worrying findings:

- Only 2 in 5 parents say they only buy games that are the correct age rating; 43% of parents admit to checking the age ratings of games but not always sticking to them.

- Of the parents who said they never check age ratings, 24% said they didn't think there was anything they could put in a game which would be unsuitable.

- 50% of parents would let their child play a game that was bought for them by a friend or relative, but had an unsuitable age rating.

- In response UKIE have launched the askaboutgames website.

Key Terms

Avatar = This is the player's representation of themselves within the game.

Narratologist = This is someone who studies narrative and narrative structure and the ways that they affect our perception.

Ludology = This is the study of games and those who play them.

UKIE = UKIE is the only trade body for the UK's wider interactive entertainment industry. They exist to champion the interests, needs and positive image of the videogames and interactive entertainment industry.

(100) What do the findings by UKIE suggest about the regulation of the computer games industry?

Task

Look at the BBFC website for decisions made about the regulation of computer games.

Main text: *Assassin's Creed III*

Industry information

- The game was launched in 2012. It is an action-adventure computer game developed by Ubisoft Montreal for Playstation3, Xbox 360, Wii U and Microsoft Windows. The format is both single and multi-player mode.

- This is the third in the series but introduces a new character and setting distinguishing it from the earlier games in the sequence, which were set in Renaissance Italy.

- However, like the earlier games, the series is distinctive in that the narrative is set in a fictional world but includes real historical events and characters. For example, it is set during the American Revolution and features key figures of the time like George Washington and Paul Revere, who interact with the fictional characters.

- On its launch it was met with generally positive reviews from gamers and the industry. *'[Its] newly refined gameplay and incredibly rich setting are captivating stuff... It improves on the underlying Assassin's Creed formula in a handful of subtle but tangible ways... And its unwavering commitment to storytelling is both rare and impressive.'*

(Official Xbox Magazine)

- *Assassin's Creed III* was the best-selling game in the United Kingdom in the week of its release, with the best sales of the series to date. It was the biggest launch in publisher Ubisoft's history and the third biggest launch of any game in the UK in 2012 (behind *Call of Duty: Black Ops II* and *FIFA 13*).

- By February 2013 *Assassin's Creed III* had sold 12 million copies worldwide representing an almost 70 per cent increase over *Assassin's Creed Revelations* at the same point of its lifecycle, according to the publisher. (www.computerandvideogames.com)

- In July 2013 it was number 8 in the computer games chart having been there for 37 weeks. This was only bettered by *FIFA 13* which was number 4 and had been in the chart for 42 weeks. (www.guardian.co.uk).

- *Assassin's Creed III* was nominated for six awards in the 2012 Spike Video Game Awards: Game of the Year, Best Xbox 360 Game, Best PS3 Game, Best Action Adventure Game, Best Graphics, and Character of the Year (Connor). GameTrailers awarded *Assassin's Creed III* Best Action-Adventure Game of the Year 2012 while Game Revolution named *Assassin's Creed III* its Game of the Year 2012. For the 2013 D.I.C.E. Interactive Achievement Awards, the game won the award for Outstanding Achievement in Animation and was nominated for Adventure Game of the Year, and Outstanding Achievement in Sound Design.

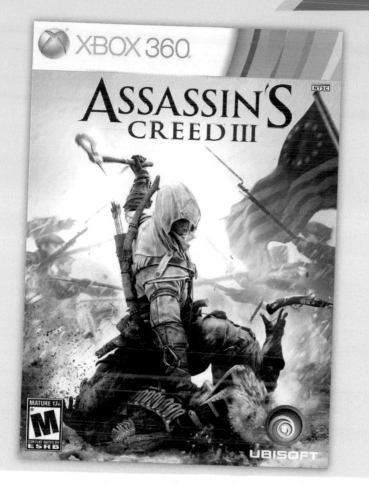

Industry: marketing

The computer games industry is adept at keeping its audience waiting for the next in a games series and Ubisoft with *Assassin's Creed III* is no exception. Part of the marketing was managed through 'leaks' early in 2012, which first suggested that the game would move away from the story of Ezio and the setting of Italy to the American Revolution. Ubisoft also stated via Facebook that an announcement about the new game was imminent. The box art for the game was then released confirming the North American snowy setting. In March 2012 CVG released screen shots that showed the game's new protagonist in a number of settings, including a town, a forest and an icy region, further whetting the audience's appetite. The focus of the marketing was also to attract an audience who are new to the series as this is a new setting, characters and storyline. Pre-order bonuses were available in chain stores across the world. Different countries created different marketing strategies for the game to ensure sales emphasising the global nature of the launch.

A cross-marketing strategy involved featuring artwork from *Assassin's Creed III* in *Assassin's Creed Recollection*, a board game app for the iPad.

Press releases were also an integral part of the pre-launch build up: *'Assassin's Creed III features the franchise's most expansive setting so far, along with an exciting new hero and exponentially more gameplay,' said Ubisoft CEO, Yves Guillemot. 'Whether you're a long-time fan of Assassin's Creed or if you're new to the franchise, you're going to be blown away by the scale and marvel of Assassin's Creed III.'*

www.guardian.co.uk/technology/gamesblog/2012

Official trailers were released prior to the launch introducing the new protagonist, the setting and the theme of the American Revolution.

Task

Watch the official launch trailer for the game on YouTube. What clues does it give for the game to follow?

Exam Tip

Ensure that you extend your knowledge of the industry beyond the game itself.

Text: genre

Categorising computer games into specific genres is a more complex task than for other media texts. By their very nature games are hybrid genres and can be classified in a range of ways, for example their themes, the interactive modes and playing experiences (first person shooter) or the type of simulation experience. The genre attributed to a specific game is usually done to aid marketing and promotion – this is easier if the repertoire of elements in a game can be linked to similar games so that the consumer has expectations and may purchase the game as a result.

Assassin's Creed III is generally placed under the umbrella genre of action adventure and as such shares some of the following codes and conventions with games of a similar sub-genre:

- Characters. They are both fictional and historically accurate. The expectation for this genre is that there will be a central character that the player will control. The two main fictional protagonists in this game are from different time zones: Desmond is from the modern story set in the 21st century and Connor is his half-English, half-Mohawk ancestor from the 18th century. As is typical of the genre, the protagonist has a goal and must overcome obstacles and challenges in order to achieve it. There is also use of actual historical characters, for example George Washington and Thomas Jefferson.

(102) What genre signifiers are apparent in the images on the game poster?

Key Term

Parkour/free running =
This is the sport of moving along a route, typically in a city, trying to get around or through various obstacles in the quickest and most efficient manner possible by jumping, climbing or running.

- Settings. These are inextricably linked to the gameplay and have been developed to broaden the opportunities and experiences of the gamer. The main setting is North America during the American Revolution, thus establishing a layer of credibility for the events that unfold. The settings include the cityscapes of Boston and New York allowing **parkour** and **free running**, a convention of this genre, as gamers can control the character as he runs from building to building. There is also a new space in The Frontier, the inclusion of this new style of terrain is a first for *Assassin's Creed* and broadens the movement opportunities. There is also The Homestead where the gamer can meet ancillary characters and is a base for the main character. A new feature is the naval setting on board a ship the Aquila which also allows for more complex gameplay as the gamer is in control of Connor, the ship and its crew.

- The iconography is specifically related to the historical time period, for example Connor's weapons are a Tomahawk and a rope dart, which makes some of the combat scenes more fluid and dramatic. The other weapons are historically accurate. Other iconography includes the uniforms of the soldiers and other signifiers of the Revolutionary War. Games of this genre will often have objects within them that are recognisable to gamers and can be used in the marketing of the game, they will be related to the theme of the game.

- Plot situations. In action adventure games the audience has an expectation of key events that will be part of the gaming experience. This will include missions and quests. Connor's mission is to keep his family safe and defeat the British. There will also be tasks including finding **Easter eggs** that allow the gamer to progress in the game. The Easter eggs in *Assassin's Creed* are feathers that the player collects. The expectation is also that there will be combat and stealth missions to test the skill of the player.

- Technical and audio. In games these aspects will mainly be related to the sophistication of the graphics and the scenes created by the makers of the game, the expectation now is that the characters will be as life-like as possible to increase the audience involvement in the game. All games of this genre also use dramatic music to build tension and increase the experience. Dialogue used will reflect the themes and time period of the game, the subject-specific lexis is evident in *Assassin's Creed III* by the use of Native American words and names of weapons, for example.

Text: narrative

As has been said earlier in this section, the analysis of computer games in terms of a traditional narrative structure can be problematic and at times controversial. *'There is a big debate over whether games are narratives that you play or games that have stories.'* (McDougall and O'Brien, *Studying Video Games*). This may depend also on the game being played. *Assassin's Creed III* has a clear plot outline that crosses other games in the series; the struggle between the Assassins who fight for peace through giving people free will and democracy and the Templars who want to establish peace through control. The game does use a range of narrative techniques within its structure. These include:

- The manipulation of time and space. The action is in the past and the present. One of the protagonists, Desmond, using a machine called the Animus, is able to relive the memories of his ancestors; his aim is to find a way to stop an apocalypse in the 21st century. The main story is set in the 18th century. The interesting point about game's narratives is that the progression of the gamer is determined by their skill and ability to be successful in the tasks and challenges; they are instrumental in the narrative itself and in some games may be able to construct their own narratives. However, ludologists will use this to assert that this is therefore play in that the narrative is fluid and not established in advance.

- *Assassin's Creed III* is set in an **open world** and is presented from the third person narrative perspective centred upon the combat and stealth of Desmond and Connor.

- Games are spatial and much of the structure is not necessarily based on the narrative but on the gameplay involved in navigating though the game's spaces.

- Another point of view may be that the narratives of games are essentially fairly basic and straightforward in structure in that, following Todorov's linear model, there is a disruption, a quest, combat and a resolution. Within this structure characters will develop and indeed, Connor goes through an arc of transformation as a result of the narrative of the game.

- In terms of narrative structure, there is also often a back-story that will enhance the involvement of the player. Whilst the characters and settings in *Assassin's Creed III* are new to the franchise, *Assassin's Creed IV*, launched in late 2013 will be linked to the narrative of the earlier game and so there will be plot links and character development.

Key Terms

Easter eggs = In the gaming world these are small secrets hidden in the games by the developer for fun. It is the aim of the gamers to find these, much like an Easter egg hunt.

Open World = In an open world game the player can move freely though the virtual world and is not restricted by levels and other barriers to free roaming.

(103) What are the main points of contention between ludologists and narratologists?

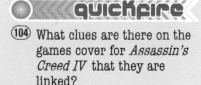

(104) What clues are there on the games cover for *Assassin's Creed IV* that they are linked?

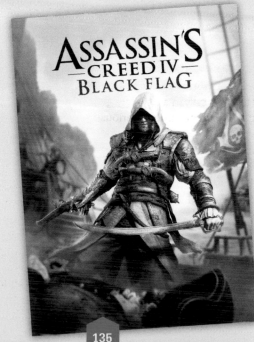

Key Terms

Side quests = These are missions that deviate from the main game and are optional. They are not required to complete the game.

Hyper-reality = This is a state where what is real and what is fiction are blended together and become indistinguishable. It may be, particularly in the case of computer games, that some gamers may feel more in touch with the hyper-real world then the physical one.

Exam Tip

Ensure that you are aware of the more sophisticated arguments regarding narrative linked to the computer games you have chosen.

- *Assassin's Creed III* also incorporates **side quests** into the narrative structure making the gameplay more interesting. These are the inclusion of naval missions that move away from the main theme and setting and give the chance to explore an optional narrative and test the skill and strategy of the gamer at a more sophisticated level.

- Computer games are said by some experts to go beyond the traditional analysis of narratives and characters. These analysts will assert that, due to the complex structure of computer games and the demands made upon the interactivity of the player, they are, in fact, post-modern texts. Evidence for this assertion is that whilst in many texts the focus is on the creation of a reality, computer games blur reality in a simulated virtual world which creates a **hyper-reality** and as such is post-modern in its structure and approach.

Text: representation

Gender

Most of the characters in *Assassin's Creed III* are male including the two central protagonists, Desmond and Connor. Connor is an interesting and complex character who develops as the game progresses. Unusually for a computer game he has an ethnic mix; he is half-English and half-Mohawk. The gamer plays as this character for most of the

Connor in Assassin's Cree III

game as he battles to support the cause of the Revolutionaries. We are introduced to his backstory in that he has witnessed the death of his mother and has been powerless to save her. This sense of powerlessness follows Connor and the gamer throughout *Assassin's Creed III* setting Connor aside from other protagonists in the franchise. Connor seems to have less ability than they to influence his future and control his destiny. He has to cope with the rejection of Achilles, a skilled Assassin and fails in some of his missions. However, this does make him a more rounded and credible character who faces moral dilemmas which are then the choice of the gamer. The high production technical codes involve the gamer completely with the character and construct his representation, his visual codes are enigmatic and mysterious, engaging the audience further as do his Native American links.

In terms of strong female representations the game struggles, apart from Kaniehti:io, Connor's mother. She is a Native American warrior from a village who is represented as brave in that she actively fights the British who want to steal Native American lands. However, she is also stereotypically involved in a romantic relationship with Templar Haytham and has his child. She is an active character who is intelligent and tactical and helps to free captured natives. Unfortunately she dies in the game having been trapped and killed by the British.

Task

Analyse other representations of gender in the game, for example Juno and Desmond. Consider how the representation is constructed and mediated within the events of the game.

Kaniehti:io in Assassin's Creed III

Representations of culture and nation

Assassin's Creed III offers a negative representation of the British colonialists and their relationship with the Native Americans. This is interesting as the game has rejected the temptation to make the Native Americans the enemy. The British, particularly Charles Lee, engage in acts of violence; for example, they burn down Connor 's town and terrorise the inhabitants of villages. In this way the representation of events and historical characters is mediated for the gamer who is always in role as Connor and therefore fighting the British.

Charles Lee in Assassin's Creed III

quickfire

(105) How is the representation of Charles Lee constructed in this image from the game?

The game also broke new ground in its representation of Native Americans who are frequently represented in a stereotypical way in computer games. Ubisoft consulted with the indigenous Native Americans in producing the characters and reconstructing the historical events in the game. They involved the Mohawks in the game's design and production, the Native American consultants provided the design team with information on buildings (Native Americans of the time lived in longhouses, not tepees), music and character behaviour. Connor was voiced by a Native American actor, Noah Watts from the Blackfeet and Crow tribe. Ubisoft also consulted language experts to ensure that the language used by the Native Americans was accurate and a correct representation of the culture.

Audience

How does *Assassin's Creed III* appeal to an audience?

- The most obvious appeal to any gamer is the interactive opportunities. This attracts the active player who can then immerse themselves in the virtual world of the game. In role as the main protagonist, Connor, the gamer is involved in a range of challenges and missions. The tests of skill and strength are another appeal of an interactive role-play game.

- The open world format will attract gamers who do not want to be restricted by levels and rules that prevent progression. This combined with the broadening of the spatial world of *Assassin's Creed* enhances the gamer's experience.

- This game, similarly to others in the *Assassin's Creed* franchise, incorporates historical accuracy in its narratives and character creation. The historical events are anchored in reality so giving the gamer information about the time and events. A young boy on holiday in Italy was reportedly able to point out landmarks and works of art on the strength of having played *Assassin's Creed*.

- The virtual world of the game offers escapism and diversion for the audience as they can involve themselves in the hyper-real world created.

- The multi-player mode offers social interaction for gamers and contrary to the stereotypical view that all gamers are loners, many enjoy the collaborative opportunities of this format and communicate regularly with gamers across the world.

- The gamer will have expectations of the action adventure genre that will be fulfilled by the content of this game.

- The game's website offers other interactive opportunities to engage with the world of the game as well as extended information about the characters and gameplay.

How may an audience respond to the game?

- Consider the literal responses to the game. These can be found on blogs and forums. The link below is to parental responses to *Assassin's Creed III*:

  tinyurl.com/l56pz85

- Stuart Hall's response theory can be applied as the game is constructed in order to elicit a particular mode of game play from the player. The gamer will therefore accept the preferred reading encoded by the game's producers.

- Oppositional readings will be mainly in response to the controversial content of games, this is often from those who have not actually played the game, but have been influenced by opinion leaders including other media texts.

Summary: The Computer Games Industry

APPEAL AND TARGETING

Interactivity

Multi-player mode and gaming experience

Open world format

Expectation of Assassin's Creed franchise

USES AND GRATIFICATIONS

Personal identity

Social interaction

Information

OTHER LITERAL RESPONSES

Games website forums

Newspaper reviews/ magazine articles

Responses on the website/blogs

Stuart Hall response theories
How can they be applied?

GENRE

Difficulty of categorisation of games

Action adventure genre

Characters are fictional and historically accurate

Typical plot situations

Sophistication of technical codes

NARRATIVE

Different nature of narrative and its structure in the games format

Ludology versus narratology

Narrative choices within the game

Techniques, e.g. manipulation of time and space

Side quests

REPRESENTATION

Consider how gender, nation and culture are represented in the game

Who is in control of the representation?

How is it constructed?

What is different about the representations in this game?

ASSASSIN'S CREED III

Developed by Ubisoft

Successful — be aware of evidence

Development from earlier games in series

Chart placing

GLOBAL APPEAL

Available on a range of global platforms

Global marketing and distribution

MARKETING and PROMOTION

Cross platform

Leaks on social networking sites

Press releases

Release of screen shots

Trailers

Game's website

Board games app

MS4 Complementary texts

As has been clearly stated at the beginning of each industry section, it is important that the main texts that you study are from a broad range. This will help you to more effectively demonstrate your understanding of the diversity of the industry and its output. Remember, there are rules to follow regarding the texts you are allowed to study:

- At least two of the chosen main texts must be contemporary (produced within the last 5 years).
- One of the texts must be British.

This book has covered one main text from each of the industries in the specification. Below are suggestions for texts that will complement that example. **These are suggestions only to illustrate a typical range for a specific industry.**

Television Industry

Example covered: *Strictly Come Dancing*
Complementary texts:

- A documentary, for example *Ross Kemp Gangs/Pirates*.
- A crime drama, for example *CSI*.

Try to ensure that the texts are not all from one channel. A combination of the BBC to show public service broadcasting issues, a commercial channel, and a channel with more minority appeal or SKY will provide a diverse range.

Film Industry

Example covered: *Skyfall*.
Complementary texts:

- A low budget British independent film, for example *Submarine*.
- A film from a different genre offering different areas of analysis from those above, for example *Bridesmaids*.

Magazine Industry

Example covered: *Men's Health*.
Complementary texts:

- A magazine targeting a different audience, for example *The Lady, We ♥ Pop*.
- A magazine from a different genre, for example *Empire Magazine*.

Newspaper Industry

Example covered: *The Independent / i*.
Complementary texts:

- A local newspaper.
- A newspaper with a different style targeting a different audience, for example *The Sun* or *The Daily Mail*.

Advertising Industry

Example covered: *Chanel Coco Mademoiselle*.
Complementary texts:

- A campaign for a British charity, for example *Barnardos*, a government health campaign.
- A campaign for a product from a different genre using different strategies, for example *GHD* hair straighteners, *Walkers Crisps*.

Music Industry

Example covered: *Ed Sheeran*
Complementary texts:

- A high profile, manufactured band aimed at a different target audience, for example, *One Direction, Little Mix*.
- An artist/s with a different image/genre of music, for example *Emeli Sande, Mumford and Sons*.

Radio Industry

Example covered: *Radio 2: Steve Wright in the Afternoon*.
Complementary texts:

- A programme from a local radio station.
- A programme with a different style, targeting a different audience, for example *The Today Programme, 5Live*.

Computer Games

Example covered: *Assassin's Creed III*.
Complementary texts:

- A game offering different gaming experiences, for example *GTA*.
- A game that offers other areas of discussion, for example *The Last of Us*.

Useful resources/texts

Both the MS3 internally assessed unit and the MS4 examination demand that you engage in independent reading around the subject in order for you to demonstrate a broad and sophisticated understanding. The more you know about the media generally and your chosen texts at both MS3 and MS4, the more sophisticated will be your response. The following is not an exhaustive list and does not cover all topics and areas but will offer a starting point.

Websites

www.theory.org.uk – this is media theorist David Gauntlett's site
www.mediaknowall.com
www.mediaedusites.co.uk – this needs a subscription
www.aber.ac.uk
www.bfi.org.uk
www.guardian.co/media
www.imdb.com
www. senses of cinema.com

Books/ Print resources

Branston, G & Stafford, R, *The Media Student's Book 5*, Routledge, 2010

Clare, A, *On Men: Masculinity in Crisis*, Chatto & Windus, 2000

Connell, B (Ed), *Exploring The Media*, Auteur, 2010

Davies, C with Bell, C, *Teaching The Music Press*, Auteur, 2012

Gauntlett, David, *Media, Gender and Identity: An Introduction*, Routledge, 2008

Inness, Sherrie, Action *Chicks: New Images of Tough Women in Popular Culture*, Palgrave Macmillan, 2004

Jackson, Peter, *Making Sense of Men's Magazines*, Polity Press, 2001

McDougal & O'Brien, *Studying Video Games*, Auteur, 2008

Tasker, Y, *Working Girls: Gender and Sexuality in Popular Cinema*, Routledge 1998

Whelehan, *Overloaded: Popular Culture and the Future of Feminism*, The Women's Press, 2000

The Media Magazine published by The English and Media Centre (subscription)

The Guardian and other broadsheet newspapers have media sections

Autueur publisher has a large catalogue of media/film texts covering a range of areas (www.auteur.co.uk)

MS4 Exam Practice and Technique

It is important that you are prepared for the MS4 examination. This does not just mean knowing your selected industries and your main texts well. Most candidates enter the examination room full of knowledge and understanding about the media – it is what you do with that knowledge that is important. Examination technique is something which must be learned and practised in preparation for what is a rigorous and challenging examination.

Preparation tips

- Look back at the MS4 past papers, be aware of what is required for each section. Consider how past questions have been worded. Your teacher may be able to show you exemplar responses provided by the awarding body which have commentaries written by examiners.

- Go over the notes/grids you have completed over the year, highlight in different colours the main points that you could use to answer different questions. There is a grid below that you can use to help you to collate your observations about your main texts. You can then highlight points you have made in the grid that may be useful for answering specific questions.

- Practise planning responses ensuring that you are using specific examples from the texts you have studied. If your texts are longer, for example films, you will need to select key scenes that best reinforce the points you want to make. For example, which scenes would be best to discuss narrative and which representation?

- Practise unpicking questions so that you are clear what a question requires you to write about.

- Revisit your main texts to remind yourself of how they demonstrate aspects of the industry; your texts will have been chosen for a specific reason. Use the grid below to help you to sort your notes into order if you have not used it when first analysing your texts.

- Be aware of how much time you will have to spend on each question. Remember to build in planning time. If you allow 45 minutes writing time, that also gives 15 minutes planning time.

EXTRACT TITLE	TEXTUAL ANALYSIS	AUDIENCE	INDUSTRY
	Genre/narrative/representation	Positioning/targeting/responses/relationship with text	Production/distribution/marketing/regulation/global

Tips for managing the examination

You must spend some time at the beginning of the examination selecting the right question for the right industry. It is essential that you get this right. You will need to fill in a grid on the front page of the paper giving your choices. You must use a different industry for each question.

- Beware of going into the examination with pre-conceived ideas regarding which industry you are going to use for which question; for example, using film for a marketing question. This is not a good way of approaching the examination paper – you need to have an open mind and make your *choices based on the questions set for that specific paper.*

- Read all of the questions. It is a temptation to only look at Section A first, answer that question and then move on. This is a dangerous method as you may find the industry you have used for Section A would have been better used to answer a Section B question.

- Unpick the question you intend to answer. Are you clear about what the focus is? Is it a question or a statement? Are there any key words that need defining in your introduction? What relevant media terminolgy will you need to include in your response?

- Plan your answer before you start writing. It may help to use a plan you have prepared in advance to give you an essay structure (see the example below). This will be time well spent and will enable you to produce a more coherent, articulate response.

- Make sure that your response is literate, intelligent and coherent. There is an expectation that at this stage in your A level studies you will have a sophisticated level of literacy that you can demonstrate in your response.

- Ensure that you refer to all three of your main texts in your answer. Failing to do so will incur a penalty. You must write at least a paragraph on each of your texts. Of course the expectation is that you will write more than this.

- You need to make the three main texts you intend to analyse clear to the examiner. It is useful to state what these are in the opening paragraph of your answer. Beware of including too many secondary texts, which may be confusing. It is acceptable, however, to refer to another text briefly to contextualise your main text and to demonstrate your broad understanding.

- Be careful with your timing. Do not 'borrow time', if you over run on each of the first two questions you have much less time for the final question, they all have the same mark allocation.

- Make sure that you answer the question that is being asked, not the one you wish had been! Avoid picking a key word, for example 'audience', and writing all you can remember. There will always be a specific focus to the question.

- If you are using theory as part of your response, make sure that you understand it, can demonstrate that understanding and can apply it to an analysis of your main texts. Avoid downloading theory without considering how relevant it is.

- Remember, this is a synoptic paper and you must demonstrate your knowledge of the subject across the whole course.

Opening paragraphs

As stated earlier, it is important that all your responses to examination questions are structured and coherent and that you demonstrate your understanding of the industry and the texts to the examiner. Having a clear structure to your essay will help you to achieve a more sophisticated response. Your opening paragraph will set the tone to your essay:

How do your chosen texts reinforce or challenge genre conventions?

All media texts belong to one or more than one genre. A genre is a category; each genre has a repertoire of elements that are recognised by audiences. These are the codes and conventions that place the text within that particular genre and these include narrative; characters; iconography and setting; technical and audio codes. Placing texts in a genre makes them easier to market to audiences. However, not all media texts can be easily placed in a specific genre; some genres are hybrid or are a subgenre. I will be looking how genre conventions have been challenged or reinforced in the television Industry using the main texts I have studied – Strictly Come Dancing; CSI Miami and Ross Kemp; Gangs.

Commentary on opening paragraph:

The candidate clearly establishes their understanding of the concept of genre. They set out what the general codes and conventions are that make a genre recognisable to audiences. This provides them with a framework with which to structure their response without repetition. They also demonstrate that they have understood that the question has a specific focus and is asking about typicality. The candidate also effectively employs relevant media terminology establishing early in their response that they have a good understanding of the subject matter. They also introduce their main texts which show a broad range.

MS4 Essay plan

Using a plan when you practise writing essays in preparation for the exam and in the examination itself will help to ensure that you produce a structured response to the question. Here is a suggested format:

Introduction

- Briefly introduce your key texts.

- Define any key terms in the question showing your understanding of what the question requires.

Main body of essay

TEXT 1 – analyse your first key text referring to the relevant concepts/theories. Remember to support your points with specific references to the texts you have studied.

TEXT 2 – as above, it may be appropriate to cross-reference. Remember to bear in mind the focus of the question. It may be that you can say something different about this text.

TEXT 3 – as above, it may be appropriate to cross-reference and to make some different points in relation to the title. Have you referred to specific examples?

Conclusion

Sum up how you have answered the question.

Understanding the questions

It is important that before you start answering the question in the examination, you consider what the question is actually asking you. The key to this understanding is to 'unpick' the key words that will allow you to establish a focus for your response.

Below are some questions from past papers with some comments on what to look out for.

Answers: commentary

This question has a specific focus. It does not ask **what** are the representations of gender in your chosen texts, so you would need to beware of giving a descriptive answer. By the use of the word 'how', you are being asked to make a judgment and come to a conclusion. The other key word is 'stereotypical'. The expectation will be that you can explain what you understand by this word in relation to the texts you have studied.

One of the key words here is 'explore', this implies a detailed analysis. You need to demonstrate your understanding of the terminology used. For example, what is meant by digital technology? Notice that the focus of the question is on the marketing of the text, not the text itself. Several candidates who answered this question in the examination had not read and understood the full question and did not look at how the texts were marketed.

'To what extent' allows you to qualify which texts are dependent and which aren't but the question also suggests you need to comment on how much they are dependent, which suggests there may be other factors that have contributed to their success. If this is the case, you will need to develop this point with examples; for example, the narrative in an independent film. You also may need to discuss what is meant by the notion of 'success', does it mean different things to different texts?

Question (Section A):

How stereotypical are the representations in your chosen texts?

Question (Section B):

Explore how your chosen texts use digital technology in their marketing?

Question (Section B):

To what extent is the success of your chosen texts dependent on stars and celebrities?

Task

Look at some past papers. Choose a range of questions and practise 'unpicking' them. Make sure you are clear about what they are asking you.

B1 question

Explore the different ways audiences/users respond to texts

Tom's answer

① Audiences can respond in many different ways to a text and, as quoted by Stuart Hall's encoding and decoding theory, all texts are 'polysemic', i.e. they have more than one meaning, this can apply to TV.

② The Wire is a stereotypical police drama. Episode 1 offers a meta-narrative within it as it does not focus on the hero or anti-hero, making it a diverse, multi-layered narrative as it makes the reader work. It is linked in with Barthes theory. It can be seen to be a complex text as it is hard to get into as it focuses on a community of characters whose narratives are inter-twined showing a multi-perspective narrative to allow the viewer to respond in many ways as it shows the point of view of many characters.

③ According to Stuart Hall's encoding and decoding theory the preferred response of the audience is that they enjoy the programme and understand the situation. The negotiated response would be that they would not particularly enjoy the text; however, they would understand most aspects of it and the oppositional reading would be the idea that the audience would not like or understand the text at all.

④ Due to the programme targeting the ABC1 audience, that audience may respond to the text in a much more acceptable and welcoming way.

⑤ This can also lead to a discussion of the uses and gratifications theory as it could be read by an audience and they may respond to it in terms of it being a diversion and escapism and as a way of seeing it as a world better than their own. Audiences may also respond via social interaction as it allows them to engage in conversation. For example, 'did you see The Wire last night?' The audience may respond to this text in that they see it as unacceptable and offensive due to the negative representations of America and the abusive language.

Examiner commentary

① The candidate begins to define the question and sets out some structure for a response. However, this introduction is very brief and could have been developed to discuss why audiences may respond in different ways. There is an introduction of theory, which should then be developed in the body of the essay, and some use of media terminology.

② The main text of The Wire is appropriate. The response at this stage focuses on the appeal of the narrative structure and there is clear evidence that the candidate has an understanding of this in relation to the text. However, the candidate needed to both link the focus to the theme of the question and include a specific example from the text to support the point.

③ The candidate introduces appropriate theory, i.e. Stuart Hall. However, at this stage in the answer they fail to apply the theory to a specific example from The Wire. If they had done this they would have more effectively demonstrated their understanding of the theory in practice. Also the response does not show that the candidate has studied a specific episode of the programme in detail as they refer to The Wire generally.

④ Here the candidate demonstrates their awareness of the target audience but could have developed their point using specific textual examples.

⑤ Here the candidate introduces the uses and gratifications theory and shows obvious understanding but they are now well into their response to this question and have not included any specific references to an episode or key scenes. However, there are good references to the idea of literal responses of an audience

Summative comment

This response is competent and there is evidence that the candidate understands the focus of the question. Although the introduction is brief, there is an attempt to define the question and to incorporate some relevant theory, i.e. Stuart Hall. The choice of the first main text is appropriate and makes a good start to the analysis of the question. The candidate also uses media vocabulary that helps to make this a more sophisticated response. However, they did need to apply the theory to specific examples from an episode of the programme to illustrate their ability to engage in detailed textual analysis. The candidate is able to broaden their discussion to comment on audience appeal and how this may elicit a response, showing their understanding of the demands of the question. The reference to literal responses is good and demonstrates their ability to think beyond the theoretical and therefore shows a more complex understanding of audience response.

A2 question

How conventional is the narrative structure of your chosen texts?

Tom's answer

① When studying the film industry and my three main films I have found many different narrative structures within them, some of which are relevant to the film's genre.

② Firstly, I'll Sleep When I'm Dead is a modern day film noir which was created in 2004 by producer Mike Hodges. It explores the narrative of Davie who is a typical 'jack the lad' who gets into the wrong crowd via the drugs trade which leads to his suicide. The storyline then follows his brother Will's fight to find why Davie killed himself. He goes on a revenge quest to kill the inflictor.

③ The film contains many narrative conventions which demonstrate Barthes theory of action and enigma codes. An enigma is the idea that the narrative constructs a mystery whereas an action code suggests an event or action sequence that will happen later in the narrative. An example of an enigma code used in the film can be seen when Will enters the scene and leaves the audience thinking 'who is he?'. This has an effect in the film as the audience will want to continue to watch to find out his role within the narrative structure. A further enigma code can be seen in the scene where Will arrives at the party and a midshot is used of a man in a suit talking on his phone looking very suspicious. This leads the audience to ask what his motives are, who he is and why he is there, again creating a narrative enigma.

④ The film also uses a non-chronological structure; this is demonstrated through the use of the flashback. The film starts where it also ends with Clive Owen walking back to his car and then the film constructs the narrative showing how the events have brought him to the key opening scene. This is effective as it allows the audience to be able to know how and why he is there and the events that led up to this.

Examiner commentary

① The introduction here is very brief. There is no evidence that the candidate has 'unpicked' the question as they do not address the focus of 'how conventional,' which is crucial in producing a satisfactory response to this question. The student also needed to define what is understood by narrative structure thus establishing a framework by which to discuss all of the main film texts. It would also have helped if the student has stated the three film texts in this introduction.

② The main text here is appropriate and the candidate does begin to focus on narrative but also falls into the trap of telling the story rather than focusing on the question and analysing the text.

③ Theory is introduced here and understanding is evident. The theory is relevant to a discussion of narrative. There is also use of relevant media vocabulary. The points made are supported with specific examples from the chosen text. There is an example of a technical code to suggest the narrative structure – this could have been further developed; however, candidates very often forget to discuss how the narrative is 'shown' through technical and audio codes. However, the candidate tends to discuss narrative generally in the film and has not yet focused on the question.

④ Here the candidate begins to implicitly discuss the unconventionality of the narrative structure and its effect upon the audience. This needed to be developed further to demonstrate a more complex understanding of the film and its narrative structure. A reference to non-linear narrative and the conventions associated with this format would have been relevant here.

Summative comment

This response is less secure and there is more limited evidence initially that the candidate has 'unpicked' the question and knows what is required. The brief introduction does not allow the candidate to show their understanding of the topic of the question. The first example is appropriate but the approach is a little descriptive; this is a common mistake with narrative based questions. However, the response gathers strength and relevant theory is introduced and is applied to an example from the main text. This is a good way to demonstrate theoretical understanding and an ability to engage in textual analysis. A more detailed discussion of how the narrative is constructed through technical and audio codes would have improved this response. The candidate is also able to demonstrate the fact that they have understood the question by examining non-conventional techniques used in their chosen text. This response has a lot of promise and improves as it develops.

A2 question

How typical are your three main texts of their genre?

Tom's answer

① Bridget Jones' Diary (Maguire 2001) falls under the genre of romantic comedy. It is a British film and was produced by a British company called Working Title. Working Title has a very successful back catalogue of films from the romantic comedy genre including Notting Hill.

② A typical convention of a romantic comedy is that it has a narrative which follows Todorov's theory. This is true in Bridget Jones' Diary. The equilibrium is Bridget's normal life at the beginning of the film; her normality is that she goes to work and believes that she will be single for the rest of her life. Bridget then starts dating her boss Daniel Cleaver. After weeks of them being together Daniel cheats on her; this is the disruption to the equilibrium. At the end of the film we see her come together with Mark Darcy, this establishes a new equilibrium, Bridget is now happy with her life and there is a resolution to the film.

③ Another way Bridget Jones' Diary fits into this genre is the fairy tale ending. At the end we see that Bridget has met the man she loves and is happy. We see this in other romantic comedies such as A Cinderella Story and Love Actually. This is a very common convention within this genre.

④ What makes this film less typical of its genre is the representation of the heroine of the film. Bridget isn't the typical skinny, beautiful protagonist audiences expect to see in romantic comedies. She drinks, she smokes, she swears and she gets herself into difficult situations which do not show her in a positive light. These elements make the film stand out from other examples of the genre.

⑤ The candidate then moved onto their next text.

Examiner commentary

① This candidate does not include an introduction but jumps straight into a discussion of their first text. This approach does not allow the candidate to demonstrate and explain their understanding of the question or to introduce their three main texts. They do show an understanding of an industry context. An introduction would have allowed the candidate to establish an understanding of the requirements of the question.

② The candidate demonstrates some awareness of the film's genre but does not discuss the codes and conventions of romantic comedies in detail. The focus is on narrative, which is a relevant code and this does link to the focus of the question as the candidate does discuss its typicality in terms of the romantic comedy genre. The examples from the narrative are related to a narrative theory, which avoids a totally descriptive response. However, the points are undeveloped. A useful comment could have been made regarding audience expectations of the narrative codes and conventions of this genre.

③ The candidate remains clear about the focus of the question and gives another example of the film's typicality within the genre. However, they also repeat a point made earlier. The brief inclusion of secondary texts from the same genre demonstrates that the candidate has a broad awareness of the genre.

④ This is a good point as the candidate has developed their response to consider the elements of the film that suggest it is not necessarily typical of the genre. They move away from narrative to discuss character and representation. To develop the response the candidate needed to analyse key scenes from the film to support the points they are making and to show an awareness of how technical codes construct the representation of a character.

⑤ This is a relatively brief analysis of this film and lacked detailed reference to key scenes – this would have demonstrated the candidate's more complex analytical skills.

Summative comment

The absence of any introduction makes it hard for the candidate to demonstrate an overview of the question. A more sophisticated response would also have discussed the codes and conventions of the genre of romantic comedies and used this as a framework to examine their chosen film text. The choice of text is appropriate and offers a range of opportunities to discuss typical and atypical elements. There is a tendency to be descriptive which should be avoided at this level, but there is reference to narrative structure which relates to the question. The candidate does develop their response by discussing the typicality of their text and comparing it to other examples. They do then move on to discuss other elements of the genre conventions effectively. More specific references to scenes from the film would have allowed the candidate to show more sophisticated analysis skills.

the head of MI5, but at the end she is seen to be old, tired and vulnerable and is replaced by a man.

Quickfire 32

Other examples of national identity in the film include Scotland, which is represented as bleak and isolated. The character associated with this representation is the gamekeeper who fulfils a stereotypical role as the caretaker of Bond's childhood home. His accent and codes of clothing reinforce the stereotypical representation. There is also a representation of the East in the form of Shanghai, apparently included to attract a broader audience for the film.

Quickfire 33

A literal response may be how many people went to see the film evidenced by box office data. A negotiated response may come from a female audience who may not be fans of action films but may be attracted by Daniel Craig.

Quickfire 34

Here you will need to make specific reference to the layout, design and content of the website for the film, or, for example, the music video that accompanied Adele's song for the film.

Quickfire 35

Magazine front covers are important because they are a main selling feature. They are what the reader will see first when they look along the shelves. The front cover main image, layout and design, visual codes, cover lines and sell lines will rapidly communicate the genre of the magazine to the consumer. The front cover will also establish the house style of the magazine that will be recognisable to the reader.

Quickfire 36

The contents page of a magazine is as complex as the front cover. In its design, layout and font styles, for example, it will replicate the house style of the publication and the particular themes of the front cover. The magazine's producers will have selected the pages to include in the content that will most clearly appeal to the reader; this will also reinforce the house styles and discourse of the title.

Quickfire 37

A reader may be attracted to the regular pages within the magazine as they know what to expect. They may be accustomed to the style of a particular journalist and this will be part of the reason they buy the magazine. However, they will also want something different and new from the inner pages and this will be fulfilled by the features and articles that will only appear in this issue of the magazine. The inner pages may be highlighted on the front cover through enigmatic headlines to persuade the consumer to buy the magazine and find out about the article. Some magazines are packaged so that it is no longer possible to have a look inside before buying, a strategy to ensure that the magazine is bought.

Quickfire 38

Narrowcasting is an advantage to advertisers as it means the magazine can be very specific about the demographic and lifestyle of its readers, thus ensuring that the advertisers can be sure that they are reaching their target audience.

Quickfire 39

Bauer Media has a broad range of titles to attract a wide audience including *Heat*, *Kerrang!* and *Empire*. Advertisers will be attracted to this publisher because through their publications they can target a broad audience. Conde Nast with titles like *Vogue* and *Tatler* clearly has an interest in magazines at the high end of the audience spectrum, they are more expensive to buy and target a higher demographic. IPC media has a range of more traditional magazines.

Quickfire 40

Sales are falling because readers are accessing more convenient and interactive ways to 'read' magazines including phone apps and the magazine's own website.

Quickfire 41

For publishers, online magazines are more cost effective as they do not have to pay for printing of a glossy magazine. This means they have to sell less advertising and can concentrate more on the magazine's content. For readers,

the magazine website offers more interactive opportunities including blogs, emails and audio-visual links. The navigation bar and related links allow the user to make choices about what they want to read and in how much detail.

Quickfire 42

The central image used on the front cover may need to be changed to someone who is more recognisable or reflects the culture of the country of publication. The content may have to be changed as it may not be suitable for some countries; for example, overly sexual content. Some countries will change the magazine's title into their language – ¡Hola! became *Hello!* in the UK version. The overall house style and brand identity will tend to stay the same.

Quickfire 43

To answer this question you will need to be familiar with the whole magazine, not just the front cover. Remember that the discourse is not the individual stories but the themes and topics that are indicative of the magazine's ethos and identity; for example, quick fix problem solving or concern for the environment.

Quickfire 44

Magazines use a range of marketing strategies including: cross-platform marketing, for example billboards and radio. They may advertise in other magazines published by the same company. The inclusion of free gifts with the magazine is another popular marketing device. Be aware of how your chosen texts are marketed.

Quickfire 45

Here you need to give specific examples of the codes and conventions of your texts that place them in the specific genre. The texts you study should be from different genres so that you have different points to make about them. Consider elements like the layout and design, visual codes and technical codes.

Quickfire 46

A narrative structure in a print text like a magazine is important as the publication relies on regular, loyal readers who have an expectation of where certain elements of the magazine are situated. This allows them to navigate around the magazine easily and fulfils their expectations.

Quickfire 47

Women do figure in *Men's Health*, although are not the main focus of the articles and features. As the representation of masculinity is linked to the notion of the 'new man', then women are often still seen as a goal, but one that can be won through understanding their behaviour and meeting their needs, which do focus on sex! Where women are featured they tend to be beautiful but also strong, they are not going to be easily won over. The sexual objectification of the female form is less explicit, but is still there; this can be seen in the articles in the magazine featured.

Quickfire 48

The positive implications are that the magazine encourages men to consider healthy eating, to be concerned about health issues and offers advice on issues of concern to men that may not be easily accessible, for example discussion of prostate cancer. However, the magazine does also offer very aspirational images of men, similar to those in women's magazines that have led men to feel inadequate about their bodies and lifestyles. Men's magazines of this genre have been blamed for the rise in male anorexia.

Quickfire 49

The advertisements suggest that the magazine is constructing an idea of who the *Men's Health* man is – someone who can afford luxury products like those in the advertisements. In actuality the *Men's Health* reader will find the advertisements aspirational, or, in a negotiated response, will ignore them and focus on the features or articles that have more resonance with them personally.

Quickfire 50

This would encourage the advertisers for more upmarket products to place their adverts in the magazine as they are assured of targeting consumers in the higher demographic brackets who are likely to have more disposable income.

Quickfire 51

Aspirers would be likely to buy the magazine due to the lifestyle represented in the magazine. Also possibly succeeders who are happy with what they have achieved, but want to maintain their health and fitness and are interested in the articles and features related to modern men.

Quickfire 52

Newspaper front pages are important in attracting readers as their headlines and main images suggest the main stories of the day. The choice of headlines will often be enigmatic and will encourage the consumer to buy the newspaper. The style and content of the front page will also clearly suggest the genre of the newspaper and what it can offer an audience.

Quickfire 53

Some newspapers are owned by multi-conglomerates and are among several titles owned by the company/individual. This means that they are in a stronger financial position as any losses can be offset by the company's other assets. Other titles are more vulnerable as they are part of a smaller company. Others are owned by a trust, which suggests that they will be more autonomous and democratic in their organisation.

Quickfire 54

The story involves personalisation as it revolves around what has happened to an individual whose photograph is the central image. The story is also ethnocentric as it has immediate relevance to the people who live in and around Newcastle as this is a local paper. The story is also unambiguous and this is reinforced by the dramatic but informative headline.

Quickfire 55

Some readers like the physical experience of choosing and buying a newspaper according to the appeal of the front page; they also like holding and flicking through the newspaper. The print version of the newspaper can be put down and picked up by other members of the family, for example, who may be attracted by aspects of its content.

Quickfire 56

The advantages of curbing press freedom are that this will protect the privacy of individuals, and scandals like that of phone hacking would be less likely to happen again. Newspapers would have to be more circumspect about the methods they use to get a story. The disadvantages would be that real investigative journalism, which often uncovers issues that are of serious concern to the public, would be curtailed.

Quickfire 57

The i presents serious, quality news in a concise way. It allows readers who have less time to keep up to date. Its design and layout makes it easy to find the key news items. The price of 20p is also an attraction.

Quickfire 58

Readers of newspapers will often tend to buy the same genre of newspaper regularly; they therefore need to easily see the genre, which will be apparent through the construction of the front page.

Quickfire 59

Without a caption the image is an open text and can be interpreted differently by different audiences. The inclusion of a caption tells the audience the context of the image and therefore an individual interpretation is less likely. The text becomes closed, anchored by the caption.

Quickfire 60

The newspaper will reflect the ideology of its producers and will fulfil the expectations of its readers. This means that certain social groups will be represented in a particular way as this is what the readers expect. For example The Daily Mail tends to present a negative representation of young people as they and their readers believe that young people are out of control and problematic. The Sun, with the inclusion of Page 3, offers a negative view of women and sexually objectifies them.

Quickfire 61

The other representation included in newspapers may be issues and events. Some events are of interest to all readers regardless of the style of the newspaper; for example, the arrival of the royal baby in July 2013 was covered in different ways by all newspapers.

Quickfire 62

Elements of the paper's front cover reflect the style and target audience including the choice of the main image – a popular paper will be more likely to include a celebrity on the front cover. The headlines on quality front pages will tend to be informative and less dramatic. The plugs will also differ. Quality papers will include content that attracts the audience, for example lifestyle articles. Popular newspapers will have fewer stories and are more image-led, whilst quality newspapers will be text-led and include a range of stories to appeal to the interests and concerns of the audience.

Quickfire 63

It is visually appealing as it clearly sets out, in a matrix style, the main stories and features with easy-to-read headings. The central image is usually related to a lighter story or feature thus offering the reader more diverse content beyond serious news. The use of graphics and images makes the page more interesting and enables the reader to skim over the content.

Quickfire 64

Many people find the online version of the newspaper more accessible and suited to their lifestyles. They can view it on a range of devices including mobile phones and computers and wherever they happen to be at the time. The interactive opportunities also appeal to users.

Quickfire 65

The newspaper constructs the idea of the reader through the content it includes, which suggests to the reader what they should be interested in reading about in terms of news items and features. The actual reader may have a range of reasons for buying the newspaper; women may buy The Daily Mail to read the articles and features that are of interest to them and may not be interested in the news items. Some readers may buy a paper for a specific item, for example sport.

Quickfire 66

This suggests that the newspaper is less impartial and more likely to offer their views about a particular news story rather than an unbiased account.

Quickfire 67

An audience will use a newspaper for information; they may also use it for surveillance to keep up to date with what is going on in the world. When a particular newspaper has an 'exclusive', an audience may use it for social interaction using the story to engage in a discussion with others.

Quickfire 68

Advertisers can use a range of different formats to ensure that their product/service reaches its intended audience. These include: radio and television adverts; billboards; magazines and newspapers; placements at events, for example, around the sides of a football pitch; the Internet; mobile phones and public places, for example, the sides of bus shelters.

Quickfire 69

A successful advertisement attracts the attention of its audience through a range of strategies including: use of music and other audio effects; celebrity endorsement; particular appeals, for example to our need to keep up to date; use of colour; offers related to the product; a memorable slogan; language and mode of address; selling tactics and other persuasive devices.

The success of the advert can then be monitored, for example, by collecting data on how many products were sold during the period when the advertisement was released.

Quickfire 70

As advertisements already use a range of tactics to ensure that we buy into the product or service, some of which can be ruthless, it is very important that the industry has a regulatory body to ensure that the producers of the adverts are not making unfair and unreasonable claims for their products/services. The ASA aims to ensure that all adverts adhere to their code of practice and are legal, honest, decent and truthful so that the consumer is not misled.

Quickfire 71

The Chanel Mademoiselle campaign is a global brand. Evidence for this is the launch of the campaign which was centred across key cities in the world including Paris, New York and Tokyo. The images used in the campaigns suggested that there was already global recognition of the brand and the iconic endorser Keira Knightley. The website also has global access and the fan sites have contributions from a global audience.

Quickfire 72

The concept of a marketing campaign advertising itself is relatively new and is related to the need to create a global buzz around the launch of a new product for a recognised brand. Where the campaign is high profile and has a large budget it is important to generate early interest through a range of teaser strategies like those used in the *Chanel Mademoiselle* campaign. This then creates anticipation for the campaign.

Quickfire 73

The main codes and conventions of a perfume advertisement include: a glamorous setting; a beautiful woman; the iconic representation of the perfume bottle; music suggesting the style of the fragrance; a slogan related to the product; a narrative often including some romantic attachment and high production values demonstrated through technical and audio codes.

Quickfire 74

The setting of the advert in Coco Chanel's apartment reminds the audience that this is a well-established and long-running brand that has links to the high profile and sophisticated fashion designer who is world renowned. The choice of setting also helps to give the campaign a narrative in which Knightley seems to be a reincarnation of the young Coco Chanel. Some of the shots used including the mirrored staircase will be recognised and associated with the life of Coco Chanel.

Quickfire 75

With regard to narrative, both adverts in the campaign employ a linear structure revolving around a central character created by Keira Knightley. Her story evolves in the advert and the choice of audio track reinforces her role within the narrative. The setting is also important in establishing the romantic element involved in both storylines and the sophistication of the product. In both adverts the audience is positioned within the narrative either physically through the use of technical and audio codes or emotionally to empathise with characters within the narrative.

Quickfire 76

1. The long shot of Keira Knightley on her own riding the motorbike along a deserted Paris street. This reinforces her independence.

2. The close-up shot in which there is direct mode of address with the audience. Her code of expression is confident and self-contained.

3. In the apartment on her arrival there is a reverse tracking shot where Knightley walks confidently towards the audience at the head of a small group, one of whom is carrying her helmet, the other is the photographer. They are in her wake suggesting her importance and dominance. The shot is also at a slightly low angle thus reinforcing her position.

Quickfire 77

In the 2011 campaign the representation of place is presented through the shots of Paris. The connotations of Paris are as a city of romance and this is the representation constructed here. The choice of shots included ones of the old traditional buildings and iconic settings in the city, for example, the Place de la Concorde. The cream of the buildings links to the colour of Knightley's clothing. The streets are deserted giving the city a surreal quality and emphasising her control over herself and her surroundings. The second main setting is the apartment with connotations of the opulence and luxury of Coco Chanel's lifestyle.

Quickfire 78

The campaign would appeal to Aspirers as this group of consumers want brands that suggest their status in society, they may be particularly attracted to celebrity labels. As such, Chanel is an established brand that has connotations of sophistication and exclusivity. They are also stylish and dynamic and can be persuaded by celebrity endorsement.

Succeeders already have status and control and have nothing to prove but they feel that they deserve the best and will be attracted by reliable established brands that are recognisable and have quality.

Quickfire 79

The audience for *Chanel Coco Mademoiselle* is targeted through firstly, the choice of Kiera Knightley as the spokesperson of the brand. She has resonance with the target audience and a large fan base. The romantic themed narrative showing a dominant female character will also attract the younger demographic – the target of the product. The advert will appeal to Aspirers as it creates a luxurious lifestyle based on beautiful people and surroundings.

Quickfire 80

A range of elements may affect how an audience responds to any text. These may include: gender; age; culture; experience; ethnicity and cultural competence. Also, the way in which the text is constructed may also position the audience and so elicit a particular response.

Quickfire 81

Digital technology has greatly helped the distribution of music. Music can now be accessed across a range of platforms including computers, mobile phones and MP3 players. This has facilitated the distribution of music by artists and recording companies. Listening to music is cheaper than in the past even when purchased legally. The devices used to listen to music have also advanced, offering sound of a high quality.

Quickfire 82

Independent labels are important for artists as they will take chances with and sign unknown bands that the major companies would not be interested in. They also offer a range of services to such bands which will bring them to the notice of a potential audience.

Quickfire 83

Digital technology has helped music performers in that their music is easily downloaded across a range of formats and platforms. Owing to the easy accessibility of music, an audience is more likely to listen to a wider range of artists and music as they no longer have to commit to purchasing the whole CD, they are therefore more likely to discover new artists. Download stores, unlike retail stores, can stock a wider range of music including the back catalogues of artists. Some artists may release their music only as a download thus creating a buzz around the release date (e.g. David Bowie).

Quickfire 84

The music industry is very global, mainly because it is easy to access due to technological advances. Global download sites mean that music can be easily listened to and social networking sites can help to promote music from different genres and cultures. This also facilitates the distribution of music from indigenous cultures across the world. Mainstream artists like Shakira have also attempted to introduce different cultural aspects in their music thus making audiences aware of the music of different cultures.

Quickfire 85

Ed Sheeran is different from other artists in that in the early days he did not sign to a record label but used other promotional strategies to get noticed including social networking sites and public appearances. He managed to achieve success without a record label, he recorded and released EPs independently. Although he has shunned the more commercial outlets for his music, he does admit that there are advantages to being signed to a major label and acknowledges the importance of their services.

Quickfire 86

Ed Sheeran is recognisable as belonging to the indie genre in that initially he was less concerned about commercial success. He is also a musician and his music plays to his talents as a guitarist and singer, he could not be said to be manufactured. His appearance and the settings and narratives of his music videos also suggest that he is less concerned about his image and more concerned about the music. The lyrics of his songs are related to real-life experiences and will relate to young people today, they are not escapist.

Quickfire 87

His other songs also feature real-life experiences and are largely reflective as he tends to sing from the first person perspective. The themes of the songs are often gritty and hard hitting. In *Drunk* Ed Sheeran sings about someone whose relationship ended because of his own inability to change. The main character in the song's narrative feels sorry for himself and the only way he can handle the pain is by drowning his sorrows in drink. *Give Me Love* is about trying to mend a broken relationship. *Kiss Me* is about a boy who has a history of broken relationships and is unsure of how to start a new one.

Quickfire 88

Other narrative techniques used in the video include point of view shots which position the audience to experience the narrative through the protagonist's perspective. Enigma codes are also used as the audience are offered a restricted narrative in the video and are only gradually given information about the main character and his role. There is also an example of a privileged spectator position as the audience see inside the character's house and so become aware of his obsession.

Quickfire 89

The target audience is those who are interested in 'serious' music and Sheeran's constructed representation reflects this. There has been no effort to construct an artificial image as is the case on some magazines; he is represented through iconography – in casual clothes with his guitar, emphasising that he is a real musician. The accompanying copy further reflects the indie genre which would appeal to the audience; it appears to be handwritten and is informal suggesting his 'no frills' style – again an appeal to the audience of this magazine.

Quickfire 90

They do this through the replication of the codes and conventions of the indie genre. These include, casual clothing and an unkempt appearance suggesting informality and a lack of the need to construct an image (bearing in mind that this in itself creates a particular image). The hoodie is worn in both texts; this has connotations of rebellious youth. The iconographic guitar also features, signifying that Sheeran is a genuine musician, a convention related to other indie performers. The copy of both texts gives an assertion suggesting that this performer is to be reckoned with and is about to make his mark.

Quickfire 91

One of his main appeals is his music which is refreshing in its authenticity and relates to the young target audience. He also does not seem to be hampered by commercial pressures suggesting his independence as a musician. This approachability and sense that he is genuine may also explain his female fan base. His YouTube videos suggest that he values his fans and makes time to interact with them.

Quickfire 92

BBC Radio fulfils its public service remit by producing content that appeals to a broad target audience. Its programmes cross a broad spectrum following the remit to inform, educate and entertain and are both speech and music led. They also produce programmes for a less mainstream audience.

Quickfire 93

As radio is a listening medium, the website offers the audience a chance to view images of the presenters. Some programmes have a live webcam operating so the programme can be viewed as it is being broadcast. The websites also offer interactive opportunities including blogs and the chance to email the programme. They also offer the listeners the chance to catch up on missed programmes or listen to podcasts of the 'best bits' of a week's shows.

Quickfire 94

The Big Show is typical of the magazine style radio programme. It is made up of a range of different elements that are conventional of this genre. These include serious and celebrity news; traffic bulletins and regular features, for example, the non-stop oldies. The programme adopts a zoo format which is again conventional of this style of programme. It also plays music that will appeal to the older Radio 2 listener.

Quickfire 95

Social groups that are under-represented on Radio 2 could be said to be ethnic minorities, this is the case in terms of programming and presenters. Young people are also under-represented but this is more acceptable as they are catered for elsewhere by BBC Radio.

Quickfire 96

The choice of guests suggests that the target audience for the show has a broad interest in the media, current affairs and lifestyle including television, film and comedy. The guests also reflect the age range of the Radio 2 audience.

Quickfire 97

With regard to the uses and gratifications theory, the programme can be said to entertain its audience by its diverse content. There are also aspects of the programme that inform the audience and keep them up to date with regard to both the media and current affairs. The blog on the programme's website could also be said to offer opportunities for social interaction between listeners as does the chance to text and email in messages and responses to topics discussed on the programme.

Quickfire 98

You may be surprised that 45% of American gamers are female; computer games are stereotypically thought to be the domain of a male user. Another surprising statistic is the fact that the average age of the purchaser is 35 years old; the assumption usually is that gamers are from the younger generation.

Quickfire 99

An audience may be attracted to the game if they are already aware of the text the game is derived from, for example a film or graphic novel. The producers of the game can also use the branding of one text within the other, for example settings, characters and logos.

Quickfire 100

The UKIE findings suggest that the problem lies with parental, not industry, control. It is clear from the statistics that parents are not aware of the content of computer games and are therefore not rigorously controlling what their children are being exposed to.

Quickfire 101

Fifa 13 is a non-controversial game that is popular with all age groups. It is one that parents are more likely to be happy with. The range of multi-player levels and the high quality graphics make it a credible real-world experience.

Quickfire 102

The poster shows the main protagonist who is enigmatic in his hood, this is a brand identifier for the whole series. He is the central image but is also featured in an action shot signifying the genre of the game. There are also clues to the time period evident in the uniforms and iconography of battle. The bleakness of the terrain is also emphasised suggesting the challenges that will face the protagonist, a key signifier of this genre.

Quickfire 103

Ludologists assert that the term 'narrative' cannot be used to describe the structure of computer games as their construction is more complex and based on the involvement of the player in the game.

Narratologists maintain that many games actually follow a more straightforward preconceived narrative construction, similar to other audio-visual texts.

Quickfire 104

The protagonist is dressed similarly to the lead character in the earlier game. Other visual codes suggest that the setting and themes are similar, for example the uniform on the dead soldier and the weapon indicative of the time period. There is a suggestion also that the naval theme may be more prevalent here and involve pirates.

Quickfire 105

The shot is taken at a low angle making him seem powerful. The lighting is low key suggesting this is not a good character; this is further reinforced by his piercing eyes and unshaven appearance. His code of expression is intimidating.

Glossary

It is very important in all your MS4 responses and your MS3 evaluation, that you employ relevant technical and analytical vocabulary. Doing so will demonstrate your understanding and allow you to produce a more articulate and informed response. The following list is not exhaustive but includes useful media terminology to help you to develop a more sophisticated analysis of texts.

A SIGN / CODE – something which communicates meaning, e.g. colours, sounds. The meaning of the sign changes according to the context, e.g. the colour red can mean passion, love, danger or speed depending on how and where it is used.

ACTION CODE – something that happens in the narrative that tells the audience that some action will follow, for example in a scene from a soap opera, a couple are intimate in a bedroom and the camera shows the audience the husband's car pulling up at the front of the house.

ADVERTISING AGENCY – a company that researches, designs and produces advertisements for a range of media platforms. The client is the company that produces the product or is staging the event, for example.

ADVERTISING CAMPAIGN – a co-ordinated series of linked advertisements with a clear recognisable theme. It will be broadcast across a range of different platforms.

ADVERTISING SPOKESPERSON – in advertising terms, someone who is employed to promote, speak about and be 'the face of' a brand. They are usually high profile celebrities who will have audience appeal, for example Keira Knightley and Brad Pitt for Chanel.

ANCHORAGE – the words that accompany an image (still or moving) give the meaning associated with that image. If the caption or voice-over are changed then so is the way in which the audience interprets the image. An image with an anchor is a closed text; the audience are given a preferred reading. A text without an anchor is an open text as the audience can interpret it as they wish. The same image of a local school in a local newspaper could run a negative or a positive headline, which would change the way in which the same image is viewed by the reader.

APPARENTLY IMPOSSIBLE POSITION – where the camera gives the audience a view of the action from an unusual position. Audiences tend to accept this view if it enhances their enjoyment of the text.

ARC OF TRANSFORMATION – the emotional changes a character goes through in the process of the narrative. The events in the story mean that they will 'transform' by the end of the story.

ASPIRATIONAL – in terms of a media text one that encourages the audience to want more money, up market consumer items and a higher social position.

AUDIENCE SEGMENTATION – where a target audience is divided up due to the diversity and range of programmes and channels. This makes it difficult for one programme to attract a large target audience.

AUDIO STREAMING – where listeners can click on a link to play the radio programme instantly. This has increased the global reach of BBC Radio as listeners abroad can tune in to hear the live programme.

AVATAR – the player's representation of themselves within the game.

BACK STORY – part of a narrative and may be the experiences of a character or the circumstances of an event that occur before the action or narrative of a media text. It is a device that gives the audience more information and makes the main story more credible.

BIBLIOGRAPHY – a list of the books, articles and websites that you have used to help you write your investigation. You should include items in this list even if you have not directly referenced them in your essay.

BINARY OPPOSITES – where texts incorporate examples of opposite values; for example, good vs evil, villain vs hero. These can be apparent in the characters or the narrative themes.

BLIPPAR – the first image-recognition phone app aimed at bringing to life media texts like newspapers and magazines with augmented reality experiences and instantaneous content. The company launched in the UK in the summer of 2011 and will be expanding globally throughout 2013.

BOOM MICROPHONE – a directional microphone mounted on a long pole. It is very sensitive, can block out extraneous noise and can be positioned to pick up specific sound, for example dialogue in a busy street.

BRAND IDENTITY – the association the audience make with the brand, for example Chanel or Nike; built up over time and reinforced by the advertising campaigns and their placement.

BROADSHEET – a larger newspaper that publishes more serious news, for example The Daily Telegraph has maintained its broadsheet format.

BUZZ MARKETING – this can also be termed more simply 'buzz' and is the term used for word of mouth marketing. It is the interaction of consumers which creates a positive association, excitement or anticipation about a product or service.

CAPTION – words that accompany an image that explain its meaning.

CARICATURE – a comically exaggerated representation that makes the person appear 'larger than life'.

CHANNEL IDENTITY – that which makes the channel recognisable to audiences and different from any other channel. Presenters, stars, programme genres and specific programmes all help to contribute to a channel's identity.

CHOSEN CONCEPT – this is the media area you have decided to focus upon. You must choose from narrative, genre or representation.

CIRCULATION – how many copies of a magazine are produced each week/month.

CONNOTATION – the meanings attached to that description, e.g. the red car in the advert suggests speed and power.

CONSUMABLE INCOME – the money left when bills, etc., are paid, which can be spent on items like luxury goods and non-essentials. The people with high consumable incomes can be targeted by advertisers.

CONTRASTING TEXTS – here this refers to films that allow you to demonstrate a broad knowledge of the industry. For example, different genres or diverse production concepts.

CONVENTIONS – what the audience expects to see in a particular media text, for example the conventions of science fiction films may include: aliens, scientists, other worlds, gadgets, representations of good and evil, etc. Useful headings to discuss conventions are: characters, setting, iconography, narrative, technical codes and representation.

CONVERGENCE – the coming together of previously separate media industries; often the result of advances in technology whereby one device contains a range of different features. The mobile phone, for example, allows the user to download and listen to music, view videos, tweet artists etc. All this can be done through one portable device.

COVER LINES – these suggest the content to the reader and often contain teasers and rhetorical questions. These relate to the genre of the magazine.

CROSS-PLATFORM MARKETING – in media terms, a text that is distributed and exhibited across a range of media formats or platforms. This may include film, television, print, radio and the Internet.

CRPG – computer role-playing game.

DAB RADIO – digital audio broadcasting allows the listener greater choice and makes the selection of radio stations easier. The digital sound quality is better and free from the interference common with analogue transmission.

DEFENSIVE SCHEDULING – where a channel may not feel that their programme can gain higher ratings than a programme on a rival channel. They may decide to save the programme for a time when they can gain a larger audience, therefore adopting a defensive strategy.

DEMOGRAPHIC CATEGORY – a group in which consumers are placed according to their age, sex, income, profession, etc. The categories range from A to E where categories A and B are the wealthiest and most influential members of society.

DENOTATION – the description of what you can see/hear in a media text, e.g. the car in the advert is red.

DIEGETIC SOUND – sound that can be seen, for example the sound of a gun firing, the cereal being poured into the bowl in an advert, etc.

DISCOURSE – the topics and language used by a media text. The discourse of lifestyle magazines tends to revolve around body image and narcissism.

DISPOSABLE INCOME – the amount of money available to a person after they have paid taxes, bills, etc. It is their money to spend as they wish.

DISTRIBUTION – this includes the organisation of the stages of the film's release, production of DVDs and Internet strategies.

EASTER EGGS – in the gaming world these are small secrets hidden in the games by the developer for fun. It is the aim of the gamers to find these, much like an Easter egg hunt.

ENIGMA CODE – a narrative device which increases tension and audience interest by only releasing bits of information, for example teasers in a film trailer. Narrative strands that are set up at the beginning of a drama/film that makes the audience ask questions; part of a restricted narrative.

ETHNOCENTRIC – this means that the newspaper will be more concerned to cover stories that are closely related to the reader and their concerns. Tabloid and local papers only tend to cover international news stories if they can relate them specifically to their readers.

ETHOS – what the channel believes in and what it sees at its role. The ethos is usually set out in the channel's charter.

EVENT TELEVISION – used to describe high profile programmes like, for example, the final of *Strictly Come Dancing*, which attract a large audience for the actual broadcast. It is highly promoted and therefore is seen as an 'event'.

EXHIBITION – the means by which a film is 'shown', for example in multiplex or independent cinemas, on television or on the Internet.

FACTOID – this has come to mean pieces of true but insignificant and sometimes strange, bits of information. Originally, the term meant information that was presented as fact but without the evidence to support it.

FEATURE – in magazine terms, the main, or one of the main, stories in an edition. Features are generally located in the middle of the magazine, and cover more than one or two pages.

FILM FRANCHISE – the entire catalogue of films belonging to a series, for example the original *Bond* film and all the films made subsequently.

FLAGSHIP PROGRAMME – a programme that is important to a channel as it has high ratings and is recognised by audiences as belonging to that channel. It may also signify the ethos of the channel.

FLEXI NARRATIVE – a more complex narrative structure with layers of interweaving storylines. This challenges the audience and keeps them watching.

FLY ON THE WALL – this technique of filming aims to be as unobtrusive as possible so seemingly producing a 'true' representation of reality. The camera is therefore as if it were a 'fly on the wall', watching events without being noticed.

FORMAT – the way in which the media text is constructed and presented to the audience.

FORMULAIC NARRATIVE – this means that the story conforms to a clear, recognisable and expected structure that often relates to the genre of the text.

FOUR Cs – this stands for Cross Cultural Consumer Characteristics and was a way of categorising consumers into groups through their motivational needs. The main groups were mainstreamers, aspirers, explorers, succeeders and reformers.

FRANCHISE – an entire series of the film including the original film and all those that follow.

GATEKEEPERS – the people responsible for deciding the most appropriate stories to appear in the newspapers. They may be the owner, editor or senior journalists. They will only let the stories most appropriate for the ideology of the paper 'through the gate'.

GENRE – media texts can be grouped into genres that all share similar conventions. Science fiction is a genre, as are teenage magazines, etc.

GENRE-SPECIFIC LEXIS – where the media text includes language that an audience would associate with that particular genre.

GLOBAL IMPLICATIONS – the importance of the film in a worldwide context.

GRID – for MS4 this appears on the front on the examination paper and must be completed after you have read the questions. It is there to ensure that you think about your choices and that you only use one industry for each question.

HEADLINE CIRCULATION – includes lesser rate sales, subscriptions, bulks – copies sold to airlines, rail companies, hotels and gyms for a nominal fee and given free to the public – and distribution in Ireland and overseas.

HEGEMONIC MALE REPRESENTATION – this derives from the theory of cultural hegemony by Antonio Gramsci. Simply put, it asserts that the dominant social position in society is taken by men and the subordinate one by women.

HIGH CONCEPT FILM – a film that can be summed up in sentence or two. It is recognisable to audiences, easily marketable and high budget.

HORIZONTAL INTEGRATION – where the conglomerate is made up of different companies that produce and sell similar products. For example a film producer, a TV company, a magazine and a newspaper.

HOUSE STYLE – what makes the magazine recognisable to its readers every issue. The house style is established through the choice of colour, the layout and design, the font style, the content and the general 'look' of the publication

HYBRID GENRE – media texts that incorporate elements of more than one genre and are therefore more difficult to classify. *Dr Who* is a science fiction/fantasy television drama.

HYPER REALITY – a state where what is real and what is fiction are blended together and become indistinguishable. It may be, particularly in the case of computer games, that some gamers may feel more in touch with the hyper-real world than the physical one.

HYPODERMIC NEEDLE MODEL – generally acknowledged to be an out of date theory which suggests that an audience will have a mass response to a media text. The idea is that the media injects an idea into the mind of an audience who are assumed to be passive and as a result they will all respond in the same way.

ICONIC REPRESENTATION – the actual image of the product appears in the advert so that the audience knows what it looks like, for example a perfume bottle.

ICONOGRAPHY – the props, costumes, objects and backgrounds associated with a particular genre; for example, in a police series you would expect to see, uniforms, blue flashing lights, scene of crime tape and police radios.

IDENTS – the channel's '**ident**ification'. The ident is a short visual image that works as a logo for the channel. It appears before the programme on channels like BBC1 and 2. BBC2 is famous for its animated '2' ident.

IMPARTIAL PROGRAMMING – that which offers a balanced viewpoint which does not pander to the interests of a particular group.

INDEPENDENT FILM – a film made outside of the financial and artistic control of a large film company. A truly independent film should be privately conceived and funded. However, few films made are really 'independent'. This more commonly refers to a film that is made by a smaller film company on a low budget.

INDEPENDENT RECORD LABEL – a record label that operates without the funding of and is not necessarily linked to a major record label.

INDIE – a term used to refer to artists that are not linked to a major record label and are therefore seen to be more 'independent'.

INDIGENOUS – originating and produced in a specific region or country, for example Britain.

IN HOUSE ADVERTISING – where the producers of the product also create the advert and do not recruit an external agency.

INTELLECTUAL PROPERTY – a legal concept which refers to creations of the mind for which the owner's rights are recognised. These rights cover such intangible assets as music, literary and artistic works; discoveries and inventions; and words, phrases, symbols, and designs.

INTERTEXTUAL – where one media text makes reference to aspects of another text within it. For example, reconstructing a short scene from a film in a television advertisement. The text chosen will usually appeal to the target audience.

LAYOUT – the way in which a page has been designed to attract the target audience. This includes the font styles used, the positioning of text and images and the use of colour.

LEXIS – the choice of words used. This may be linked to a particular genre, e.g. the lexis of science fiction can be scientific and technical.

LIBEL – the written communication of damaging false information.

LINEAR NARRATIVE – where the narrative unfolds in chronological order from beginning to end.

LITERAL AUDIENCES – this refers to examples of responses from actual audiences that can be evidenced rather than the application of theoretical models. For example, statistics of box office numbers.

LUDOLOGY – the study of games and those who play them.

MALE NARCISSISM – this literally means 'self-love' and its derivation is from the Greek god Narcissus who mistakenly fell in love with his own reflection. In media terms it suggests an obsession with body image and looking good.

MASCULINITY – the perceived characteristics generally considered to define what it is to be a man. These can adapt according to sociological variations and cultural changes.

MANIPULATION OF TIME AND SPACE – where the narrative shapes the text through space and time.

MECHANICAL COPYRIGHT – this gives the artist sole right of reproduction of their recorded work. 'Mechanical' refers to the physical or digital copy of the recorded song. The term dates back to when records were produced mechanically.

MEDIA CONGLOMERATE – a company that owns other companies across a range of media platforms. This increases their domination of the market and their ability to distribute and exhibit their product.

MEDIA PACK – produced by the magazine publishers in order to inform advertisers of the magazine's target audience. It also includes information about advertising rates within the magazine.

MEDIA PLATFORM – the range of different ways of communicating with an audience, for example newspapers, the Internet, and television.

MEDIA TEXT – a product of a media industry, e.g. a film, advertisement, television programme, magazine, etc.

MEDIATION – the way in which a media text is constructed in order to represent the producer of the text's version of reality; constructed through selection, organisation and focus.

METROSEXUAL MAN – an urban male who is narcissistically concerned with his physical appearance and fashion. He would acknowledge being sensitive, romantic and in touch with his feminine side. He first appeared in the pages of men's lifestyle magazines like *GQ* and a good example is David Beckham.

MISE-EN-SCENE – in analysis of moving image – how the combination of images in the frame creates meaning. How individual shots in a film or photograph have been composed.

MMORPG – massively multi-player online role-playing game.

MODE OF ADDRESS – the way in which a media text 'speaks to' its target audience. For example, teenage magazines have a chatty informal mode of address; the news has a more formal mode of address.

NARRATIVE – the 'story' that is told by the media text. All media texts, not just fictional texts, have a narrative. For example, magazines have a clear beginning, middle and end. Most narratives are linear and follow a specific structure (Todorov).

NARRATOLOGIST – someone who studies narrative and narrative structure and the ways that they affect our perception.

NARROW CAST – where a text, for example a magazine about sea fishing, will target a very specific, narrow audience.

NATIONAL IDENTITY – the representation of a country as a whole, encompassing its culture, traditions, language and politics. This includes the characteristics of the country that are clearly definable to other nations.

NEWS AGENDA – the list of stories that may appear in a particular paper. The items on the news agenda will reflect the style and ethos of the paper.

NICHE AUDIENCE – a relatively small audience with specialised interests, tastes, and backgrounds.

NON-DIEGETIC SOUND – sound that is out of the shot, for example a voice-over, romantic mood music.

NON-LINEAR NARRATIVE – here the narrative manipulates time and space. It may begin in the middle and then include flashbacks and other narrative devices.

OBSERVATIONAL DOCUMENTARY – where the camera follows the subject around and 'observes' their behaviour and activities.

OPEN MIC VENUE – live shows for the performance arts, for example, poetry reading, comedy and music. Anyone can turn up on the night, book a slot and then perform without payment.

OPEN WORLD – in an open world computer game the player can move freely though the virtual world and is not restricted by levels and other barriers to free roaming.

OPINION LEADERS – people in society who may affect the way in which others interpret a particular media text. With regard to advertising, this may be a celebrity or other endorser recommending a product.

PAPARAZZI PHOTOGRAPHER – a freelance photographer who aggressively pursues celebrities and royalty to take pictures to sell to magazines and newspapers for the highest price.

PARKOUR – also known as free running and is the sport of moving along a route, typically in a city, trying to get around or through various obstacles in the quickest and most efficient manner possible, by jumping, climbing, or running.

PERSISTENT WORLDS – a feature of MMORPG games. It means that the game world continues even when the gamer is not part of it. In this way the virtual world replicates real life.

PICK AND MIX THEORY – suggested by British sociologist and media theorist, David Gauntlett. He asserted the autonomy of the audience and challenged the notion that audiences are immediately affected by what they read. He maintains that audiences are more sophisticated than this and will select aspects of the media texts that best suit their needs and ignore the rest.

PLOT SITUATIONS – elements that are part of the narrative and that an audience will expect to see in a particular text.

PLURALITY – in a media context, this refers to a range of content to suit many people.

POLITICAL BIAS – where a newspaper may show support for a political party through its choice of stories, style of coverage, cartoons, etc. It may be subtle and implicit or explicit as in the case of the tabloids on election day.

PRIMARY SOURCES – the specific media texts that you choose to analyse, for example two horror films or two music videos.

PRIVILEGED SPECTATOR POSITION – where the camera places the audience in a superior position within the narrative. The audience can then anticipate what will follow.

PROFILE – for radio stations this refers to how they are defined to their target audience; includes their aims and their ethos.

PUBLIC SERVICE BROADCASTER – a radio and television broadcaster that is independent of government, financed by public money and is seen to offer a public service by catering for a range of tastes.

QUALITATIVE DATA – this data is collected from focus groups and is more concerned with the 'quality' of the responses. This will give you more specific, detailed information.

QUANTITATIVE DATA – data that is generally collated from research in the form of questionnaires. This type of data will provide you with statistics and numbers but not reasons.

QUOTATIONS – these are phrases taken from your research texts and are used to support your points. They must be enclosed within quotation marks and the source acknowledged.

RADIO PLUGGER – a radio plugger ensures that an artist's music gets included on the playlists of radio stations. They may also arrange for the artist to play live or to be interviewed on the station. They are paid for their contacts and they are the link between the artist and the radio stations, producers and DJs.

READERSHIP – the number of people who actually read the magazine. It is generally thought that two people in addition to the buyer of the magazine will pick it up and read it at some time.

RECORD LABEL – companies that manufacture and distribute recorded music and promote that music.

RED TOP – a British newspaper that has its name in red at the top of the front page. Red-tops have a lot of readers, but are not considered to be as serious as other newspapers.

REGULATOR – a person or body that supervises a particular industry.

REPERTOIRE OF ELEMENTS – key features that distinguish one genre from another.

REPLICATE – in the context of MS3 this means that you would create a text that follows closely the findings of your Research Investigation.

REPRESENTATION – the way in which key sections of society are presented by the media, e.g. gender, race, age, the family, etc. One important example in the media is how women are represented in magazines.

REQUESTS – in a media context it is when an audience 'clicks' in order to stream or download a programme.

RHETORICAL QUESTION – a question asked for effect where no answer is expected. For example, in magazines the focus of the question may encourage the reader to engage in self-reflection.

ROYALTIES – the fees paid to the owner of the music which allows another person to play, perform or record that music. The organisation of payment of royalties has been made more complex with the advancements in digital technology.

SECONDARY SOURCES – academic texts that will support your investigation. They must be from a range of different formats including books, articles, websites, for example.

SEXUAL OBJECTIFICATION – the practice of regarding a person as an object to be viewed only in terms of their sexual appeal and with no consideration of any other aspect of their character or personality.

SIDE QUESTS – missions that deviate from the main game and are optional. They are not required to complete the game.

SIMULCAST – the streaming of live radio programmes from the website at the same time as they are broadcast on the radio.

SISTER PAPER – one that is published by the same company and has links to other papers in the brand.

SOCIOLOGICAL CONTEXT – this relates to what is happening in society at the time the text is made. Texts change in order to reflect sociological changes.

SOUND BITES – short clips of dialogue or music taken from a longer text in order to communicate the essence of the narrative to an audience.

SPLASH – the story that is given the most prominence on the front page of a newspaper.

STEREOTYPE – an exaggerated representation of someone or something. It is also where a certain group are associated with a certain set of characteristics, for example all Scotsmen are mean, blondes are dumb, etc. However, stereotypes can also be quick ways of communicating information in adverts and dramas, e.g. the rebellious teenager in a soap opera, as they are easily recognisable to audiences.

STRIPPED – a technique used in radio and television whereby a certain programme is broadcast at the same time every day. In radio this attracts an audience who associate a particular programme with their daily routine, for example driving home from work.

STUART HALL'S AUDIENCE RESPONSE THEORY – Stuart Hall is a cultural theorist who researched how audiences respond to media texts. He suggested that producers encode texts, and audiences may take on the preferred meaning, have a negotiated response where they accept some aspects of the text and disagree with others, or have an oppositional response where they reject the ideology of the text.

SUB-GENRE – where a large 'umbrella' genre is sub-divided into smaller genres each of which has their own set of conventions. For example, the television genre can be sub-divided into teen drama, hospital drama, costume drama, etc.

SUBJECT-SPECIFIC LEXIS – the specific language and vocabulary used to engage the audience. Subject-specific lexis used on the front cover of the magazine will make the reader feel part of the group who belong to the world of that magazine. For example, terminology used on the front covers of gaming magazines.

SUBVERT – in the context of MS3 this means that you can use your findings to create a product that uses the conventions of the text in a different way. For example, you may find that after researching the representation of women in horror films that they are usually victims. You may decide to subvert these findings by producing a trailer featuring a woman 'villain'.

SUSPEND DISBELIEF – here, an audience may be aware that where they are positioned by the camera, for example, is impossible, but they do not challenge this and instead believe it because it enhances their involvement in the story.

SYNDICATED OUTPUT – where radio stations make and sell a programme to other stations, or buy a programme that may be available to other radio stations.

SYNERGY – the interaction and co-operation of two or more media organisations in order to produce mutually beneficial outcomes. For example, the combination of the artist and the recording company.

SYNOPTIC ASSESSMENT – encourages students to combine elements of their learning from different parts of a course and to show their accumulated knowledge and understanding of a topic or subject area. It helps to test a student's ability to apply the knowledge and understanding gained in one part of a course to increase their understanding in other areas. For example, the research and writing of the MS3 Research Investigation may help in your understanding of an MS4 text or industry.

TABLOID – refers to the dimensions of a newspaper, a tabloid is smaller and more compact in size. However, there are further connotations attached to the term and it also tends to refer to a newspaper whose content focuses on lighter news, for example celebrity gossip, sport and television.

TARGET AUDIENCE – the people at whom the media text is aimed.

TECHNICAL CODES – these are the way in which the text has been produced to communicate meanings and include:

Camera shots – for example, close-up shots are often used to express emotion.

Camera angles – a shot of a character from above makes them appear more vulnerable.

Editing – the way in which the shots move from one to the other (transitions), e.g. fade, cut, etc. This may increase the pace and therefore the tension of the text.

Audio – how is the sound used to communicate meaning – voice-over, dialogue, music, SFX, etc.?

TECHNICAL ROLE – for the purpose of this specification, this refers to filming, editing and sound. Where sound is taken on as a technical role the expectation is that you will be able to demonstrate a range of complex skills comparable with filming and editing. This may be, for example, dubbing, audio editing, lip synching, managing the recording of external dialogue, post production audio, etc.

TEXT OUT – this relates to the strategies the text uses to attract an audience rather than the 'audience in' which refers to how the audience may respond.

THEORETICAL RESPONSES – models that are the product of studies that suggest possible ways in which audiences may interact with texts.

TIME-SHIFTED VIEWING – where a programme is recorded to be watched at a later time. Some digital video recorders allow the user to start watching the programme before it has finished. Sky+ allows audiences to pause, rewind and record live television.

UKIE – the only trade body for the UK's wider interactive entertainment industry. They exist to champion the interests, needs and positive image of the videogames and interactive entertainment industry.

UNDERGROUND – made up of a range of musical genres that operate outside of the commercial, mainstream music scene. These music genres tend to be more creative in their expression and promote individuality rather than a formulaic style.

UNPICKING QUESTIONS – many students make mistakes in their responses because they have not read the question carefully. Unpicking the question may involve underlining key words or phrases to ensure that your focus is appropriate.

USES AND GRATIFICATIONS THEORY – suggests that active audiences seek out and use different media texts in order to satisfy a need and experience different pleasures.

VERTICAL INTEGRATION – vertically integrated companies own all or most of the chain of production for the product. For example a film company that also owns a chain of multiplex cinemas to exhibit the film and merchandise outlets.

VIRAL MARKETING – where the awareness of the product or the advertising campaign is spread through less conventional ways including social networks and the Internet. Viral marketing is so named because many of the messages use 'hosts' to spread themselves rapidly, like a biological virus.

VISUAL CODES – the clues in the text to help the audience analyse and understand it. Visual codes are split into:

Code of clothing – what is worn says something about the character and makes them easier to understand, e.g. uniforms, followers of football teams and bands, etc.

Code of expression – facial expressions give clues to emotions, e.g. a smile, a frown, etc.

Code of gesture – the way that bodies are moved communicates messages, e.g. a wave, thumbs up.

Code of technique – specific to media texts and is about the way in which the image is presented, e.g. the use of black and white suggests sophistication, the use of soft focus suggests romance, etc.

WATER COOLER TELEVISION – an American term which describes an immediate audience response to a programme where it is talked about around the water cooler the next day.

WINDOW ON THE WORLD – the idea that media texts, particularly those that present aspects of reality, for example news programmes, are showing the audience the real world as it happens.

WORD OF MOUTH ADVERTISING – where someone recommends a product or service they have used to someone else.

ZOO FORMAT – this refers to the style of the programme where there is a main presenter who hosts the show but he/she is supported by other regular co-presenters. This team then chat, joke together and give opinions. This creates an informal feel to the programme.

Index